AF594552

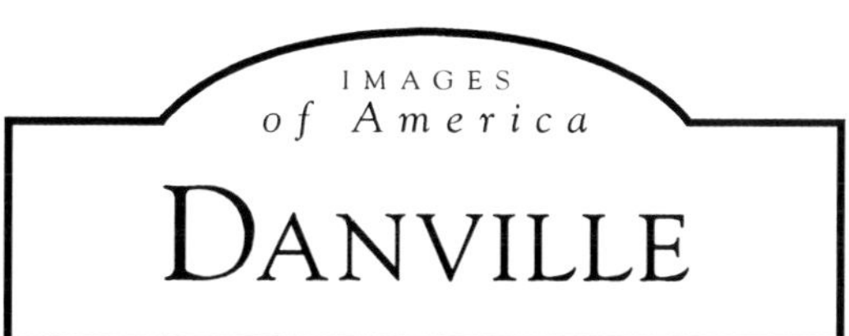
IMAGES
of America
DANVILLE

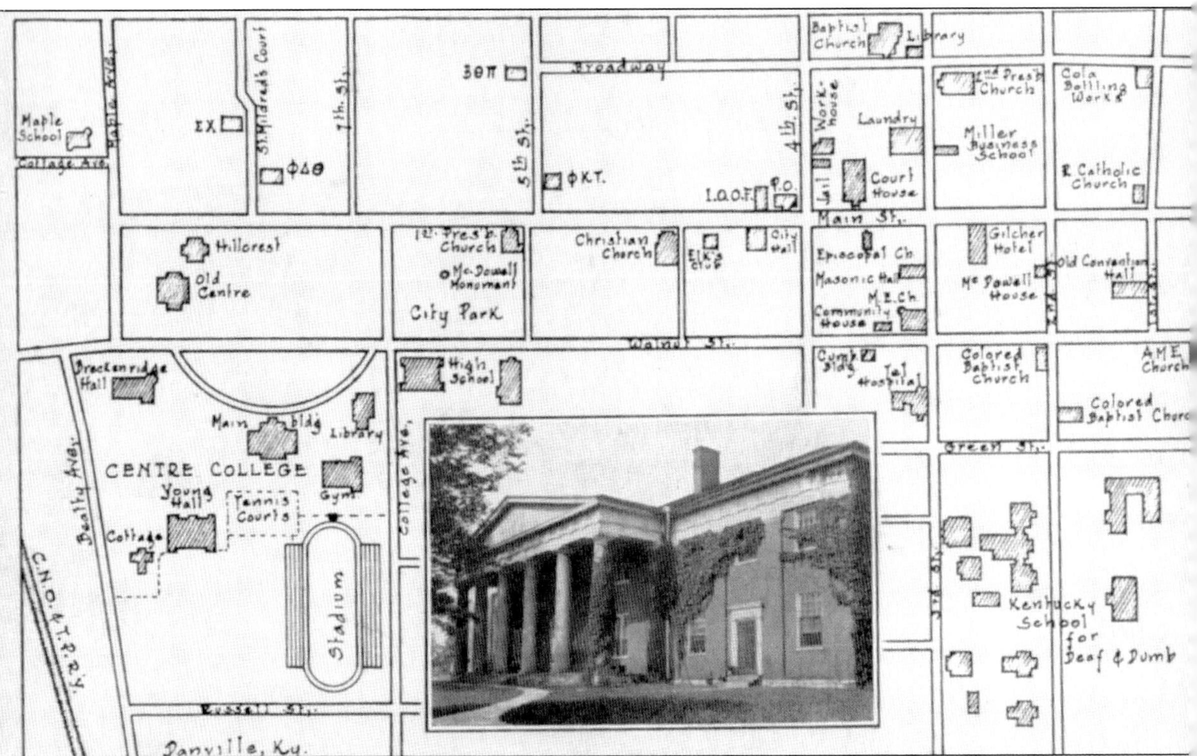

This undated postcard depicts Old Centre over a map of Centre College's campus and downtown Danville. Key historical locations are visible on the map, including the Ephraim McDowell House, the Kentucky School for the Deaf, the Gilcher Hotel, and a number of churches. (Courtesy of Centre College Special Collections.)

**On the Cover:** The Danville Motor Company's men and cars line the streets in a parade to honor the Centre College football team's victory over Harvard University. A rivalry between the two schools culminated in a Centre victory of 6-0 in 1921; graffiti celebrating the occasion still remains peppered throughout Centre's campus in the formula "C6-H0." This picture can be seen in full on page 56. (Courtesy of Centre College Special Collections.)

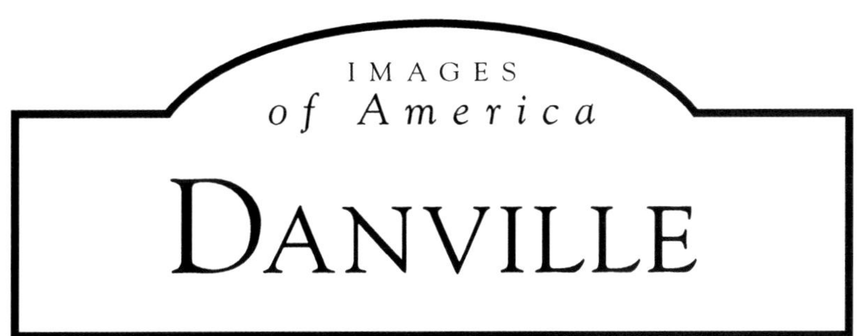


Lindsay Merritt with a foreword by
Carol Johnson Senn and Clarence Wyatt

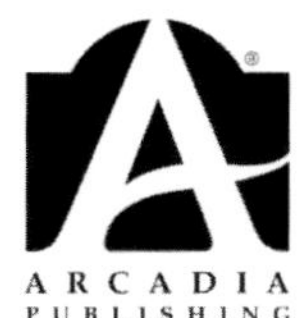

ISBN 978-0-7385-8767-7

Published by Arcadia Publishing
Charleston, South Carolina

Printed in the United States of America

Library of Congress Control Number: 2011921038

For all general information, please contact Arcadia Publishing:
Telephone 843-853-2070
Fax 843-853-0044
E-mail sales@arcadiapublishing.com
For customer service and orders:
Toll-Free 1-888-313-2665

Visit us on the Internet at www.arcadiapublishing.com

*To Tyler, the reason I came to Kentucky.*
*Your support and love mean everything to me.*

# Contents

# Foreword

Danville has always been a place of pride for its citizens. Early in Danville's history, its residents founded Centre College and Kentucky School for the Deaf (KSD), and hosted the Kentucky Constitutional Conventions. Today, the community is proud to have 10 National Register historic districts and a strong advocate for preservation, the Heart of Danville Main Street Program. Many of the buildings from the early 19th century remain as well-preserved and wonderful examples of early Kentucky architecture. Today, Danville is still home to Centre College, one of the top private liberal arts colleges in the nation. Ephraim McDowell Regional Medical Center provides the residents of more than 10 counties with the finest in medical care through the services of over 100 physicians as well as other health care professionals. The Main Street historic district is a vital combination of retail, professional, and residential properties. Danville is the only Great American Main Street City in Kentucky, thanks to the award-winning Heart of Danville program. Tourism brings visitors to Danville every day to visit McDowell House Museum, the Norton Center for the Arts at Centre College, Constitution Square State Historic Site, Pioneer Playhouse, the Great American Dollhouse Museum, and Jacobs Hall on the KSD campus.

The respect for history and preservation can be observed every day as you drive through Danville, where 200-year-old homes are well maintained on tree-lined streets. The downtown district is overseen by an Architectural Review Board under the auspices of the City of Danville. New construction downtown, such as the City Municipal Building, is done with forethought to blend into the historic district. Come and see for yourself what history awaits you in this historic community.

—Carol Johnson Senn
Executive Director, McDowell House Museum

—Clarence Wyatt
Claude D. Pottinger Professor of History, Centre College

# Acknowledgments

An undertaking of this magnitude could not have been accomplished alone. I would like to extend my grateful appreciation to all who assisted me in the creation of this book. Bob Glass, head of Special Collections at Centre College: thank you for sharing your institution's amazing photograph collections, and thank you for the many hours you put into this project. JoAnn Hamm, Sylvia Manning McGaughey, James McGaughey, Rhonda Bodner, and Roger McCowan of the Kentucky School for the Deaf: thank you for providing me with wonderful photographs and stories to share with readers. McDowell House Museum staff and docents: thank you for the use of your photographs, for teaching me the history of this treasured landmark, and for helping me edit my work. Guy Ingram: thank you for your photographs—they add so much personality and character to this book. Michael Wiser: thank you for sharing your extensive photograph and postcard collection and your knowledge of local history. Michael Denis: thank you for sharing your scanner, your teaching stories, and your expertise on publishing. Clarence Wyatt and Carol Senn: thank you for writing the foreword to this book—having it written by two people so in touch with this town's history is a real privilege. Brenda Edwards, Art Moore, and H. Kenneth Alcorn: thank you for sharing your valuable knowledge about this town and its historic buildings and inhabitants. Amy Perryman: thank you for your support through this whole process and answering my never-ending stream of questions. Mom and Dad: thank you from the bottom of my heart for instilling a love of history in me at an early age. Tyler Chelf, you cheered me on from start to finish—thank you for your unwavering support.

# INTRODUCTION

In his 1941 book *Early Days in Danville*, Calvin Fackler writes, "Our town occupies the central portion of a rich, undulating plain which lies between the waters of Clark's Run (south) and Wilson's Run (north). Some cynic, whose name is now happily lost, once remarked that its location spoiled the best farm in Boyle County."

Driving through downtown Danville, Kentucky, one might be able to imagine how the City of Firsts once looked when it was still an early settlement, when heated debate occurred in Grayson's Tavern and the log courthouse in Constitution Square, when carriages and riders on horseback traveled the main thoroughfare, and when young men with their schoolbooks walked across the gentle hills of Centre College's campus.

Danville is a one-of-a-kind town where pioneer history mingles with modern-day life. New buildings sit alongside old structures, and it is not uncommon to find an 18th-century silversmith shop located near a modern graphic design studio, or a preserved 18th-century apothecary shop within a block of a brand-new pharmacy. Students go to classes and parishioners attend church services in buildings that were once used as military hospitals following the bloody Battle of Perryville during the Civil War. The juxtaposition of old and new only serves to heighten the appreciation Danville residents have for the fascinating story of their town. There is a deep sense of respect for the town in which Kentucky successfully declared its statehood, a doctor performed a lifesaving surgery that had never before been accomplished, and deaf children attend a school that was the first of its kind in the nation.

Danville was home to many famed Kentuckians, a number of whom were recognized on national and international levels. John C. Breckinridge was vice president under James Buchanan, a presidential candidate, a Confederate general, and the Confederate secretary of war; John Marshall Harlan was a US Supreme Court justice known as the "Great Dissenter;" Robert P. Letcher and William Owsley were governors of Kentucky; and Theodore O'Hara was a soldier whose famed poem "Bivouac of the Dead" adorns markers in Arlington and Gettysburg National Cemeteries. They are among the dozens of great citizens who once resided in this Kentucky town.

Danville was part of the Great Settlement Area around James Harrod's Fort, which is now present-day Harrodsburg. John Crow, one of the settlers in Harrod's 1774 exploration team, claimed land to the south of Harrod's Fort, building Crow's Station in 1782. Within a year, Crow sold land to another pioneer, Walker Daniel, who founded Danville in 1783–1784. In the spring of 1783, Kentucky County, Virginia, became a district, and it was granted a supreme court that initially met in Harrodsburg on March 4, 1783. Justices John Floyd and Samuel McDowell presided, John May was named court clerk, and Walker Daniel was named attorney general. Harrodsburg's accommodations proved insufficient, so the court moved its meetings to the Dutch Meeting House, several miles from Harrodsburg. The court authorized Daniel and May to find a location for a log courthouse to be built near John Crow's station, and sessions were held at Crow's Station until the new courthouse was constructed. In the middle of March 1785, the Kentucky District

Supreme Court met for the final time at Crow's Station, and its minutes state, "Adjourned until Monday ten of the clock, then to meet at New Buildings erected for the use of the Court by Isaac Hite . . . Monday the 14th of March, at the New Buildings in Danville."

Danville's convenient location on the Wilderness Road, plus the proximity of three taverns, made the small town a hot spot for political discussion—namely, the separation of Kentucky from Virginia. Between 1784 and 1792, ten conventions were held in Danville, and a constitution for an independent commonwealth was created. During one of the conventions, Gen. James Wilkinson proposed that Kentucky secede from both Virginia and the United States and join the Spanish Empire; his idea was defeated, and it likely came as no surprise to his colleagues that, after his death, he was discovered to have been an agent of Spain. In 1786, the Danville Political Club, comprised of key town citizens, began meeting at Grayson's Tavern to discuss the most pressing political issues of their day. Members Joshua Barbee, Robert Craddock, Christopher Greenup, Harry Innes, Samuel and William McDowell, James and Thomas Speed, Thomas Todd, and almost two dozen others have descendants still living in the Danville area. The Political Club was instrumental in securing Kentucky's statehood. On June 1, 1792, Congress accepted Kentucky's constitution and admitted it as the nation's 15th state.

With a population of great thinkers, it is no wonder that institutions of higher learning began springing up in Danville. Transylvania University, the 16th college in the United States and the first west of the Allegheny Mountains, was chartered in 1780. Its first classes were held on the outskirts of Danville, in the small cabin of Presbyterian minister David Rice, before moving to nearby Lexington in 1789. Centre College, whose campus and administrative building Old Centre are the oldest continually operating west of the Allegheny Mountains, was founded in 1819. The Kentucky School for the Deaf, established in 1823, was the first state-sponsored school for deaf students in the nation and the first school for the deaf west of the Allegheny Mountains. John William Bate, born into slavery in Louisville, established the first public school for African Americans in Danville, and Danville was also the location of the first African American home school in Boyle County, taught by Willis Russell. Leaving their marks on the town to this day, Danville Theological Seminary, Bell Seminary, Hogsett Academy, Danville Classical and Military Institute, and the Kentucky College for Women are among the institutions that have come and gone in Danville's long history.

The 1860s were a difficult period for the burgeoning town. A devastating fire spread through Danville in 1860, destroying 64 buildings and causing more than $300,000 in damages. The town lost churches, businesses, homes, and even its twenty-year-old county courthouse. The Civil War from 1861 to 1865 meant fewer students at schools, more costly materials needed for construction, and heartbreak for families who lost loved ones in battle. Prior to the bloody Battle of Perryville, ten miles from town, Confederate forces occupied Centre College's Old Centre; after the October 1862 battle, Confederate soldiers fled through Danville, pursued by the Union force. Old Centre was taken by Union forces and turned into a military hospital, as were many other buildings in Danville. Centre College's president Lewis W. Green, who served from 1857 to 1863, refused to shut down his school during the war, despite his campus being used by both the Union and the Confederacy. Green cared for sick and wounded soldiers after the Battle of Perryville, and eventually succumbed to typhoid fever, a disease that had spread rapidly through the military hospitals in town.

In the middle of the 19th century, Danville and Boyle Counties backed the construction of the Lexington and Danville Railroad. Located over the Kentucky River, High Bridge was planned as a suspension bridge for the Lexington and Danville Railroad, made by John Roebling, who also designed the Brooklyn Bridge in New York City. Stone towers were erected in 1851 to hold suspension cables, but work on the bridge was abandoned during the Civil War. Despite this setback, the railroad industry continued to grow in Danville. A redesigned High Bridge opened in 1877, and lumber companies, grain elevators, and mills sprang up along rail lines in town. Danville became an important spot on the north-south line at this time, and its industrial growth continued into the next century.

The late-19th and 20th centuries saw a time of business growth and urban renewal in Danville. Many longtime residents fondly recall spending their youths in the downtown area, at a local drugstore's lunch counter for a soda, enjoying parades down Main Street, and witnessing the rejuvenation of historic buildings and districts. In 1937, Constitution Square State Historic Site, the location of the constitutional conventions, was designated a state park. Restoration of the buildings in the park began that year, interrupted by World War II. In 1939, the house of famed surgeon Ephraim McDowell opened to the public as a museum after years of restoration by the Kentucky Medical Association and the Works Progress Administration (WPA). In 1948, workers revisited Constitution Square, spending the next seven years doing renovations, landscaping, and adding walkways. Included in the park was the Governor's Circle, which honored Isaac Shelby, Kentucky's first and fifth governor. Two statues of men shaking hands—a depiction of Kentucky's state seal—are surrounded by plaques honoring each governor of Kentucky. Governor Shelby was said to have inspired Kentucky's state motto, "United we stand, divided we fall." This line was in one of Shelby's favorite pieces of music, John Dickinson's "The Liberty Song," as "They join in hand, brave Americans all, / By uniting we stand, by dividing we fall." In the 1970s, urban renewal led to the razing of a historic African American business district, which was built on the side of Constitution Square facing Ephraim McDowell's home. The district included the Doric Lodge No. 18, initially founded in 1888 and moved to the site in 1920. The lodge served as an important social and cultural center for African Americans in the region.

While Danville has always had a deep appreciation for its history, in recent years the community has become more involved in preserving its history. Founded in 1986, the Heart of Danville has been dedicated to the revitalization of Main Street Danville. Since its inception, the association has assisted with the restoration of the Hub-Gilcher building, administered programs and grants for building facade work, and advocated for historic preservation and streetscape improvement. Regular citizens help as well by working to keep historic museums and sites alive and running, so that the story of Danville can be shared with younger generations.

It is essentially impossible to put the entire history of a town like Danville in a book of this size; it is no easy task to even briefly touch upon it in the allotted room an author is given. However, the locals—longtime residents, historians, and institutions—have shared their stories, their photographs, and their love of this town to help paint a picture of over 225 years of Danville's history. This book is by no means a complete history of Danville, but I hope it encourages you, the reader, to dig deeper into the story of your own hometown.

# *One*

# Birthplace of the Bluegrass

In the 1770s, adventurous settlers ventured westward, eager to claim land in the untouched wilderness that would someday become the Commonwealth of Kentucky. One band of pioneers, led by James Harrod, arrived in what is now Harrodsburg in 1774, establishing the Great Settlement Area in the land around their fort. John Crow, one of the settlers, claimed over 1,000 acres of his own, naming his property Crow's Station in 1782. Initially just a palisade surrounding a log cabin and a spring, Crow's Station would soon become one of the most integral locations in the founding of Kentucky. John Crow sold a portion of his land to Walker Daniel, the first district attorney in Kentucky; in 1783–1784, Danville was established here and named in honor of its founder. Danville became the site of ten constitutional conventions that took place between 1784 and 1792. Kentucky separated from Virginia to become its own commonwealth, officially joining the Union as the 15th state on June 1, 1792. Danville's role in the independence of Kentucky earned it the nickname "Birth of the Bluegrass."

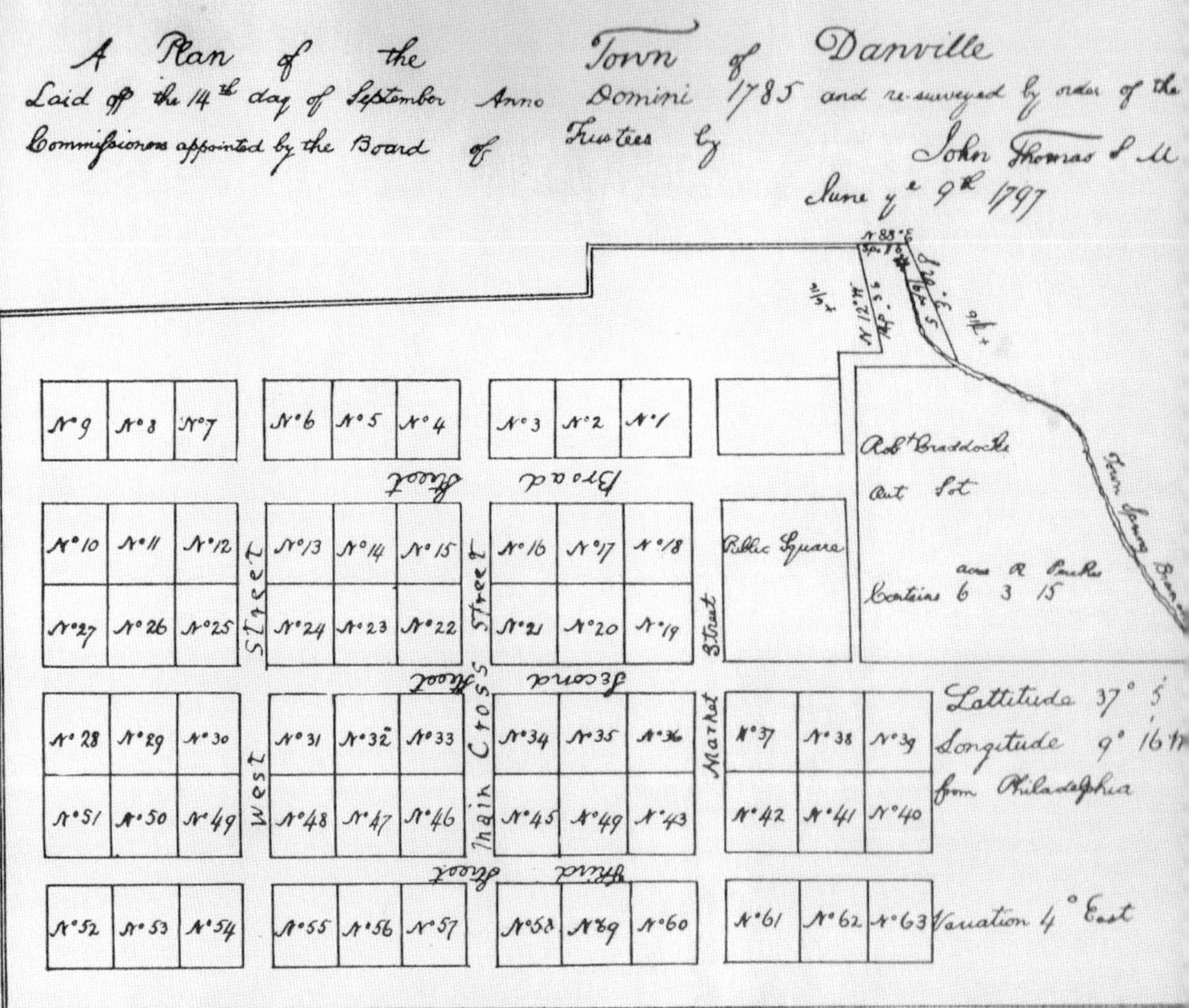


ORIGINAL PLAT OF DANVILLE, KY.

This plat of Danville, charted on September 14, 1785, shows a layout of the town that is not much different than how it looks today. Each tract of land was numbered and sold to settlers and businessmen looking to stake their claims in the new town. The public square contained a meetinghouse used by the Presbyterian Concord congregation, a courthouse where the Supreme Court of the Kentucky District met, and Grayson's Tavern, where politicians dined and discussed the pressing issues of the day. Another popular business, Barbee's Tavern, was located across from the public square in plot no. 38. Though the present-day layout of Danville is similar to the plat laid out over 225 years ago, one notable change is street names. Broad Street is Main Street today, Second Street is Walnut Street, Third Street is Martin Luther King Boulevard, Market Street is Second Street, Main Cross Street is Third Street, and West Street is Fourth Street. (Courtesy of Calvin Fackler, *Early Days in Danville*.)

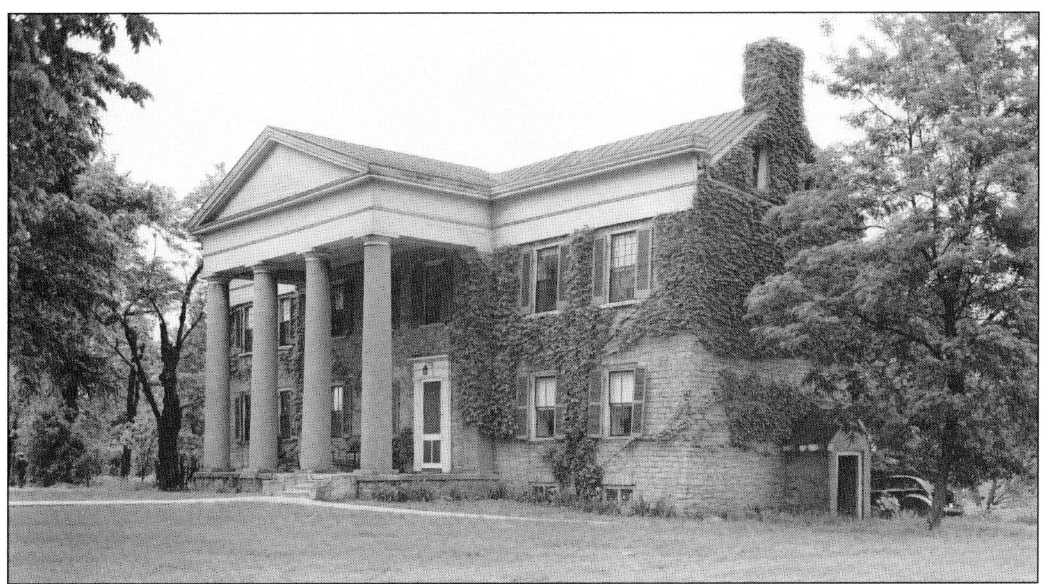

In 1774, John Crow came to the region with explorer James Harrod, founder of nearby Harrodsburg, and 32 other settlers. Crow chose land in what is now Danville, establishing Crow's Station in 1782. He then sold the land that was to become Danville to its namesake, Walker Daniel. The stone house in these 1940 photographs was built in 1784 and is the oldest existing house in the state of Kentucky. Known previously as the Crow-Barbee House and Oakland, the building recently served as a bed-and-breakfast called the Old Crow Inn. In the over 225 years since the structure was built, only six families have owned it: the Crows, the Barbees, the McCartys, the Adamses, the Moores, and the Brousseaus. (Both courtesy of the National Park Service [NPS] Historic American Buildings Survey.)

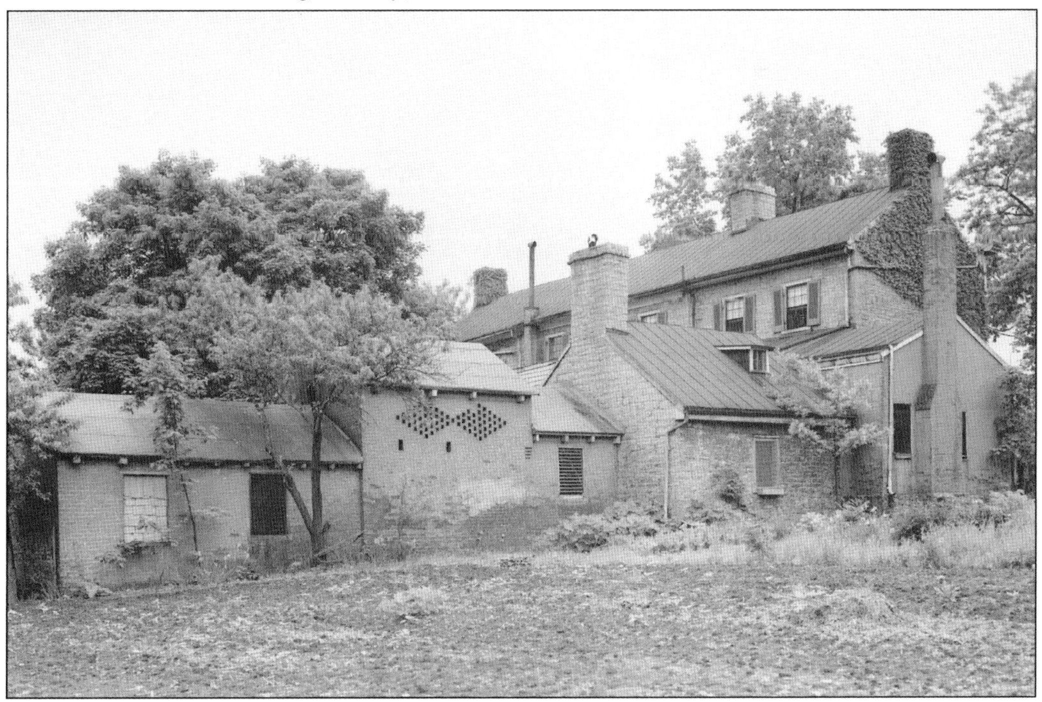

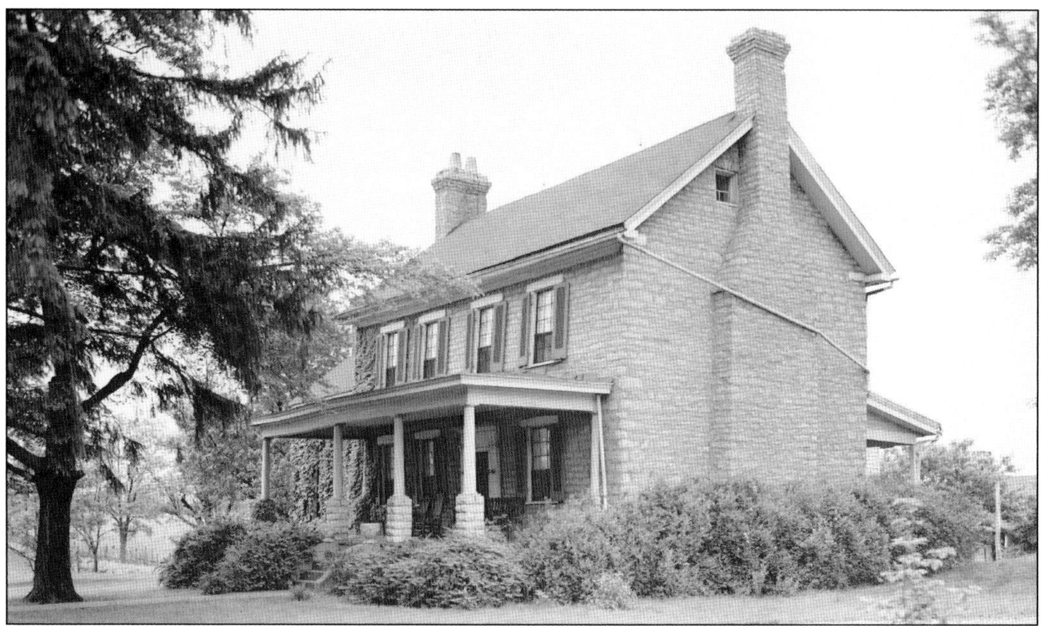

Like his brother John, William Crow arrived to the area with James Harrod and other settlers in 1774. In 1780, he established William Crow's Station, located at the headwaters of Spears Creek. Crow was known to be a wealthy but irreligious man, and there are records of him donating money to establish schools in the area. After the Transylvania Academy on the outskirts of town moved permanently to the city of Lexington, Crow donated $150 to establish the Kentucky Academy, which ended up selecting another town for its campus. In 1819, money was collected from local donors to create the Danville Academy; over $10,000 was raised, including $100 from William Crow. However, the funds to construct the academy were transferred to the new trustees of Centre College, which opened in 1820. (Both courtesy of the NPS Historic American Buildings Survey.)

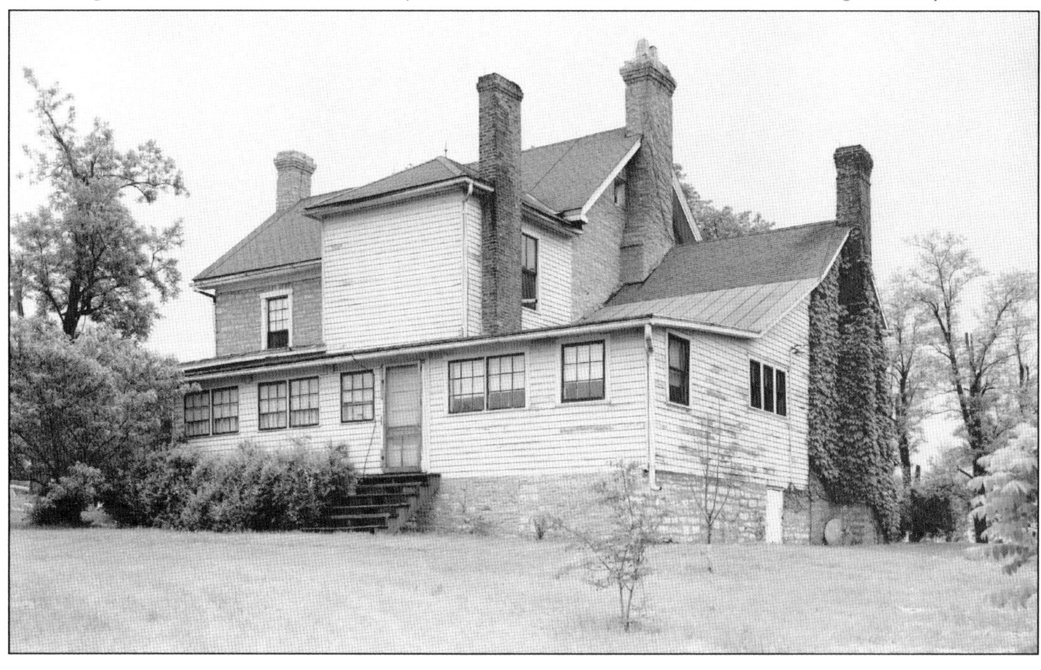

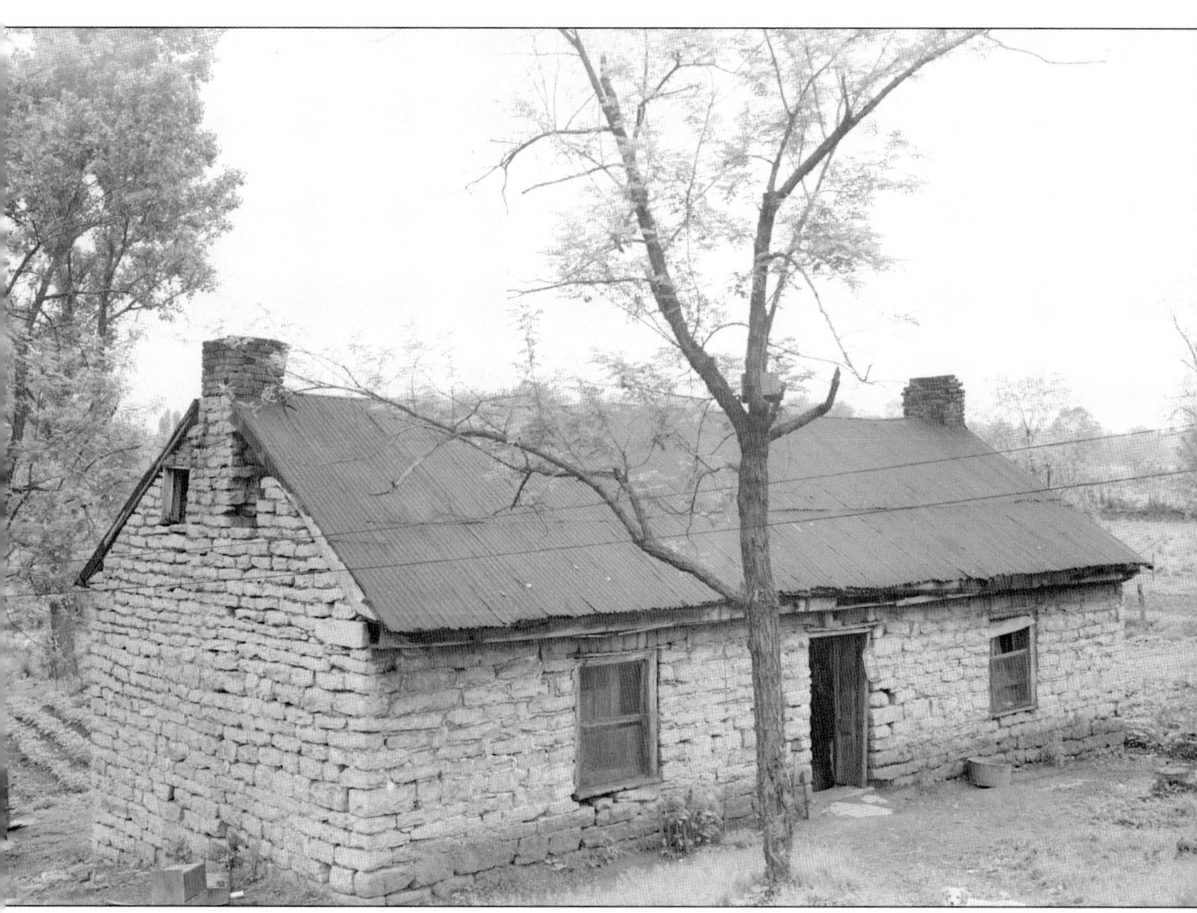

Early settlement of the region was often in the form of stations—a defensible residential site common on the late-18th-century Kentucky frontier. Danville as it is known today was nearly encircled by various stations by the end of the 1700s. Clark's Station was settled by George Clark, brother-in-law of William Whitley, famed Kentucky pioneer. Clark developed his property, known locally as "the Fort," in 1775, improved the land in 1776, and raised a crop of corn in his fields in 1777. It was one of the first stations built near the forts at Harrodsburg and Stanford. Pictured here in 1940, Clark's Station was located on Clark's Run Creek, a branch of Dick's (now Dix) River, less than two miles from the city center of Danville. (Courtesy of the NPS Historic American Buildings Survey.)

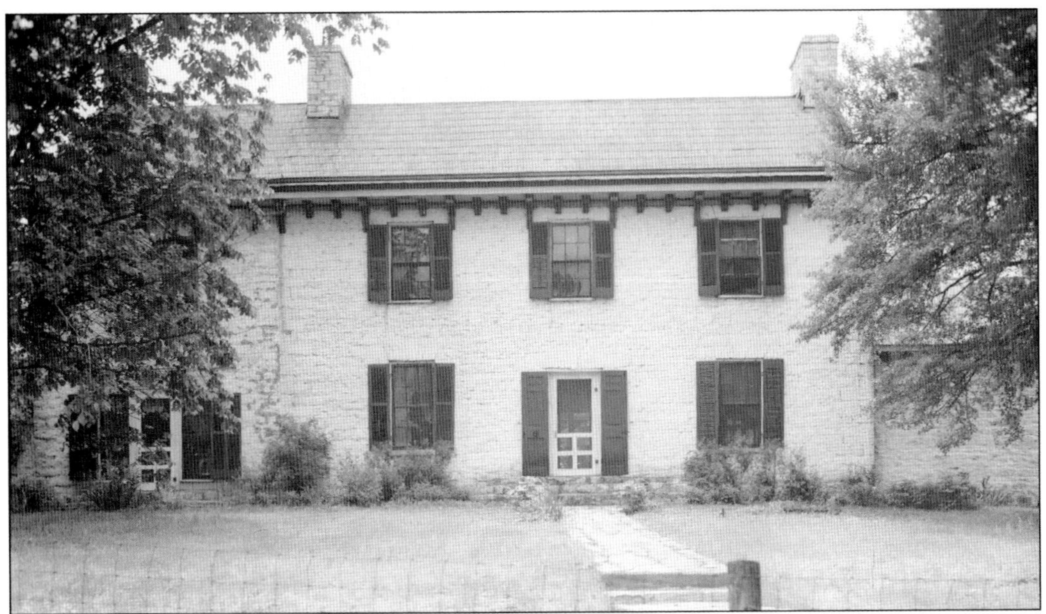

This station, built by Virginia native James Wilson between 1785 and 1794, was one of the early settlements in the region. Located at the forks of Clark's Run Creek, Wilson's Station faced the well-traveled Wilderness Road, prompting some local historians to suspect that it served the community not only as a safe haven from potential Native American raids but also as a stopping point for travelers making their way through the Kentucky frontier. (Courtesy of the NPS Historic American Buildings Survey.)

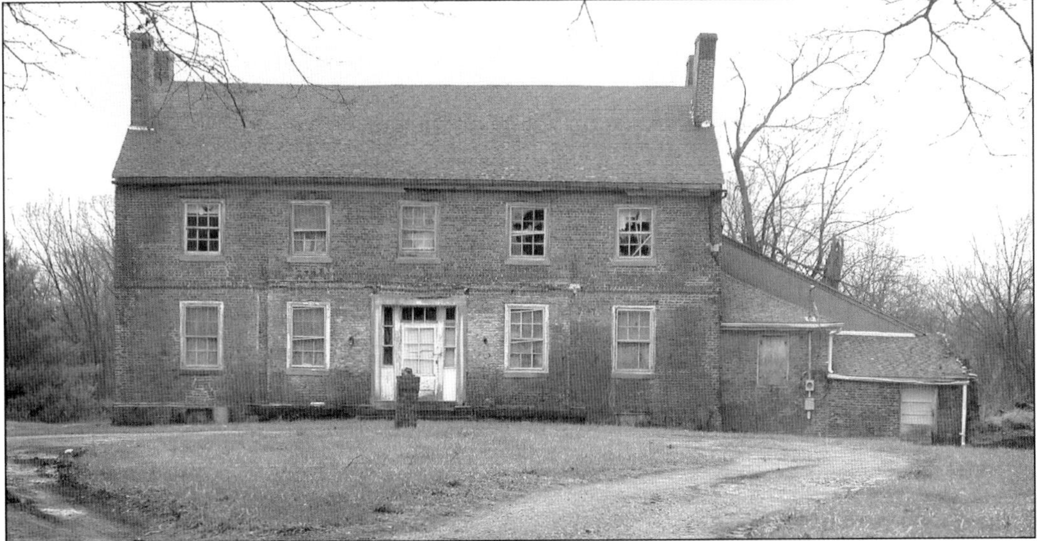

Willis Green's house was built around 1800. Initially moving to the region in 1782 as a surveyor to locate land warrants, Green chose the land several miles south of present-day Danville to build his home. Due to the gently rolling hills on which he built his home, he named his estate, fittingly, Waveland. Green was a prominent citizen of Danville, present at two of the constitutional conventions held in the town square as well as being a participating member in the Danville Political Club, whose intense debates would help pave the way to Kentucky statehood in 1792. (Courtesy of Guy Ingram.)

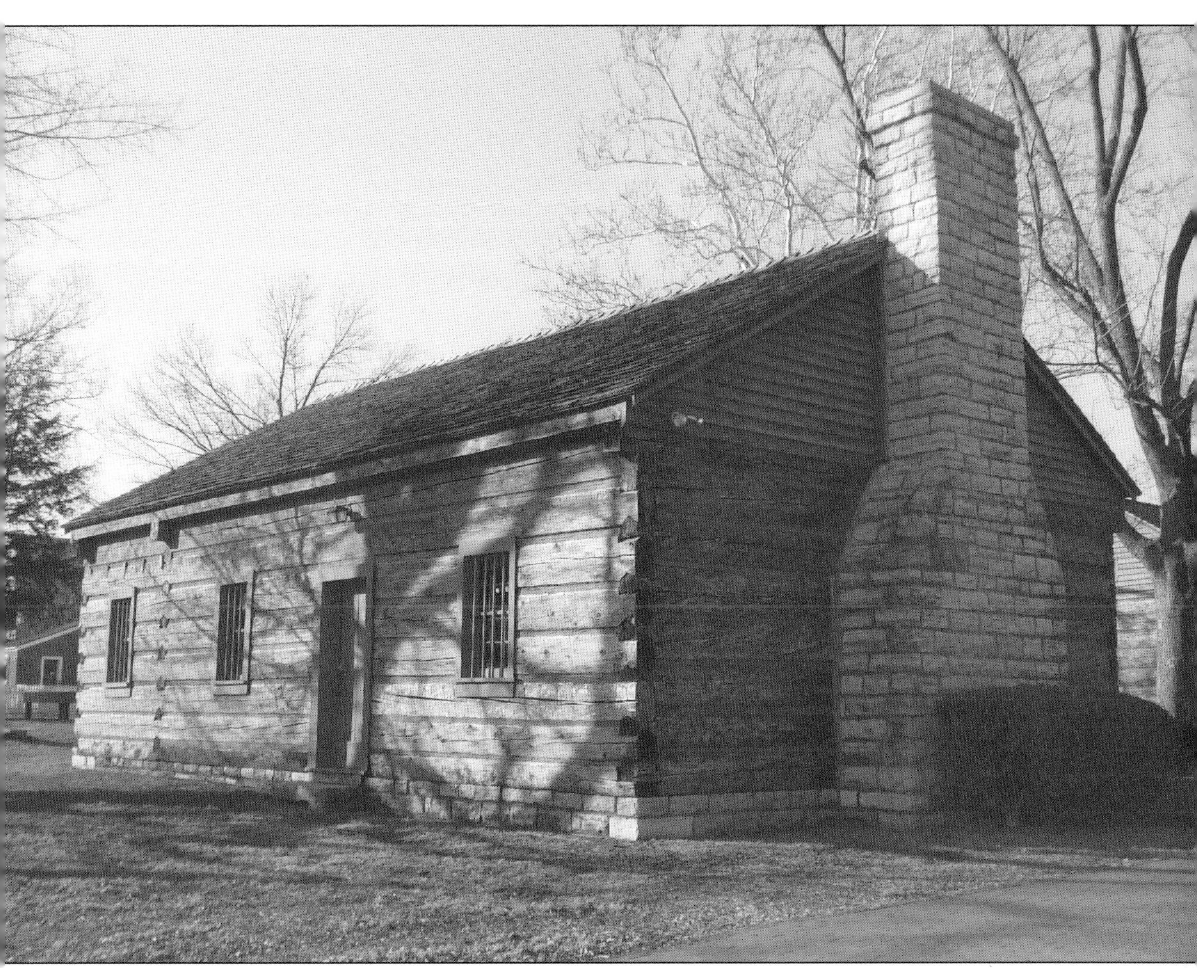

Virginia's Kentucky County became a district in 1783, and a supreme court for the district was established in nearby Harrodsburg on March 4 that year, with justices John Floyd and Samuel McDowell, father of surgeon Ephraim McDowell, presiding. However, accommodations at that location were not sufficient, and the District Court of Kentucky authorized Walker Daniel, attorney general, and John May, court clerk, to "make choice of a proper and safe place for holding their terms, somewhere in the neighborhood of John Crow's Station; and to employ persons to build a log Courthouse." While the log courthouse was being completed, court was held at Crow's Station. Upon completion of the Danville Courthouse, the court met there from March 14, 1785, until 1792. The replica pictured here stands on the site of the original building. (Author's personal collection.)

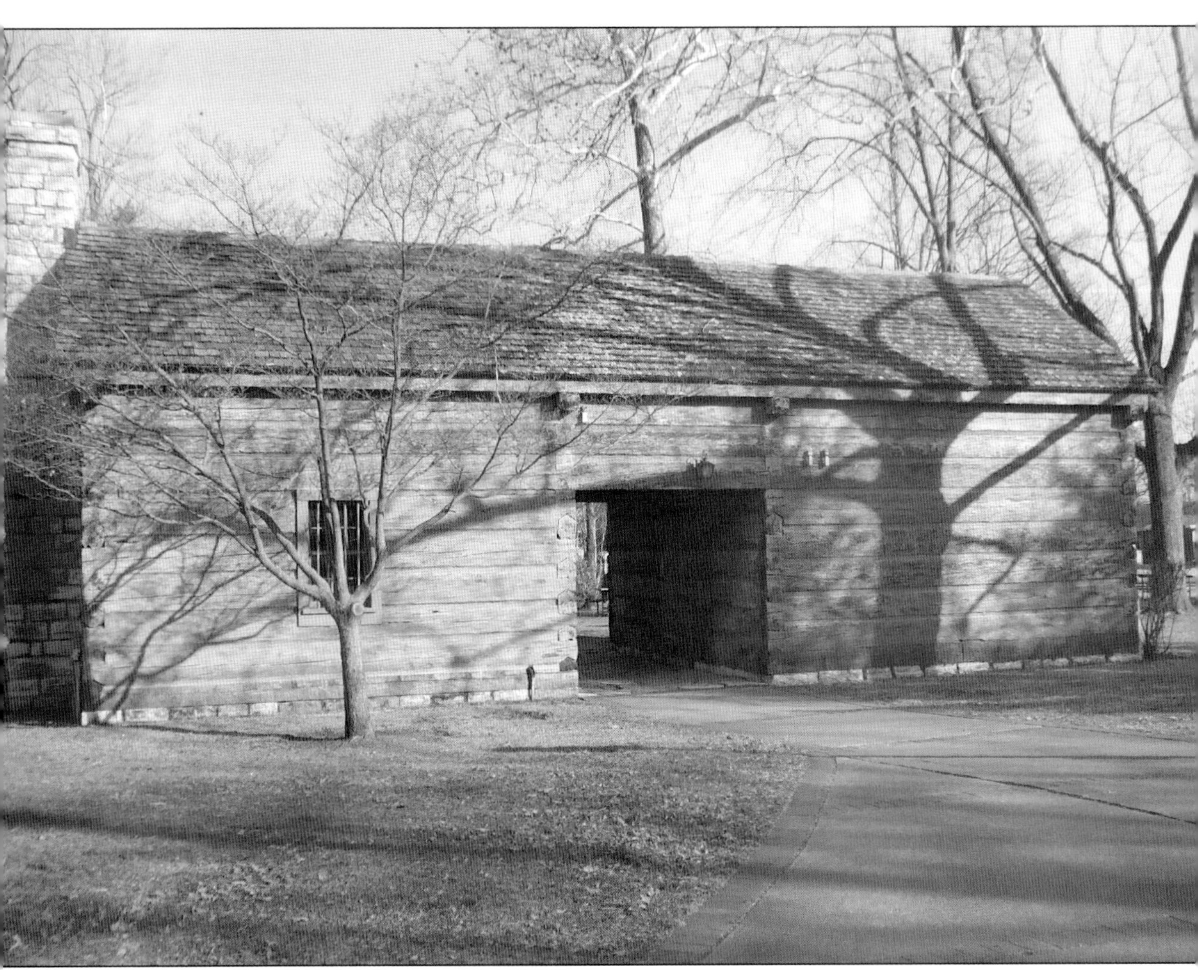

In the same order to attorney general Walker Daniel and court clerk John May to find a good location for a courthouse, the district court also asked that they ensure the construction of "a prison of hewed or sawed logs not less than nine inches thick." The jail was located near the center of the public square, close to the log courthouse. It included two rooms: one for debtors and one for other criminals. Rules for the jail were laid out in 1786 and stated that any man who was not imprisoned for treason or felony could freely leave the jail and stay within a 10-acre lot designated by surveyor Thomas Allin. Several taverns and the town spring were within the range that prisoners could wander, a concession for which many were surely grateful. This replica stands on the site of the original jail. (Author's personal collection.)

Built in 1785, Grayson's Tavern, the first tavern in Danville, was owned and operated by Benjamin Grayson. The first political club west of the Allegheny Mountains, the Danville Political Club, existed from 1786 until 1790 and often met in Grayson's to discuss political issues of the day. Unless they had an acceptable excuse, members were fined if they left a meeting early, arrived to one late, or missed it entirely; one such acceptable excuse was if a member had to be out of town to woo a woman. Including some of the most famous names in Danville—McDowell, Barbee, Speed, Todd, Muter, Greenup, and others—the club often discussed separation from the state of Virginia, and 11 of its members participated in at least one of the ten constitutional conventions that led to Kentucky's statehood in 1792. (Right, courtesy of Centre College Special Collections; below, author's personal collection.)

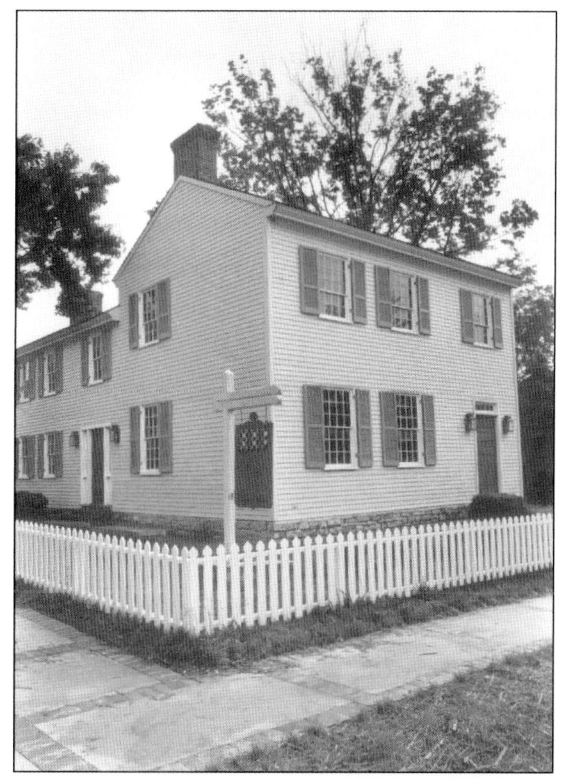

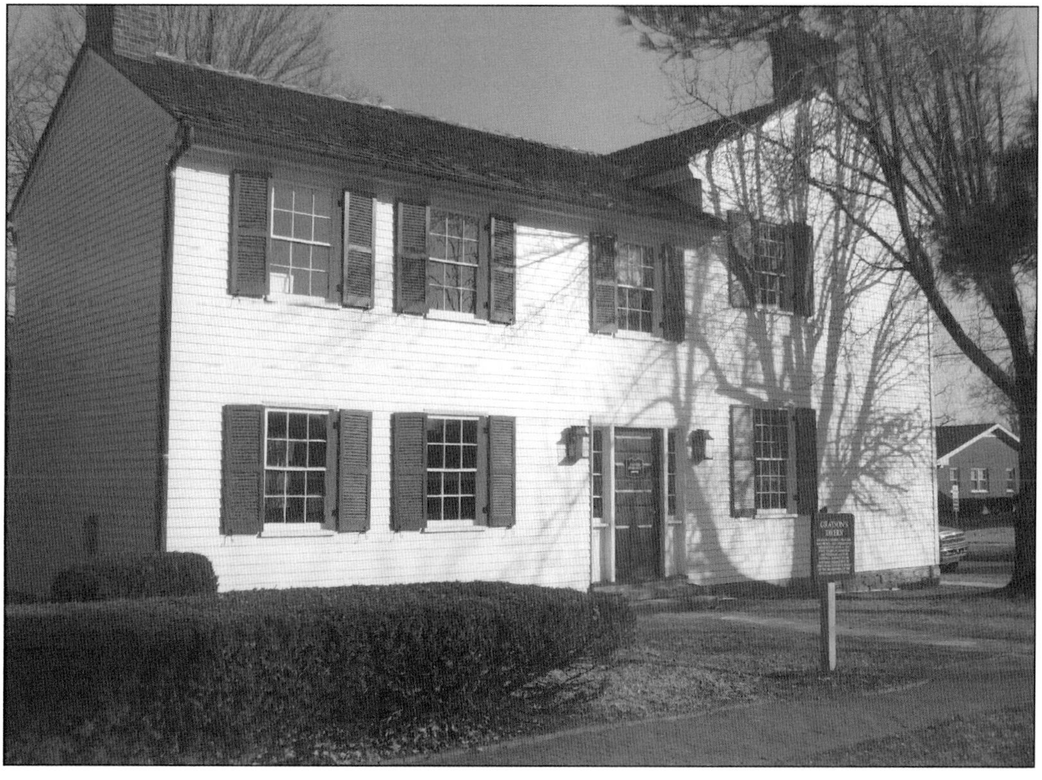

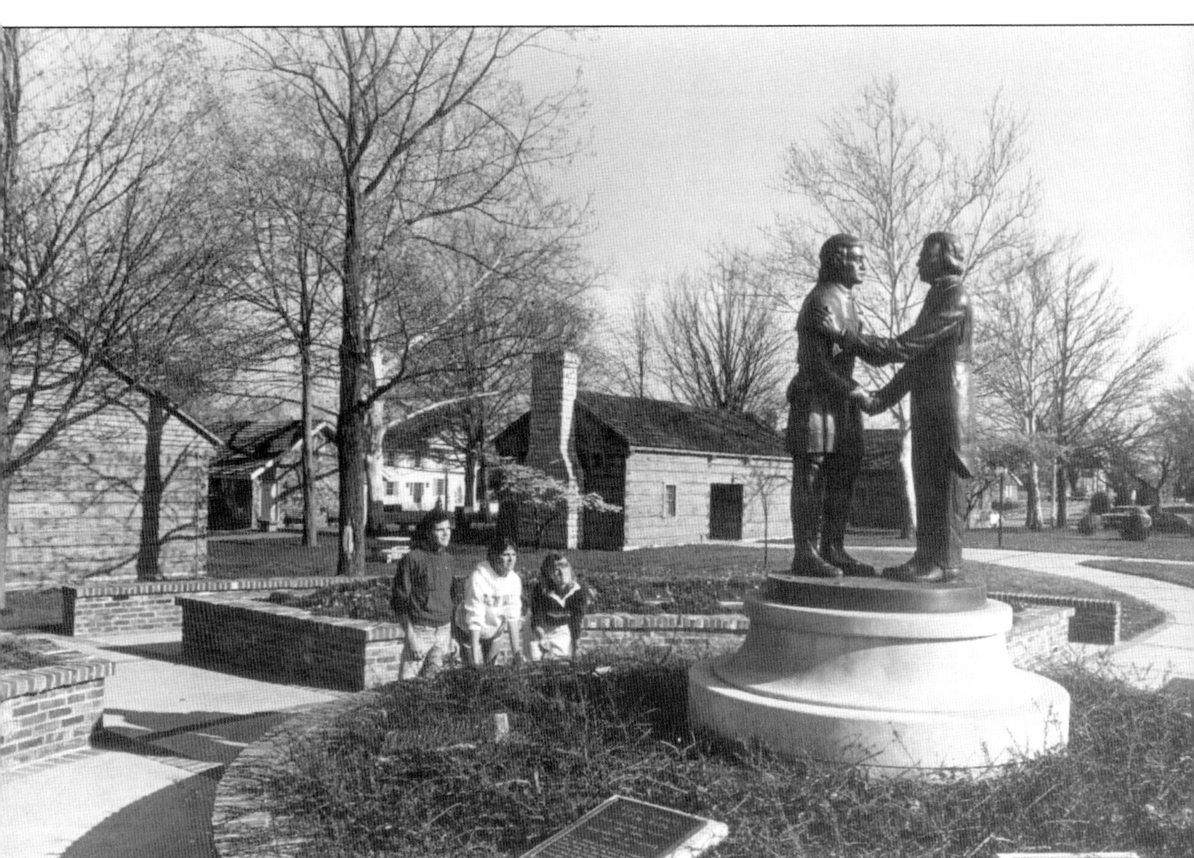

Three Centre College students stand next to the iconic statutes in Governor's Square at Constitution Square State Historic Site. Around the statues are bronze plaques honoring Kentucky's governors. Also visible in this photograph are a replica of the original Presbyterian meetinghouse (left), a replica of the first jail (center), and a replica of the courthouse (behind the two statues). (Courtesy of Centre College Special Collections.)

# *Two*

# City of Firsts

Danville's location on the well-traveled Wilderness Road allowed it to grow rapidly as a place where the educated and enlightened could flourish. These men and women established successful and prestigious schools that still stand today, founded a political club instrumental in Kentucky's statehood, and even performed a surgery that had never before been successfully completed. Danville was the first capital of Kentucky and held the first courthouse in the commonwealth. It was home to several firsts west of the Allegheny Mountains: the first post office, first political club, the first college (Transylvania University, the 16th oldest in the United States, now in Lexington, Kentucky), and the oldest continually used campus and administrative building, at Centre College. Danville also had the first Presbyterian church in Kentucky, and the Kentucky School for the Deaf was the first state-sponsored school of its type. Dr. Ephraim McDowell made medical history when he operated on Jane Todd Crawford in his Danville home, removing an abdominal tumor in a surgery that had never been successfully attempted. These historical benchmarks and others have cemented Danville's role as a "City of Firsts."

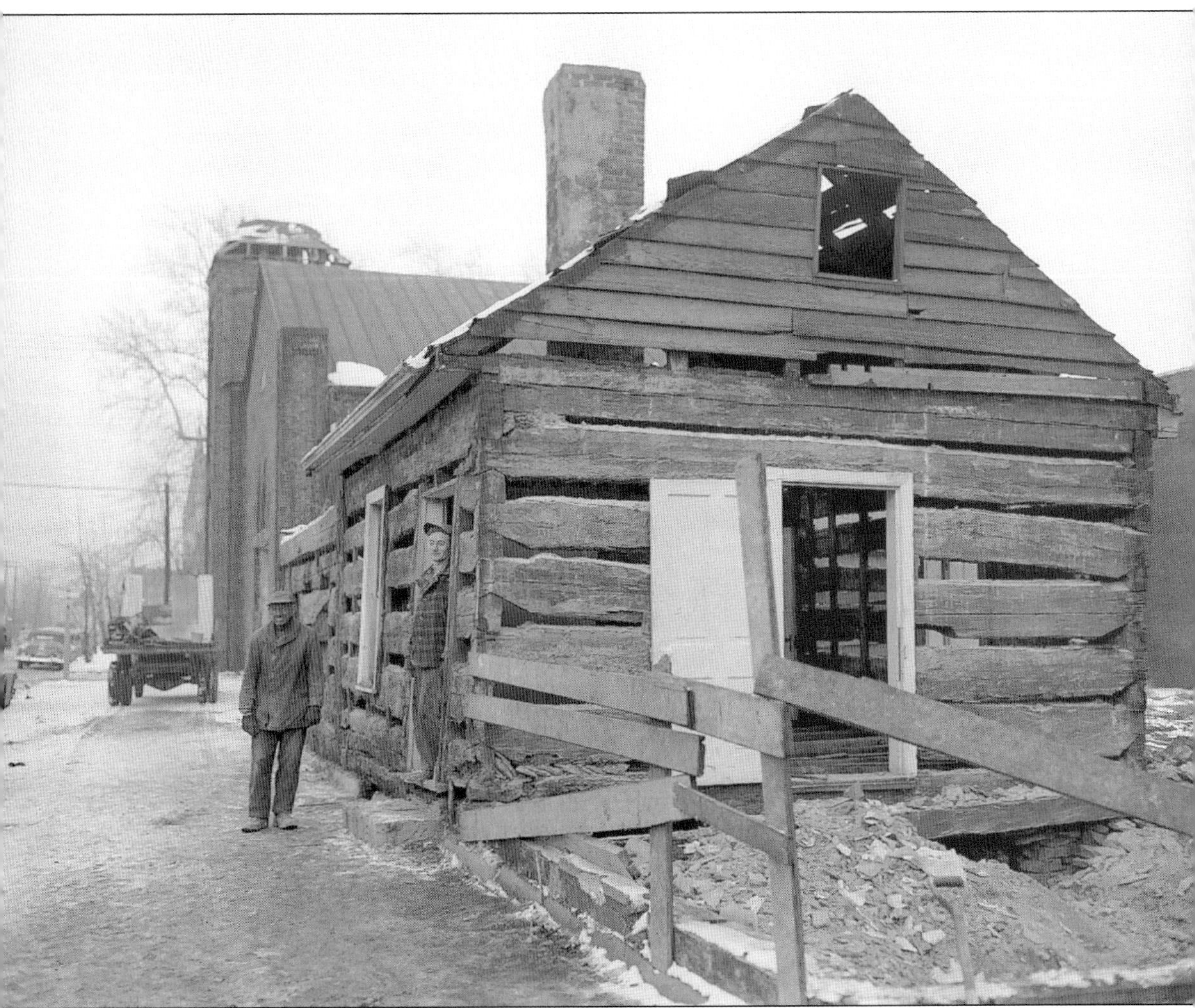

Constructed in 1792, this log building served as the first post office west of the Allegheny Mountains. Thomas Barbee was appointed the first postmaster, and the first mail was received on November 3, 1792. Several other famous Danville residents served as postmaster over the years, including Ephraim McDowell, who ran the post office out of the back room of his apothecary shop from 1799 to 1801. The post office was located on Walnut Street, and was even used at one point as a home for nurses who worked at the Ephraim McDowell Hospital, named for the famous surgeon. The post office was eventually moved to its current location on Constitution Square in 1931, where it has been renovated and decorated to look as it did in 1792. (Courtesy of Guy Ingram.)

This postcard (right) is of a daguerreotype of Jane Todd Crawford, the "pioneer patient." In December 1809, Crawford made a 60-mile journey through the Kentucky wilderness to Danville in order to receive surgery for a life-threatening tumor in her abdomen. Her doctor, Ephraim McDowell (below), was a famed physician in his time; he performed surgery on Crawford in 25 minutes without antisepsis or anesthesia, which would not be introduced until the 1840s. He successfully removed a 22.5-pound tumor from her abdomen, and Crawford made a complete recovery, living for another 32 years after her surgery. This was the first successful surgery of its type in the history of medicine, and Dr. McDowell became known as the "Father of Abdominal Surgery." (Both courtesy of the McDowell House Museum.)

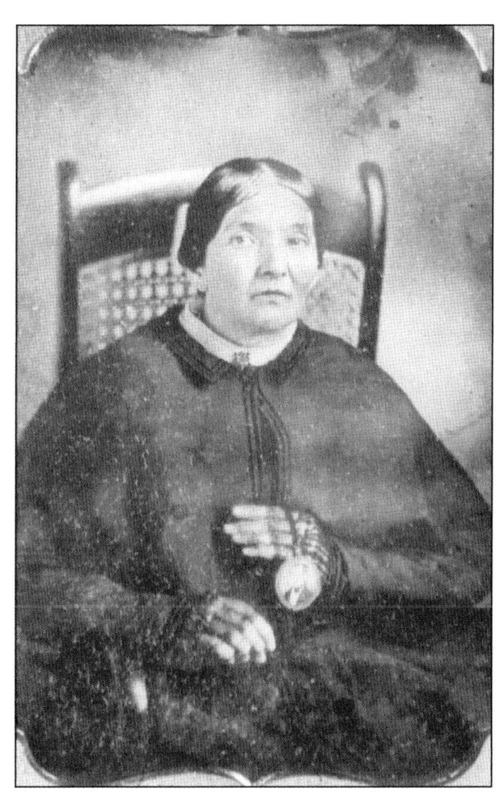

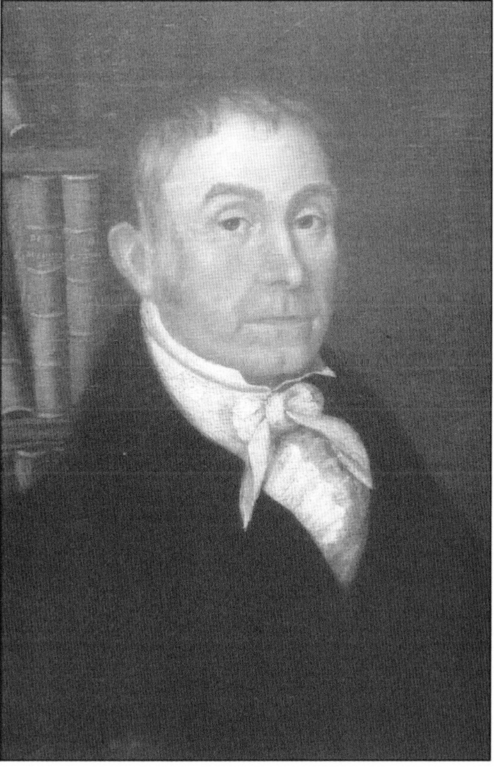

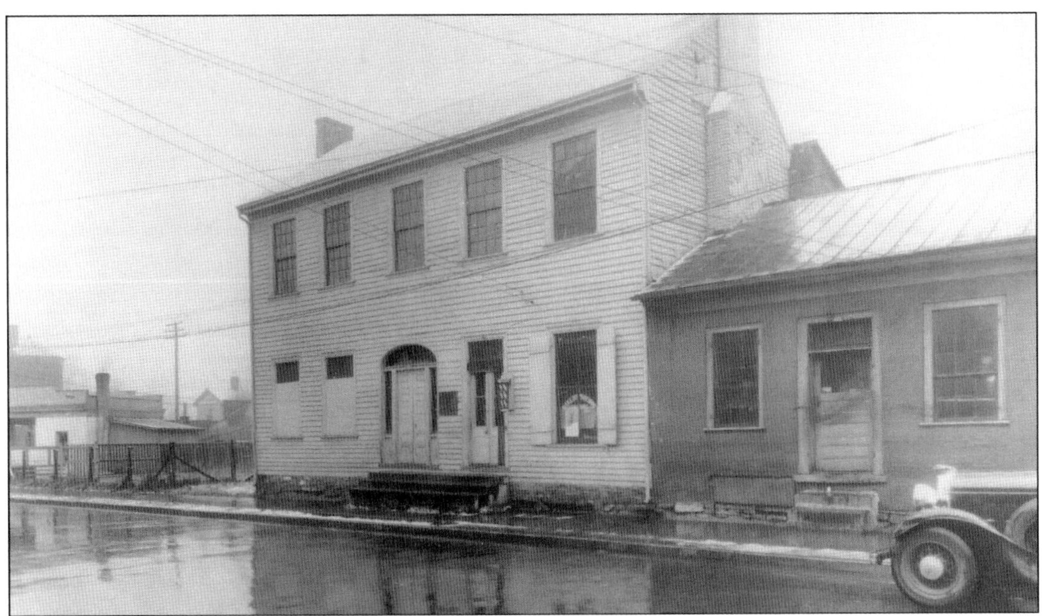

After Ephraim McDowell passed away in 1830, his wife, Sarah, sold the house and moved to their summer residence, Cambus Kenneth, several miles outside of Danville. Over the next 100 years, the house passed through many hands: it was home to a Centre College president, served as a Methodist parsonage, housed 12 families as a boarding house, and was even used as a shoe-shining shop, a barbershop, and a restaurant. The undated picture above, taken before the late 1930s, shows the state of the house prior to restoration by the WPA. An earlier photograph (below) shows a barber's pole as well as a sign above the front door advertising the restaurant inside that reads, "Meals at All Hours." (Both courtesy of the McDowell House Museum.)

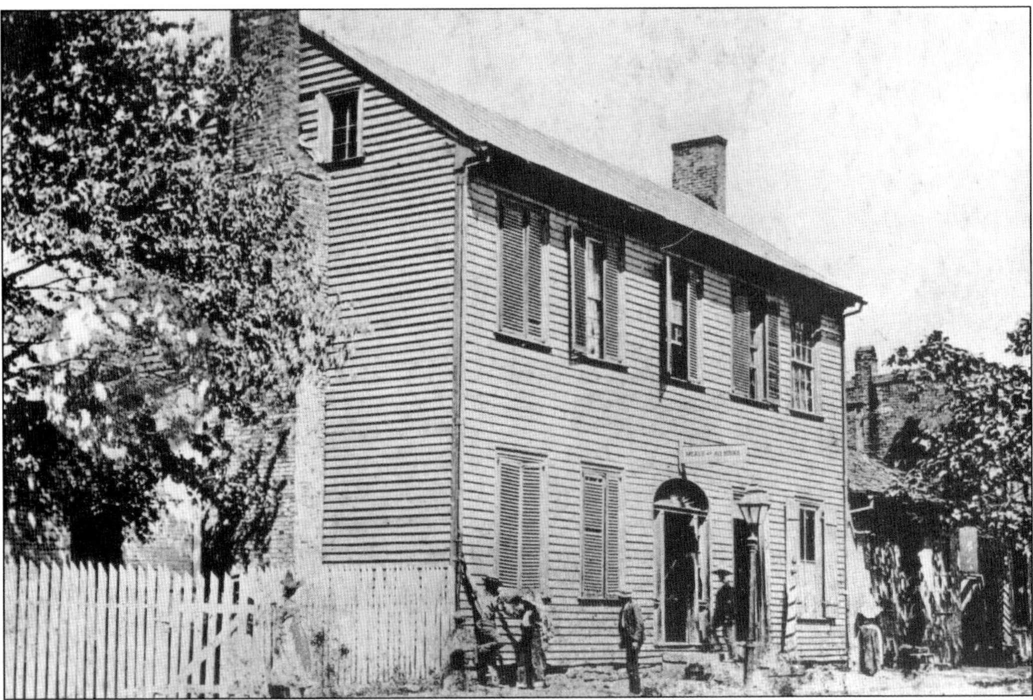

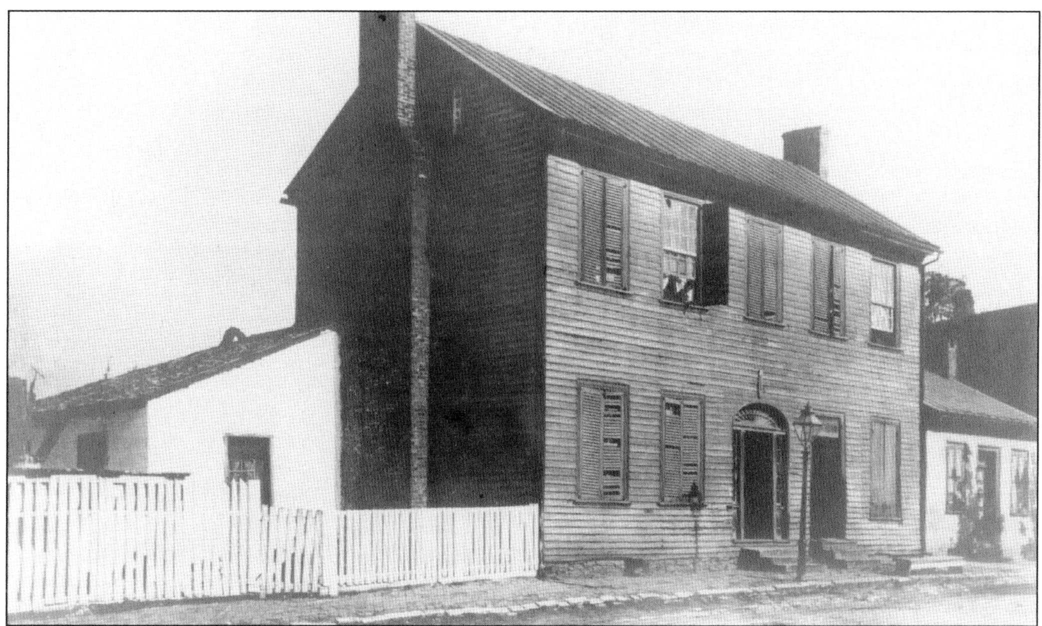

In the late 1930s, WPA workers came to the McDowell House, which had been badly damaged by decades of misuse by its residents. The room in which Ephraim McDowell's famed surgery took place was used as an ash dump for the upstairs fireplaces, and a hole was burned through its floor. Souvenir-seekers had grabbed pieces of the chair rails to make gavels for medical societies, and holes were punched through the walls for stovepipes. The state of the home and apothecary shop prior to renovation (above) left the state of Kentucky with a lot of work to do before being able to turn it into a museum in 1939. Pictured in 1973 (below), the house and apothecary shop look as they did when the McDowell family lived there. (Both courtesy of the McDowell House Museum.)

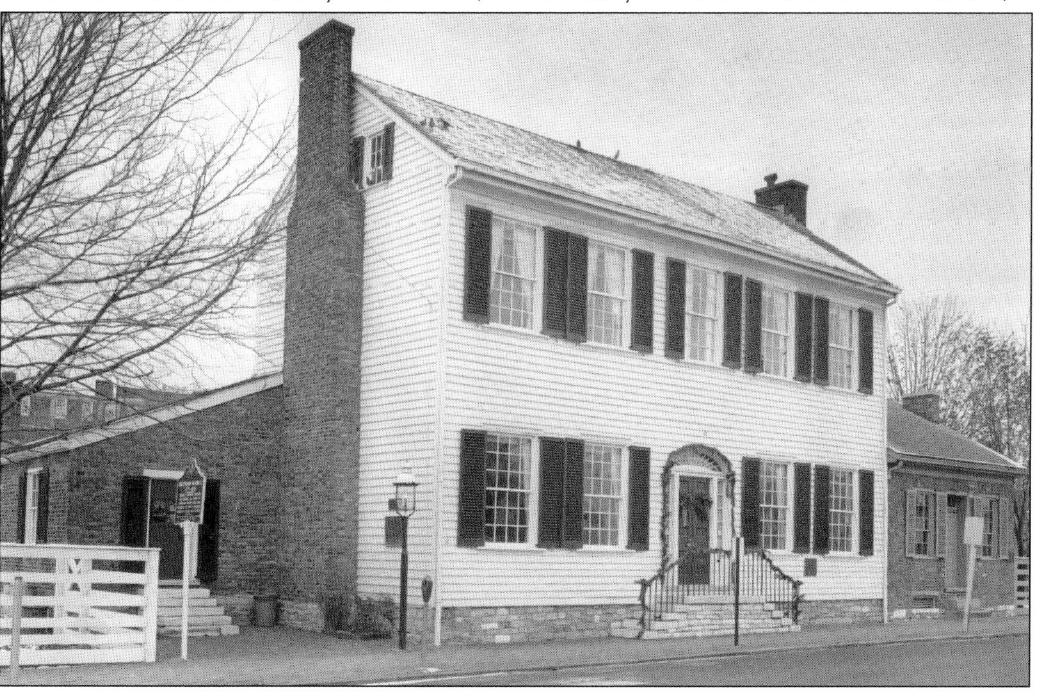

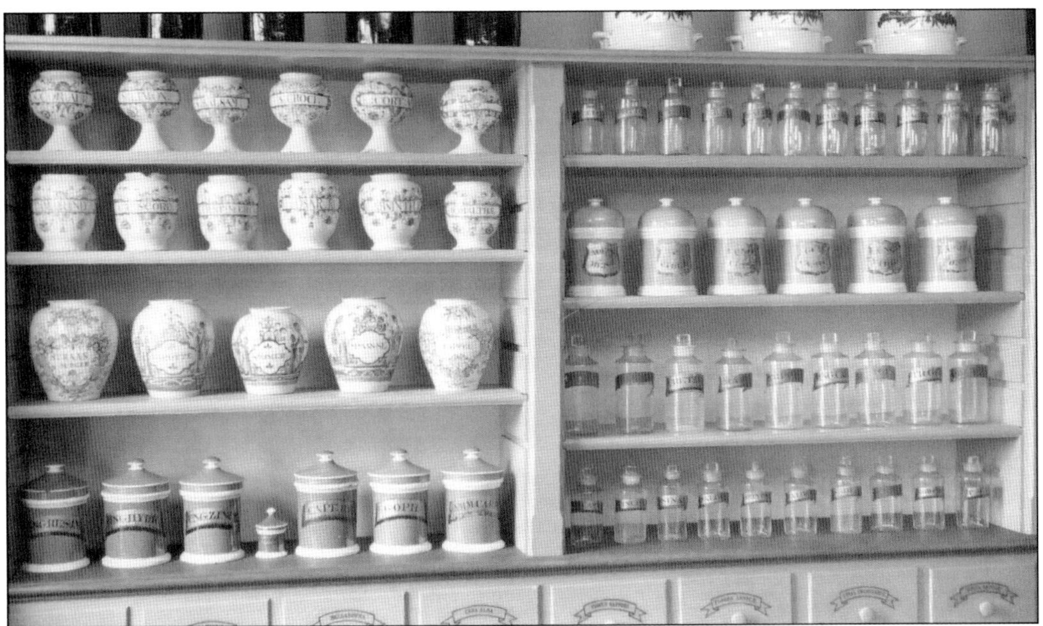

When Ephraim McDowell returned from his studies at the University of Edinburgh in Scotland in 1795, he opened an apothecary shop with a partner, Adam Rankin. He eventually took sole ownership of the business, and ran it, a small medical office, and even the post office out of the building for a number of years. After McDowell passed away in 1830, the apothecary shop passed from owner to owner, serving as a pool hall in the beginning of the 20th century. While McDowell's house was purchased by the Kentucky Medical Association and turned into a museum in 1939, his apothecary shop was not purchased and restored until the late 1950s. It is now a part of the McDowell House Museum. (Both courtesy of the McDowell House Museum.)

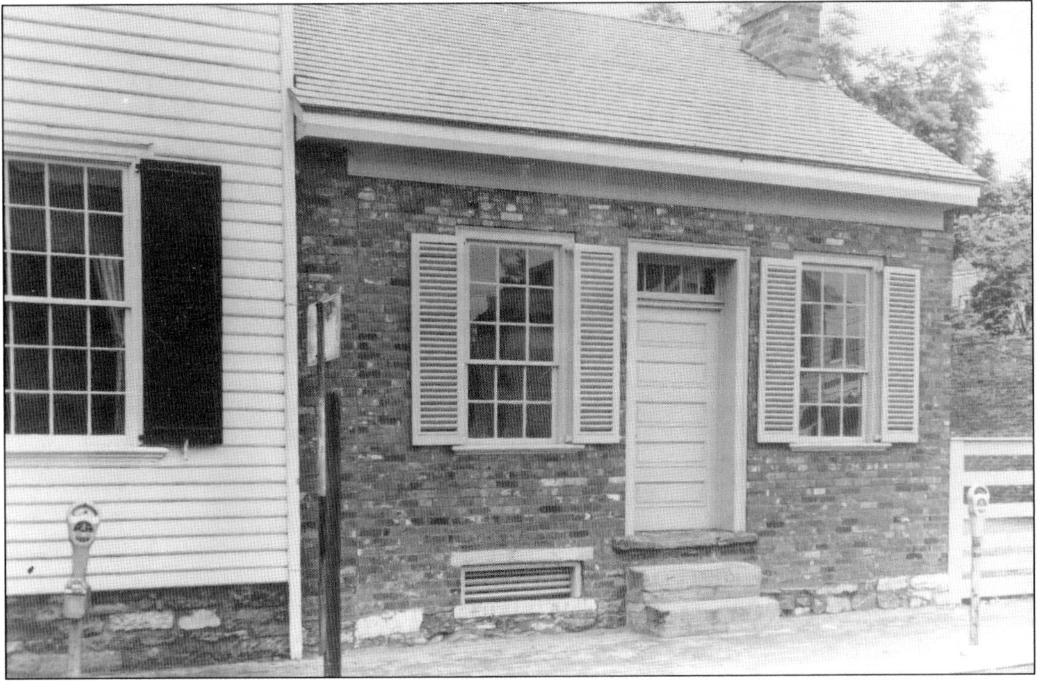

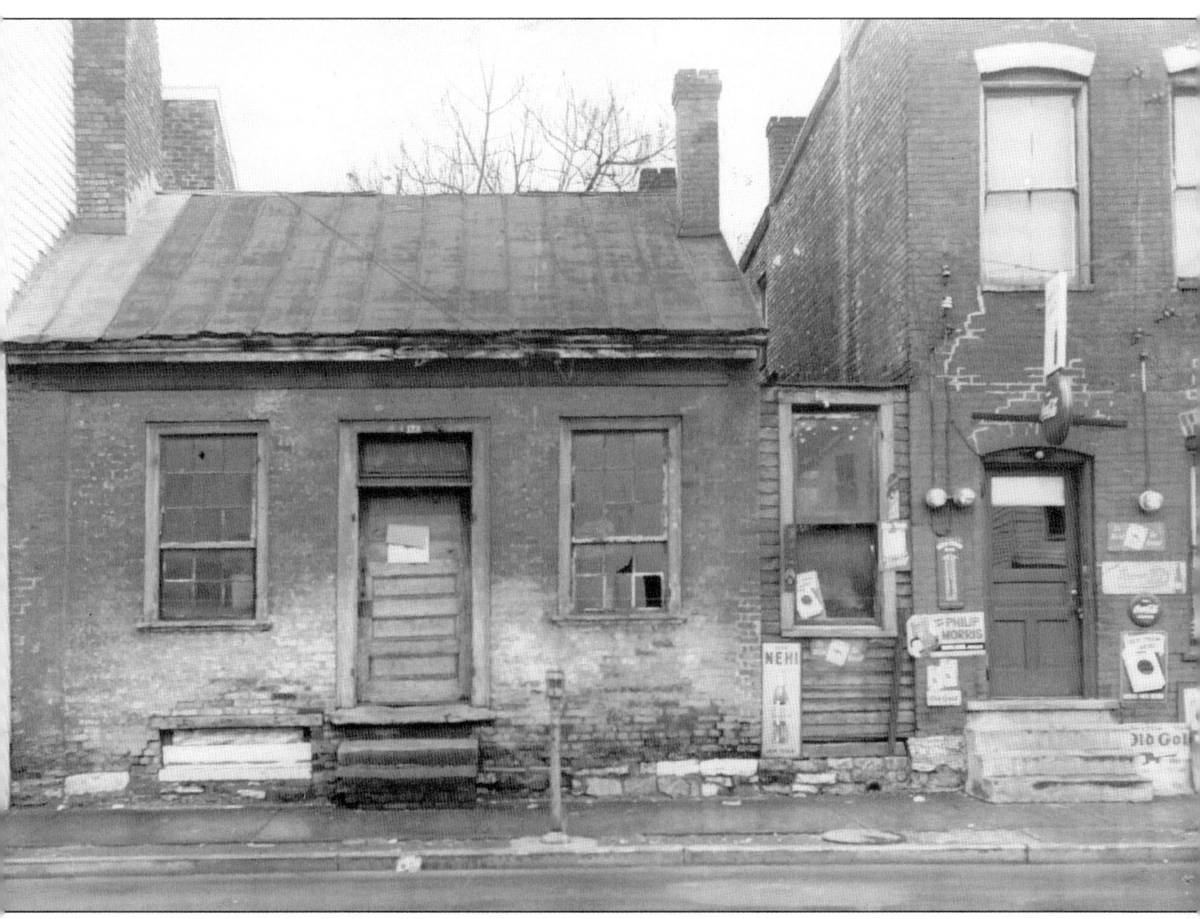


This undated photograph shows Ephraim McDowell's apothecary in a dilapidated state around the time it served as a pool hall. The building on the right was torn down, and the empty lot that remained was turned into an apothecary garden such as McDowell would have used to supply his store. Herbs would be taken from the garden, hung to dry, ground with a mortar and pestle, mixed into a malleable dough-like substance, pushed through a pill device to create equal-sized pieces, and then molded into pill form and sold to customers. An archaeological survey completed with assistance from the University of Kentucky and the Governor's Scholars program of Centre College in 2006 unearthed over 200 years' worth of artifacts. Medicine bottles, buttons, Coca-Cola bottles, brandy bottles, and even dolls were excavated in this dig. (Courtesy of the McDowell House Museum.)

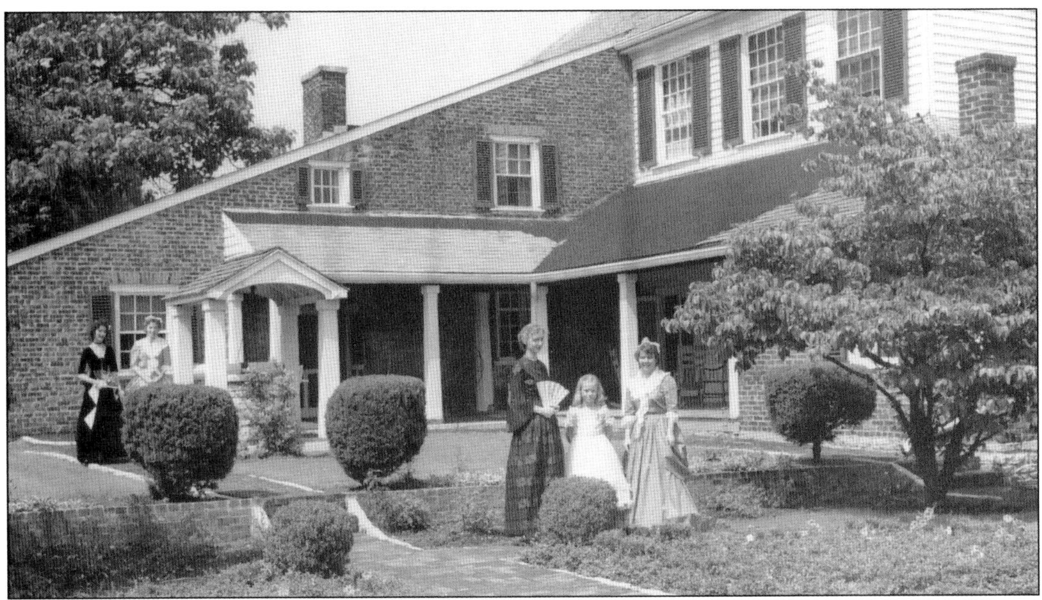

Five women pose in the McDowell House formal garden in this undated photograph. The garden was installed in 1820 for Sarah Shelby McDowell, Dr. Ephraim McDowell's wife and the daughter of Kentucky's first and fifth governor, Isaac Shelby. The three stages of house construction are visible in this image: the slanted brick building on the left was constructed in the mid-1790s, the white wooden clapboard section was added in 1803 and 1804, and the brick office, obscured by a tree on the right, was built in 1820. (Courtesy of the McDowell House Museum.)

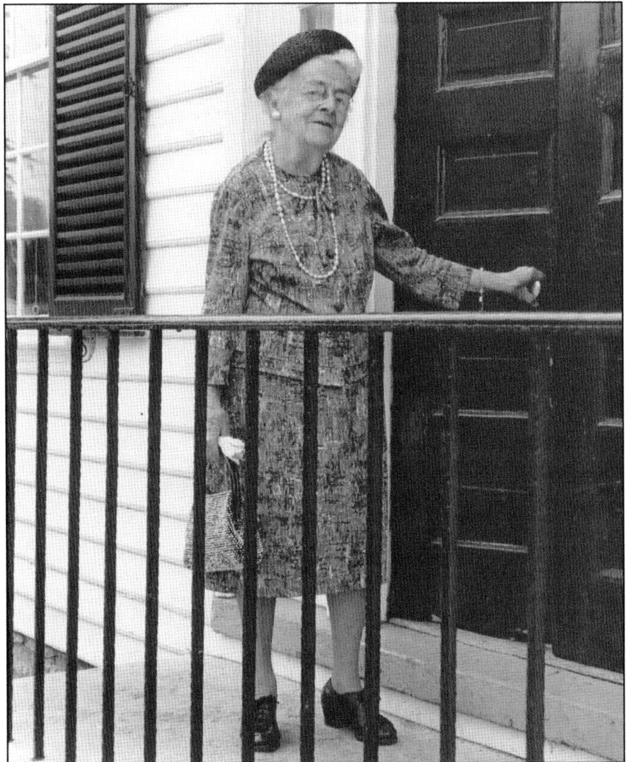

The great-granddaughter of Ephraim McDowell, 91-year-old "Willie" Shelby, stands at the front door of the McDowell House in this 1969 photograph. Willie was the daughter of Florence McDowell Shelby, whose father was William Wallace McDowell. Over the span of 22 years, the McDowells had nine children: Susannah Hart, Isaac Shelby, Mary Thompson, William Wallace, Adeline, Catherine, Sarah Letitia, Sally Ann Clay, and Alfred. Of these children, only Susannah, Mary, William, Adeline, and Catherine survived to adulthood. (Courtesy of the McDowell House Museum.)

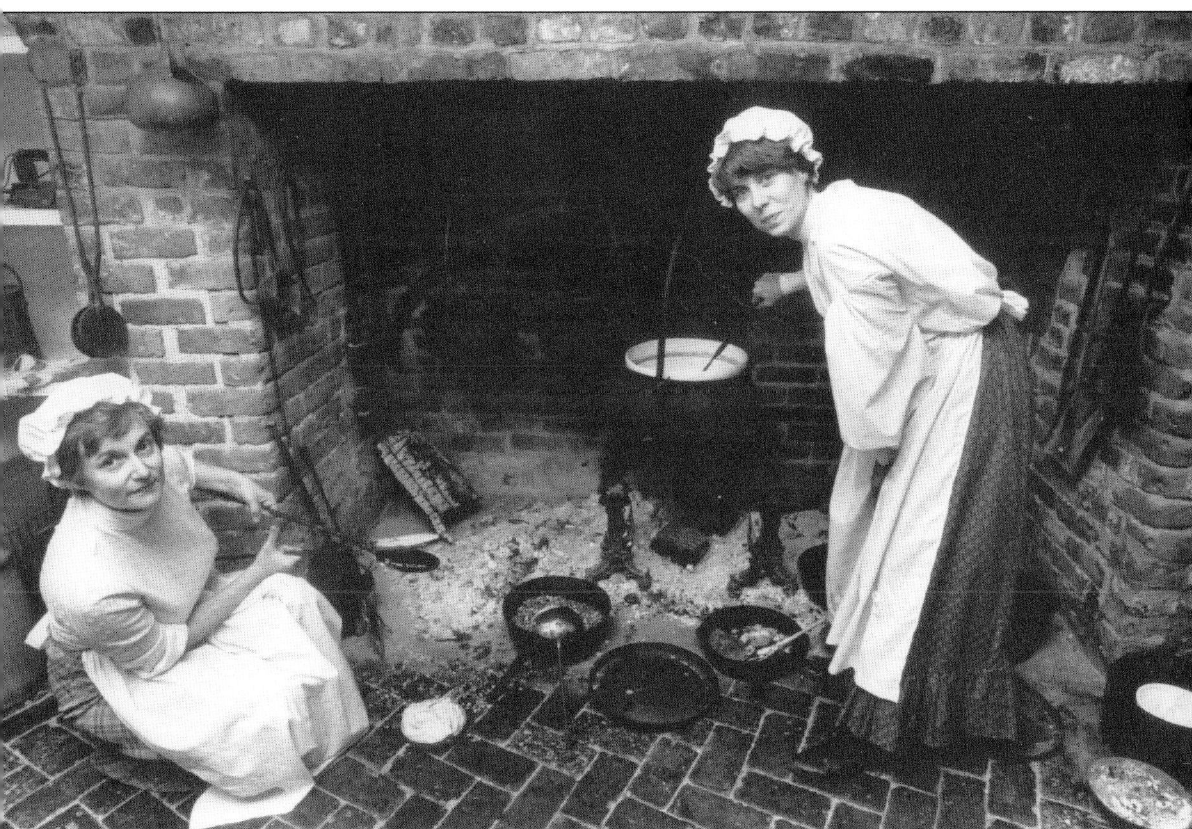

Susan Nimocks (left) and Gloria Martin are hard at work in the McDowell House kitchen preparing a meal for guests of the museum. The kitchen was often used in lessons to teach visitors how 18th-century cooking was done over an open fire. When the McDowell House was turned into a boardinghouse for 12 families after Ephraim McDowell passed away in 1830, one family chose the kitchen for its living quarters. The large fireplace proved too drafty for this family, who bricked it over; when the Works Progress Administration came to restore the house in the late 1930s, museum legend states that they tore down the brick wall and discovered pots and pans still in their original locations in the fireplace. (Courtesy of the McDowell House Museum.)

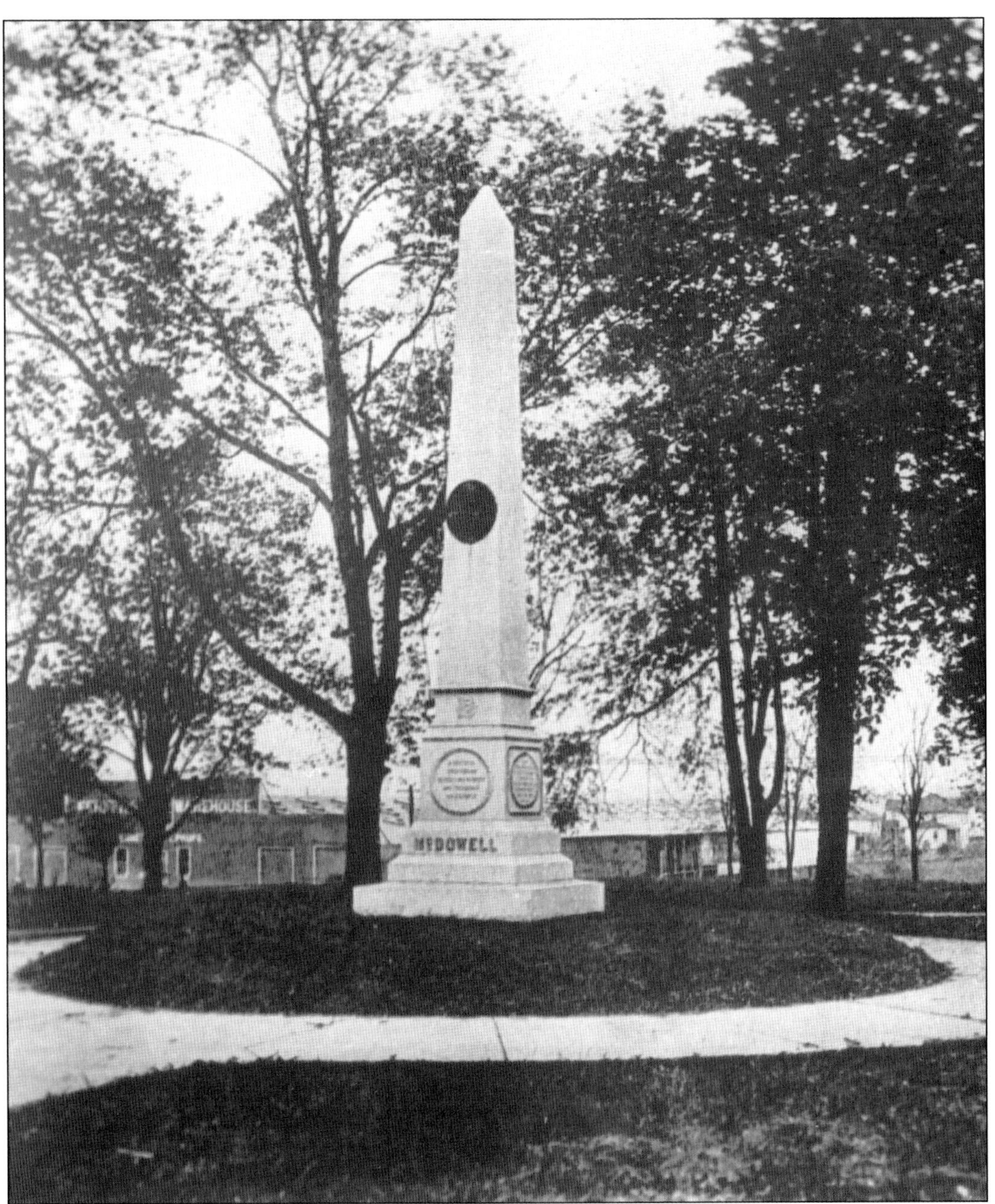


In 1879, forty-nine years after Ephraim McDowell passed away, the Kentucky Medical Association honored the doctor with a monument next to the First Presbyterian Church. McDowell and his wife were moved from their original resting place at Isaac Shelby's estate, Traveler's Rest, and reinterred at what is now known as McDowell Park. The Kentucky Medical Association took an integral role in restoring the McDowell House. In 1935, the association purchased the home, deeded it to the state to be restored by the WPA, and received the property back in 1948. The Women's Auxiliary to the medical association worked hard to refurnish the house with both original McDowell pieces and furniture from the early 19th century. The Kentucky Medical Association also dedicated a monument to Jane Todd Crawford that is now situated in the McDowell House gardens. (Courtesy of the McDowell House Museum.)

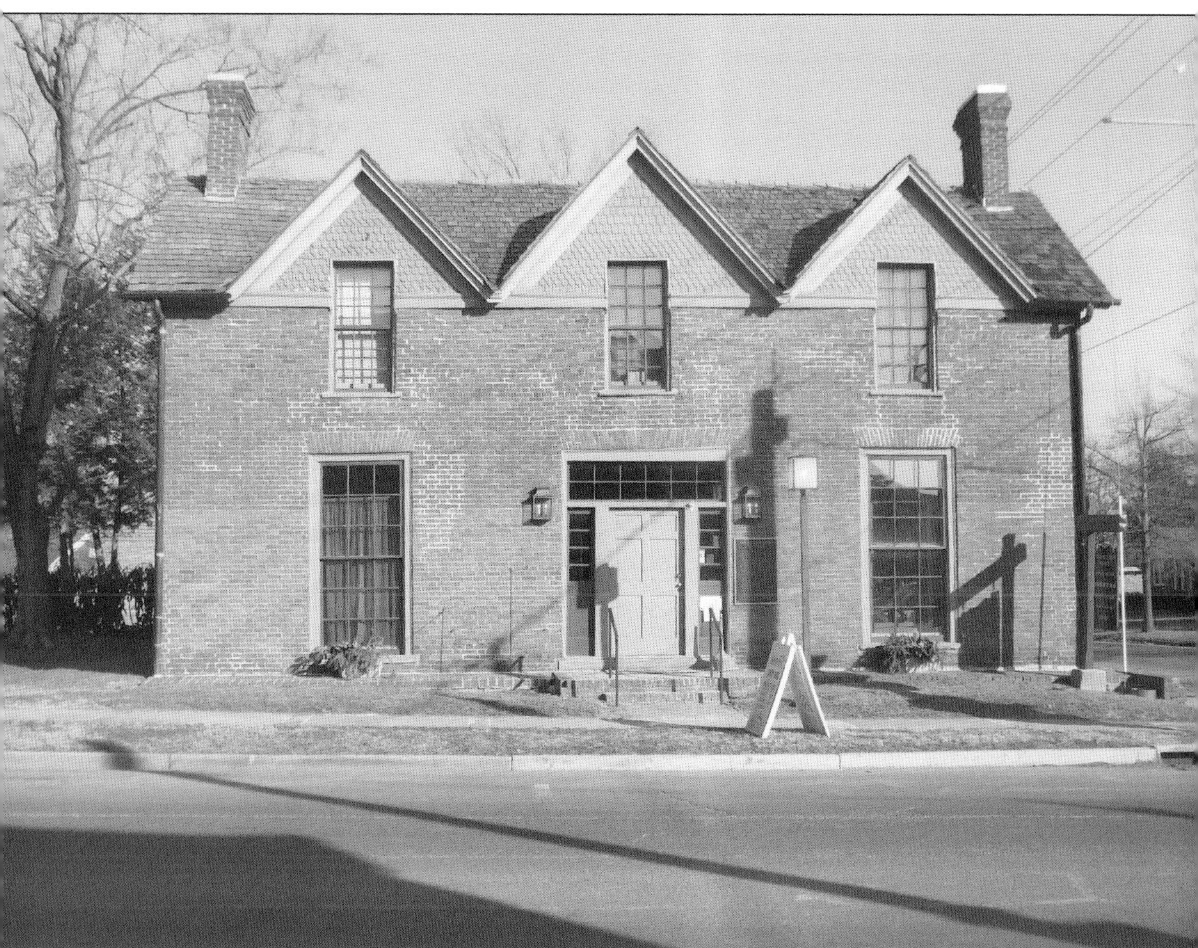

Ephraim McDowell did not undertake his historic surgery alone; his nephew James McDowell, apprentice Alban Goldsmith, and likely two other doctors assisted McDowell. On Christmas Day 1809, McDowell and his assistants brought a kitchen table into the bedroom where they were operating and placed Jane Todd Crawford on top of it. Through the duration of the 25-minute surgery, Crawford had a handkerchief over her face, singing hymns and reciting psalms to keep herself distracted. Antiseptics and anesthesia had yet to be discovered, and nowhere in McDowell's meticulous notes on the surgery did he mention giving her anything to dull the pain. Goldsmith, a pupil of McDowell's and later a notable doctor in his own right, built this brick house across the street from his instructor around 1820. It currently houses the Constitution Square Museum's gift shop. (Author's personal collection.)

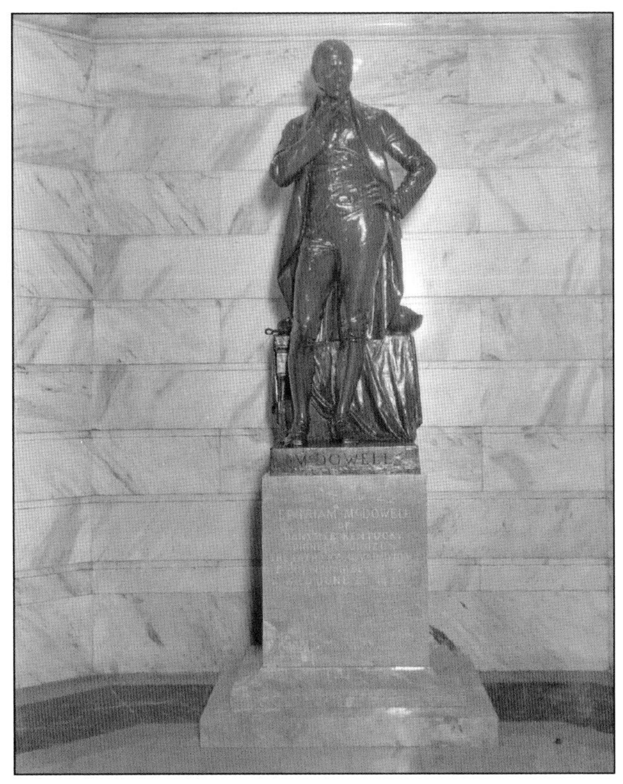

In the US Capitol, statues of famous men and women are on display, representing the best and brightest sons and daughters of each state. Kentucky is represented by Ephraim McDowell, the Father of Abdominal Surgery, and Henry Clay, the "Great Compromiser." A copy of the McDowell statue, sculpted by artist Charles Niehaus, sits in the rotunda of the Kentucky State Capitol in Frankfort (left). Ephraim McDowell's likeness joined the statues of other famous Kentuckians, Abraham Lincoln, Jefferson Davis, Alben Barkley, and Henry Clay, in a dedication ceremony (below). (Both courtesy of the McDowell House Museum.)

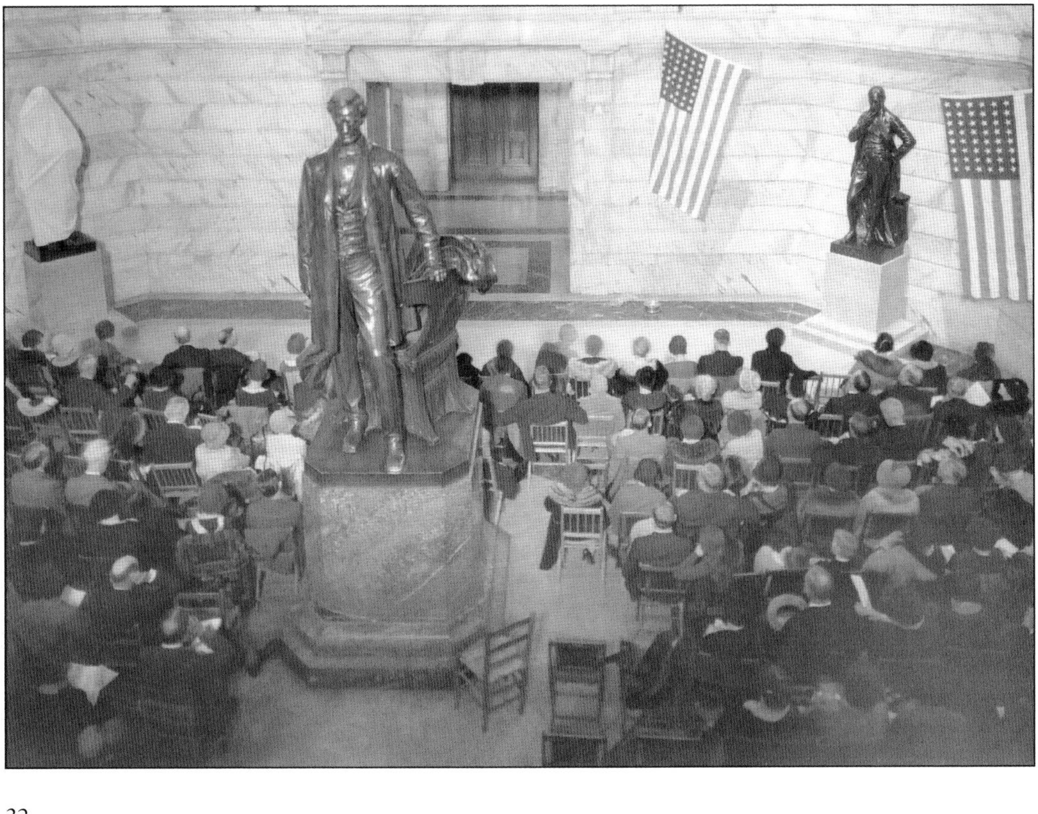

# *Three*

# Houses of Worship

In its earliest days, Danville citizens felt a need for organized religion. Presbyterian minister David Rice had been asked by residents to move permanently to the small settlement, but he refused to do so until he "received a written call by a substantial number of sincerely religious people." He received a petition with 300 names on it, including key pioneer families such as the McDowells, the Irvines, the Shelbys, the Caldwells, and the Cowans. Rice organized the Concord congregation in Danville in 1784, holding services at the meetinghouse in the public square. Since then, churches from other denominations have made their marks on Danville—Catholic, Baptist, Methodist, Episcopalian, and more. Many of the original church structures still stand today, and some are even in use as their original purposes. When fires devastated their places of worship, or religious schisms caused a divide in a congregation, devout Danville residents would find other places to convene, including private homes, the county courthouse, and even an out-of-use jail. To this day, the faithful in Danville are an integral part of the community, and their church histories have an everlasting presence in the collective memory of this town.

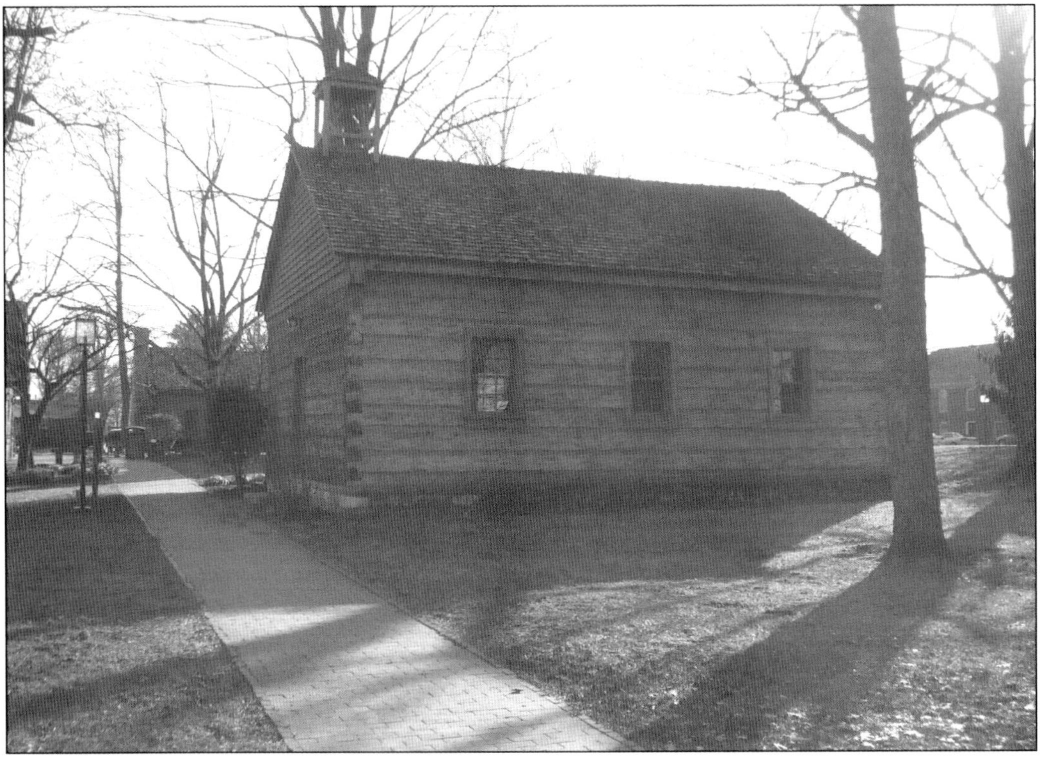

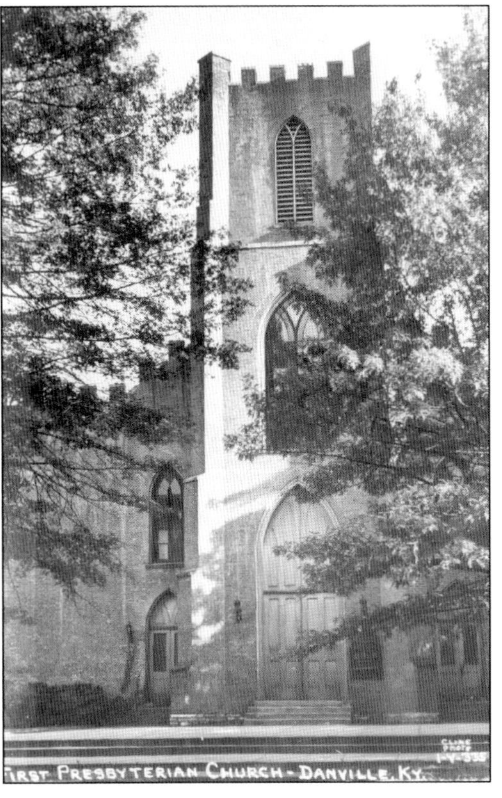


In the spring of 1784, David Rice, a Presbyterian minister from Hanover County, Virginia, organized congregations in Danville, Cane Run, and the Forks of Dix River. His Danville congregation was given the name Concord, and worshipers gathered in a log meetinghouse (replica above) on Constitution Square; this was reputed to be the first house of Presbyterian worship in Kentucky. In 1831, the congregation moved to a new place of worship at the corner of Fifth and Main Streets, at the location where the present-day First Presbyterian Church stands (left). (Above, author's personal collection; left, courtesy of Michael Wiser.)

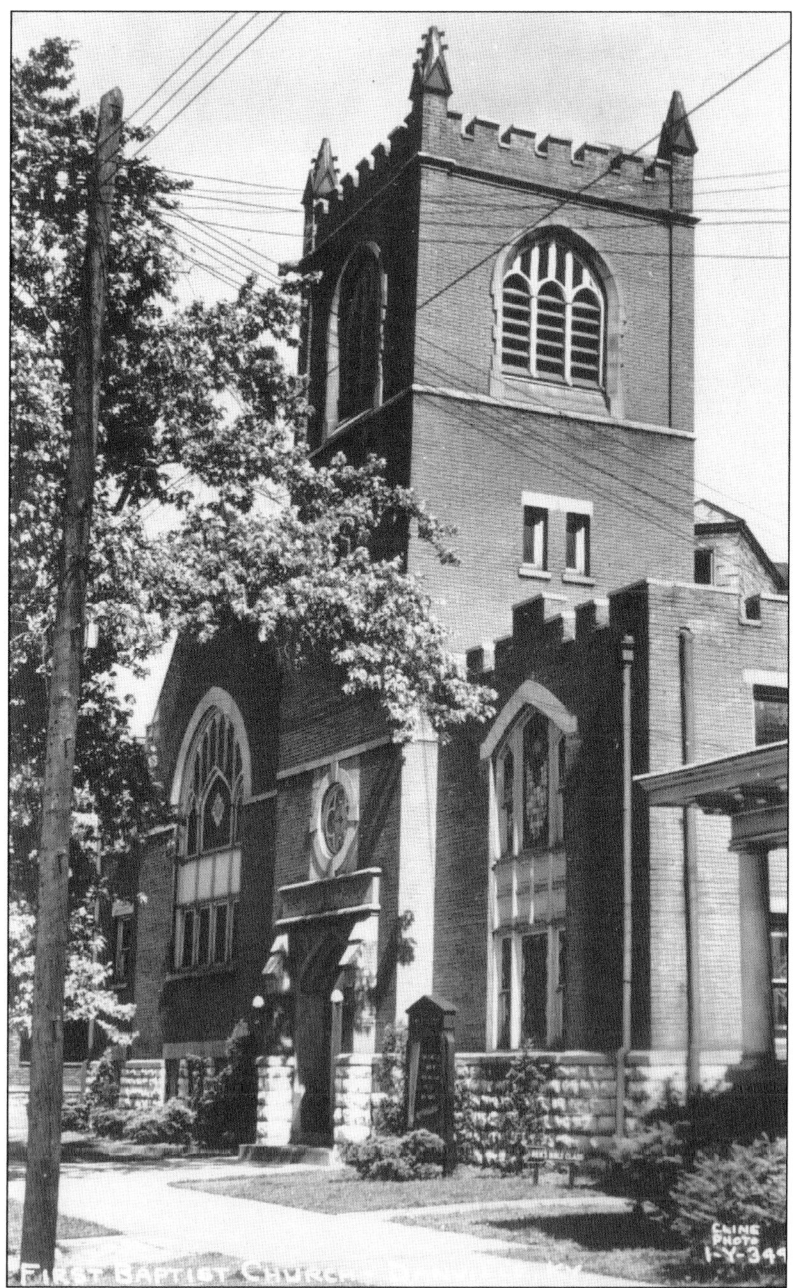

In 1823, nine Baptist parishioners convened at a local home and organized the First Baptist Church, selecting elder Thomas Hand to be their pastor. The group purchased land on Broadway Street, and a small log cabin was built there to hold services. A larger brick building was later constructed with two sets of doors, one for men and one for women. In 1861, the church opened the Baptist Female Seminary, and in 1881, the brick building burned down, and a new church was constructed within a year. Between the 1920s and the 1950s, seven Baptist churches opened in Danville. In 2000, the First Baptist congregation relocated to a larger facility, and the church was sold to the Danville Public Library and demolished to make way for an expansion. (Courtesy of Michael Wiser.)

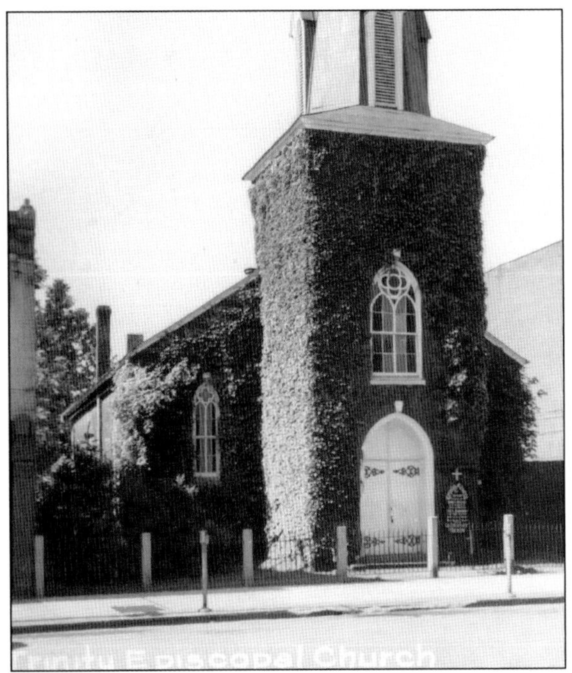


In 1829, eight laymen and a minister met to discuss creating an Episcopal church in Danville. At this meeting, famed local physician Ephraim McDowell introduced a resolution to organize a parish, given the name Trinity Episcopal in the week after Trinity Sunday. The congregation initially met in the old stone jail in town, which was no longer in use at that point, and then moved into its current building in 1831. The church was gutted in the fire of 1860, but it was rebuilt almost immediately using plans that transformed it into a Gothic Revival structure. In 1862, Trinity Episcopal, along with many other churches and buildings in town, served as a hospital for casualties from the nearby Battle of Perryville. The building is the oldest continually used church in Danville. (Courtesy of Michael Wiser.)

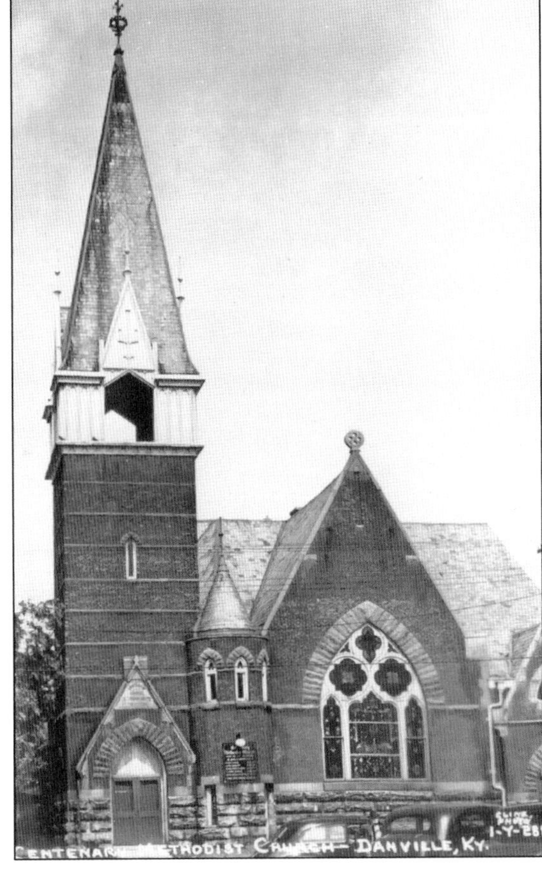

The first Methodists in Danville met around 1789 in a small log cabin at the location of the church's present-day downtown site, on the corner of Third and Walnut Streets. A small brick church was built nearby in 1835 but proved too small for the growing congregation; the church pictured here was constructed in 1888 and is still in use today. (Courtesy of Michael Wiser.)

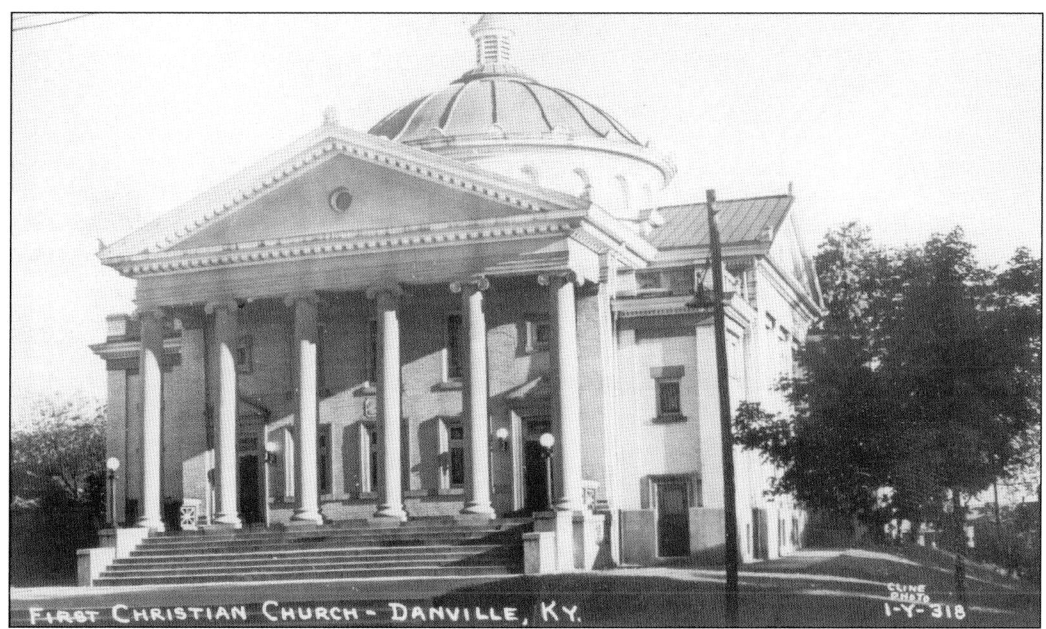


The original First Christian Church was built in 1847 with Rev. Curtis Smith as its first pastor. When it was destroyed in the 1860 fire that devastated much of Danville, the congregation built a new church at the corner of Fourth and Walnut Streets in the late 1860s. In 1914, the building was sold and turned into an apartment complex, and the congregation moved into a new Main Street location (pictured here). The building stood until burning down in 1965, and the First Christian Church now meets at its current location on Lexington Avenue. (Courtesy of Michael Wiser.)

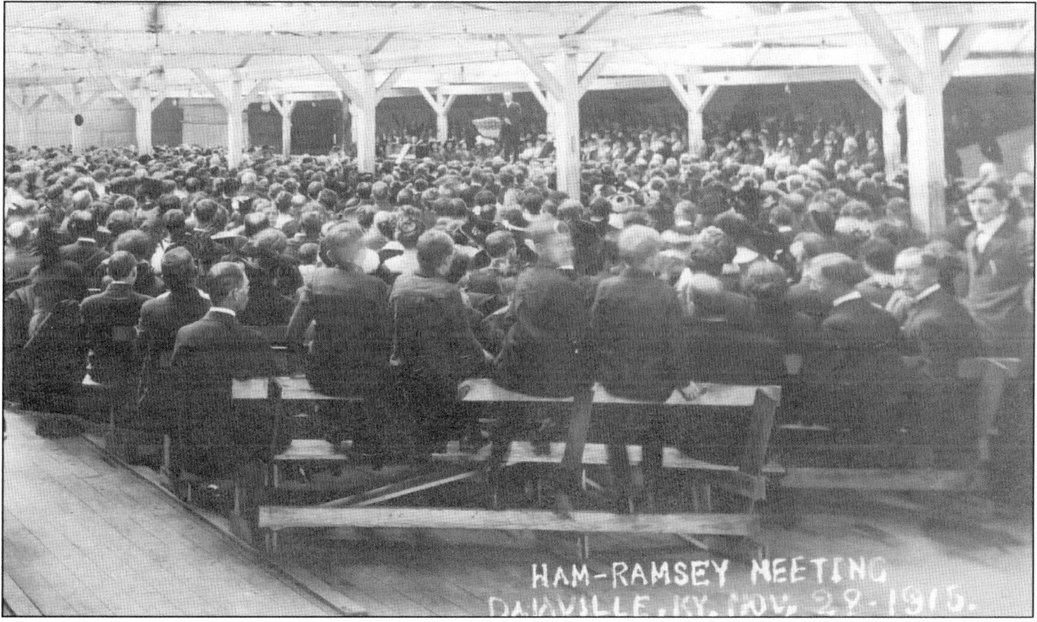


Mordecai Fowler Ham Junior, an American Independent Baptist evangelist and temperance movement leader, along with his music director and fellow evangelist William Ramsey, came to Danville in 1915 to lead a revival. The meeting, which nearly 5,000 people attended, was one of 289 such revivals that Ham led between 1901 and 1941. (Courtesy of Michael Wiser.)

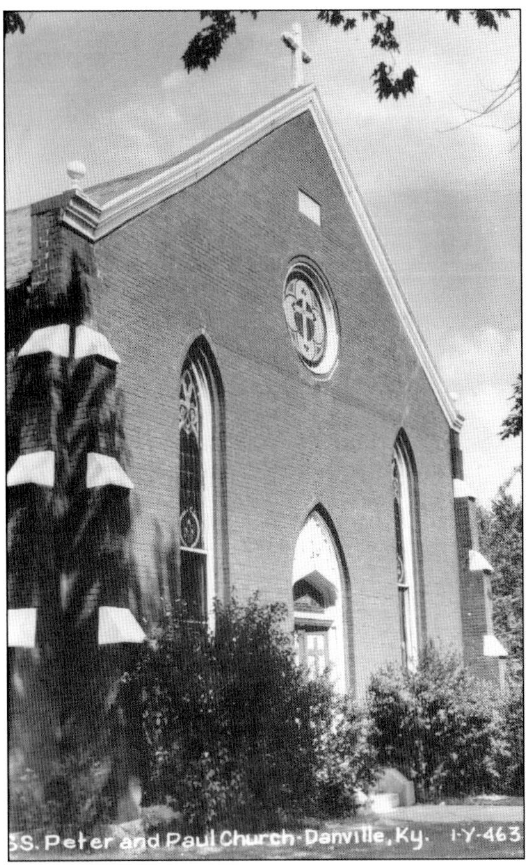


Father Stephen Badin, the first Catholic priest ordained in the United States, began leading Danville Catholics starting in 1798. In 1807, work began on a church, St. Patrick's, which was dedicated by Father Badin in 1810. The original church stands today on North Fifth Street as a private residence, and is the oldest standing former Catholic church in Kentucky. The parishioners left St. Patrick's in the 1820s, and, according to church history, attended mass in the courthouse and in private residences. In 1866, construction began on SS. Peter and Paul Church, at the site of Gill's Tavern, one of the early meeting places for pioneer Kentuckians. Dedicated in 1871, the church still serves the Catholics of Danville to this day. (Left, courtesy of Michael Wiser; below, author's personal collection.)

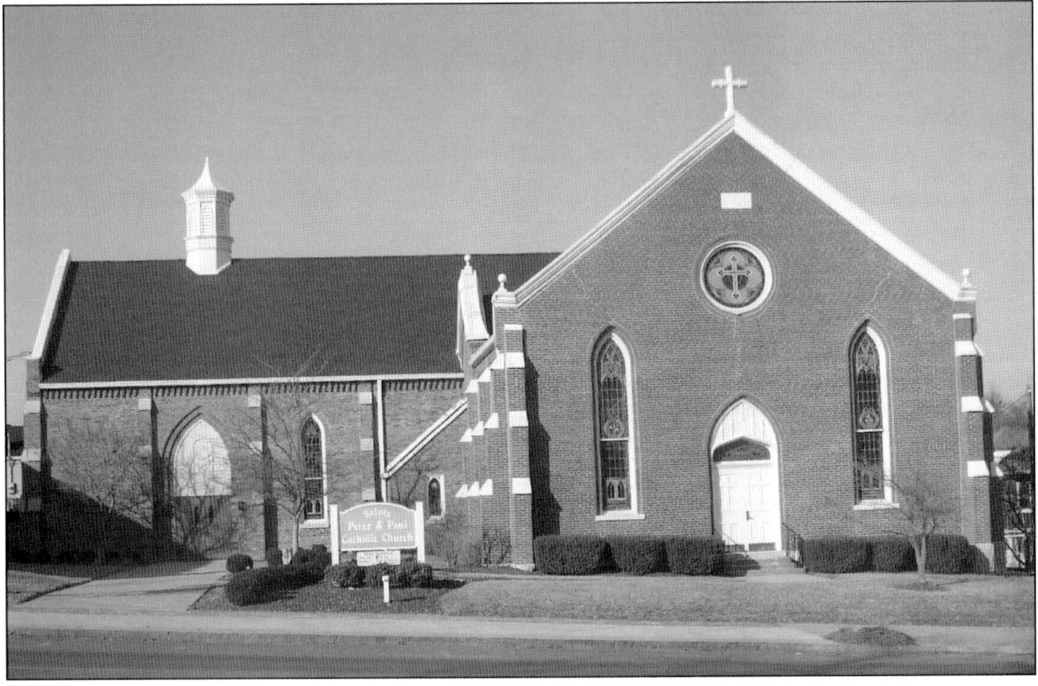

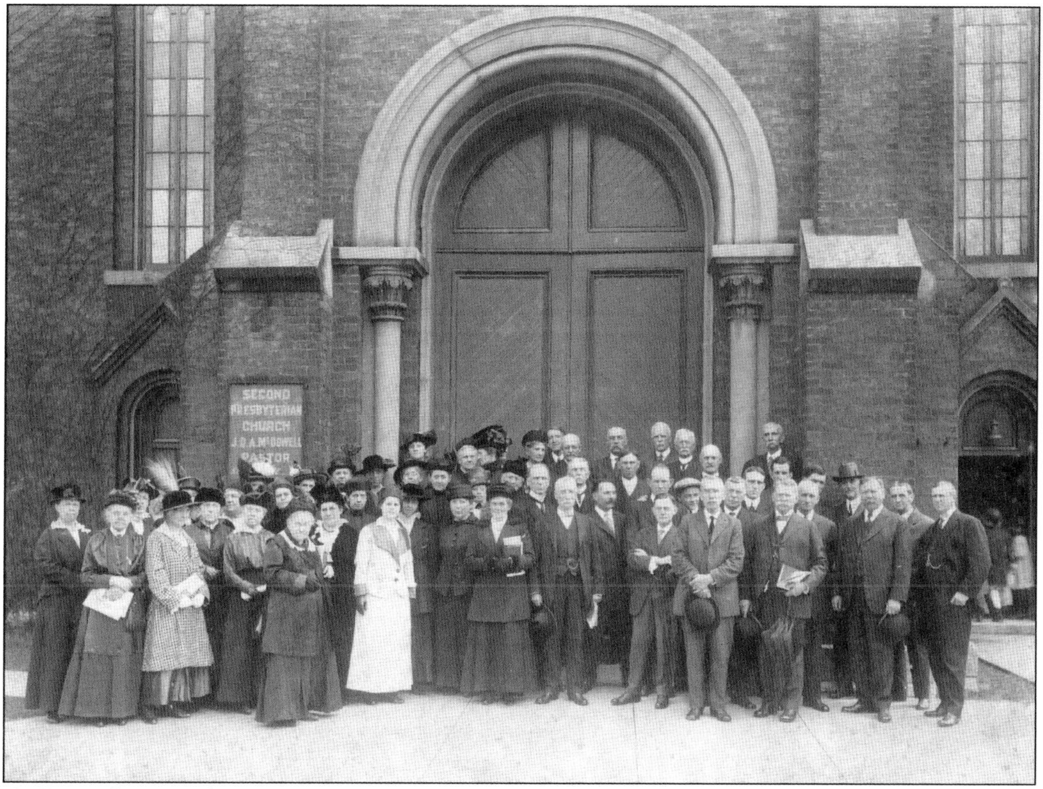

As Danville's population increased in the mid-19th century, a need arose for another Presbyterian church. In 1853, the Second Presbyterian Church was built on Third Street to accommodate the growing congregation. In 1865, when the national body of the Presbyterian Church divided, the First Presbyterian Church aligned with the Presbyterian Church, US, while the Second Presbyterian Church joined the Presbyterian Church, USA. After over 100 years of being apart, the two churches reunited in 1969, and the Second Presbyterian Church congregation moved back into the First Presbyterian Church. The Second Presbyterian Church building still stands today, having served as the much-loved Tea Leaf restaurant, and currently as a café and antiques store. (Both courtesy of Centre College Special Collections.)

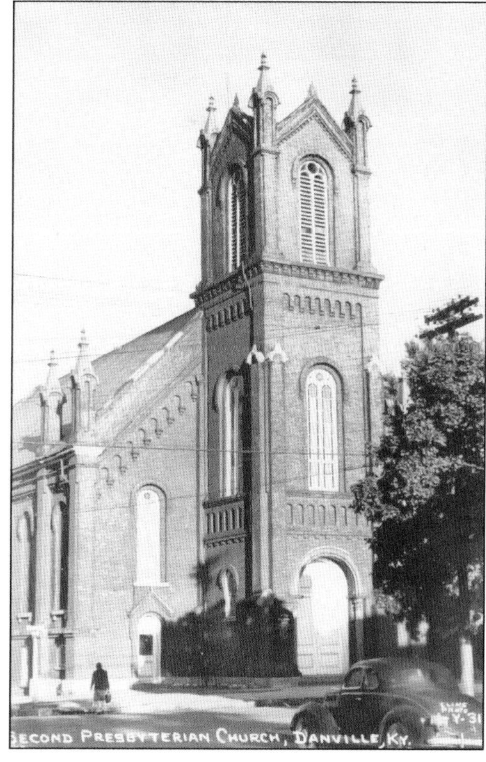

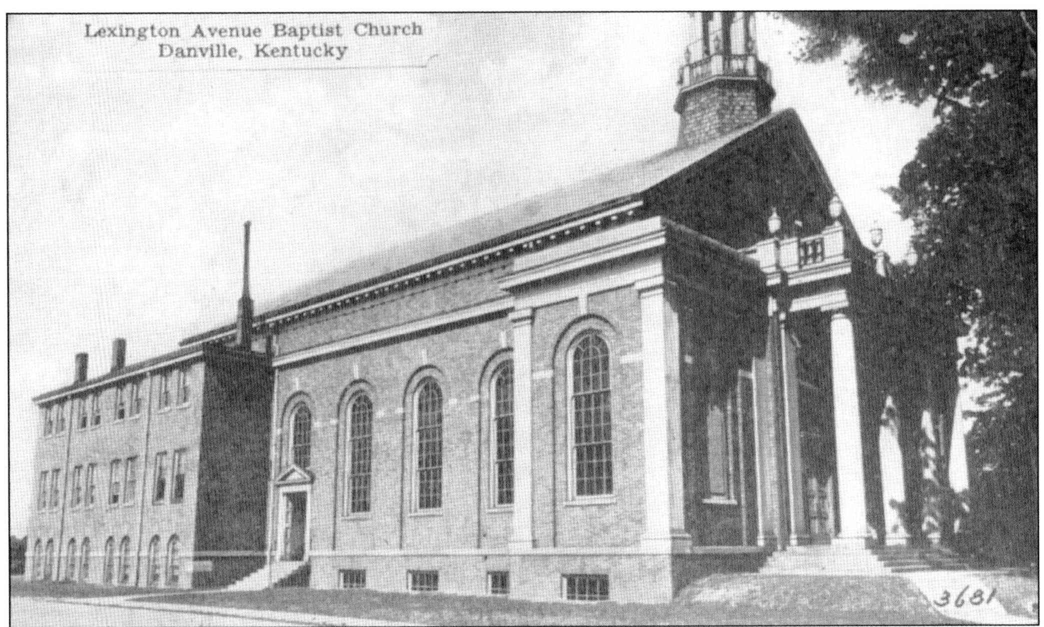


In 1927, the Boyle County Courthouse was the meeting place for 127 Baptists, many from the First Baptist Church in town. They had been convening in various homes throughout the community for several weeks, and had finally decided to form their own church. The congregation purchased a lot at the intersection of Fourth and Lexington Streets and began to raise money for construction through bake sales and other fundraisers. The cornerstone for the Lexington Avenue Baptist Church was laid on May 19, 1929. On January 12, 1930, the congregation held its final service at the courthouse and then walked down the street in double file to the newly completed church. (Both courtesy of Centre College Special Collections.)

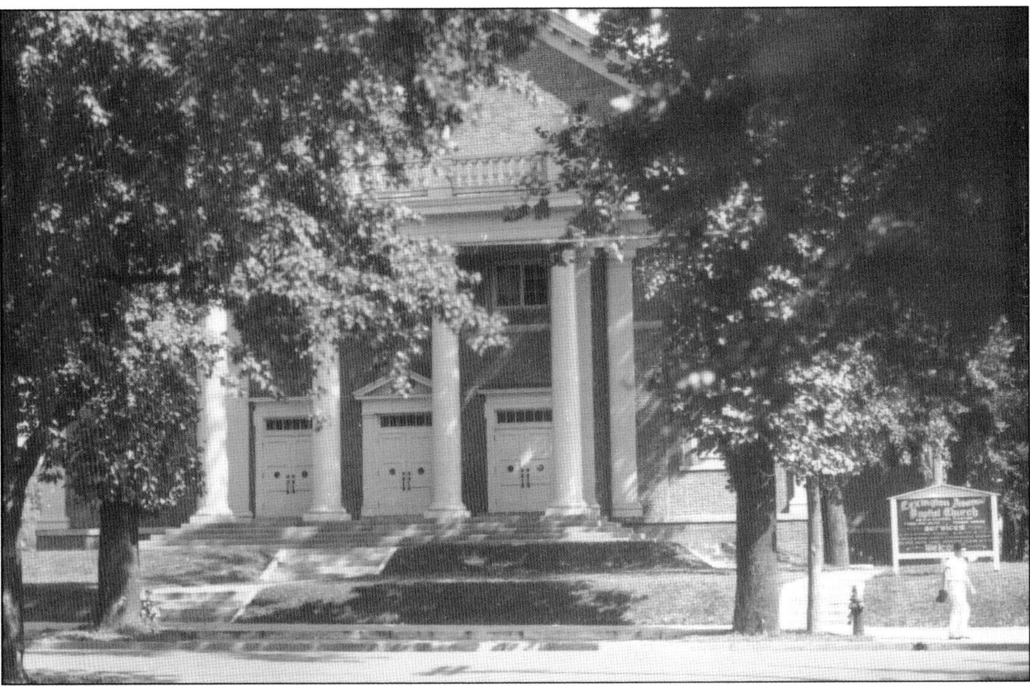

# Four

# Centre College

Centre College was founded by the Kentucky Legislature on January 21, 1819, under the order that it "shall at all times be conducted upon liberal, free, and enlightened principles." The school's board of trustees included famous Kentuckians Isaac Shelby, the first and fifth governor; Ephraim McDowell, the Father of Abdominal Surgery; and Rev. Samuel K. Nelson. Old Centre, the oldest continually used college administrative building west of the Allegheny Mountains, opened as a dormitory and classrooms in 1820. The first graduating class of 1824 had only two students; the class of 1829 had five students. Over the next few decades, the college grew in size and wealth, interrupted only by the Civil War. Prior to the bloody Battle of Perryville in October 1862, Confederate forces occupied Old Centre. After the battle, the Confederates retreated through Danville, pursued by the Union soldiers, who took Old Centre and turned it into a military hospital. In 1901, the college merged with Central University in Richmond, becoming the undergraduate liberal arts college of what was then called Central University of Kentucky. This merger was dissolved in 1918, eight years prior to Centre College becoming coeducational and forming a partnership with the Kentucky College for Women. The two schools completely merged in 1962, and Centre College has continued to grow as an institution, producing many illustrious alumni in its nearly 200 years of operation.

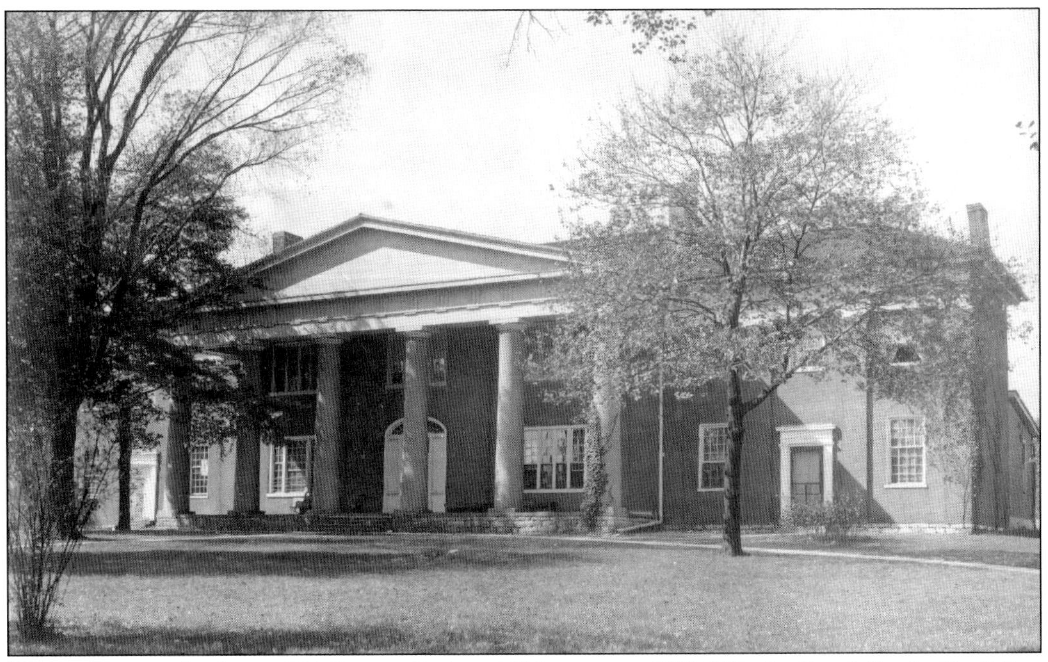

These photographs depict Old Centre. Built in 1820 at a cost of $10,000, the Greek Revival building opened its doors that fall to two professors and five students. As the school grew, Old Centre housed classrooms, libraries, dining rooms, and laboratories as well as serving as a dormitory, a preparatory school, and a Civil War hospital after the nearby Battle of Perryville. It is listed in the National Register of Historic Places and included in the Smithsonian Guide to Historic Places. (Both courtesy of Centre College Special Collections.)

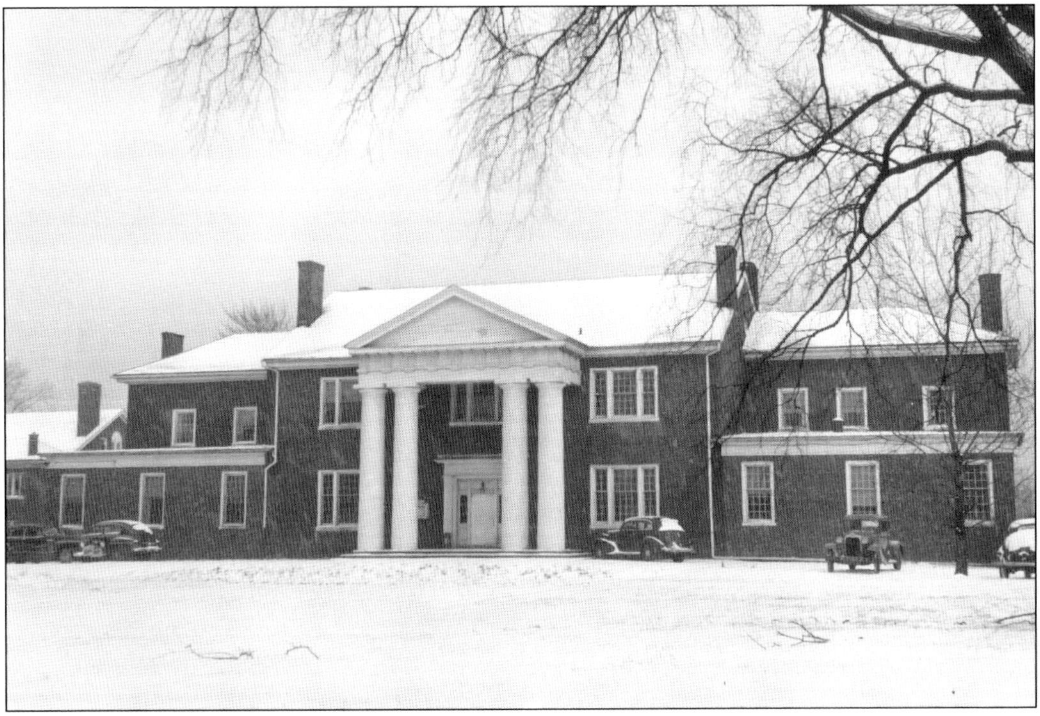

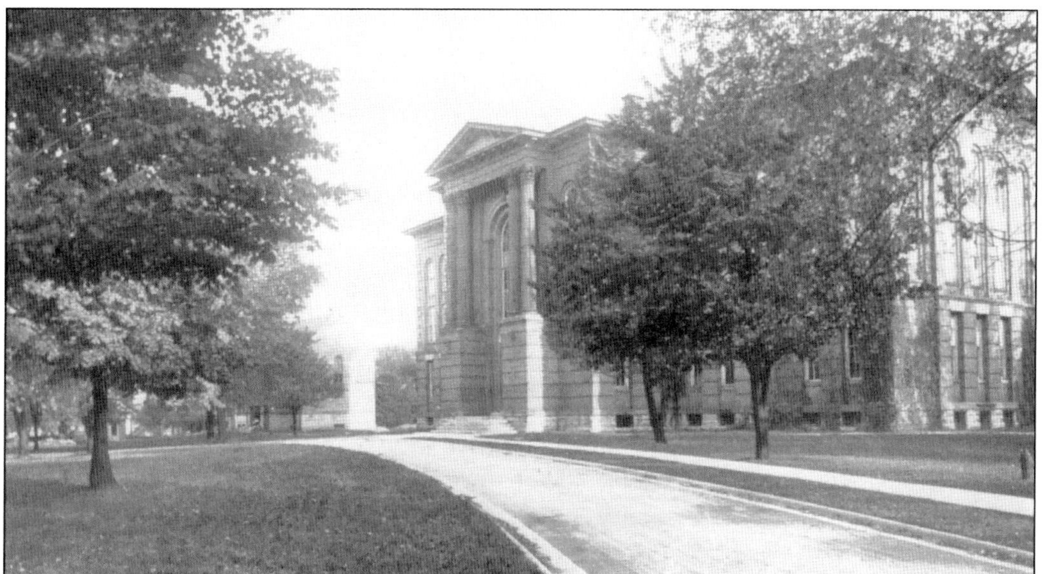

Old Main, as seen in 1915 (above) was built in 1871. It was originally slated to be built in 1863 for $32,000, but the Civil War greatly affected the availability of labor and materials, and the college's board of trustees voted to postpone construction until prices stopped fluctuating so wildly. Old Main served as the college's primary academic building until it was torn down in 1965 to provide space for the new Grace Doherty Library. Students from the classes of 1878, 1879, and 1880 line the steps and walkways in front of Old Main in an 1878 photograph (below). (Both courtesy of Centre College Special Collections.)

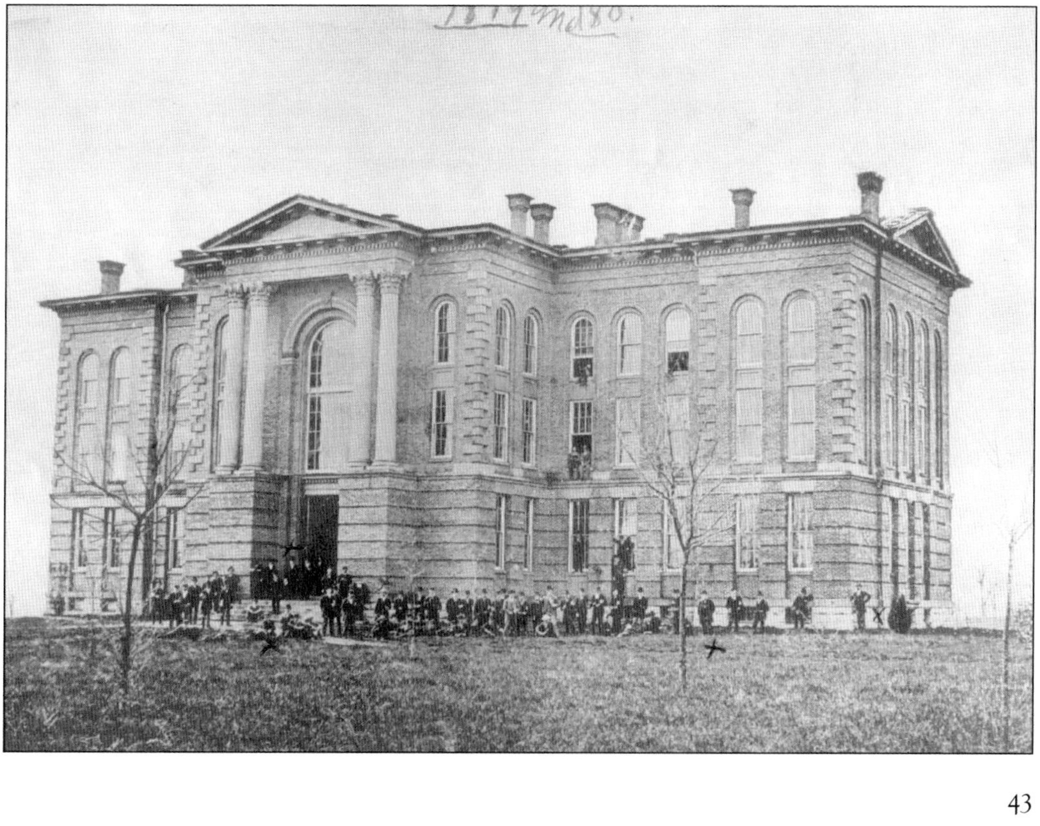

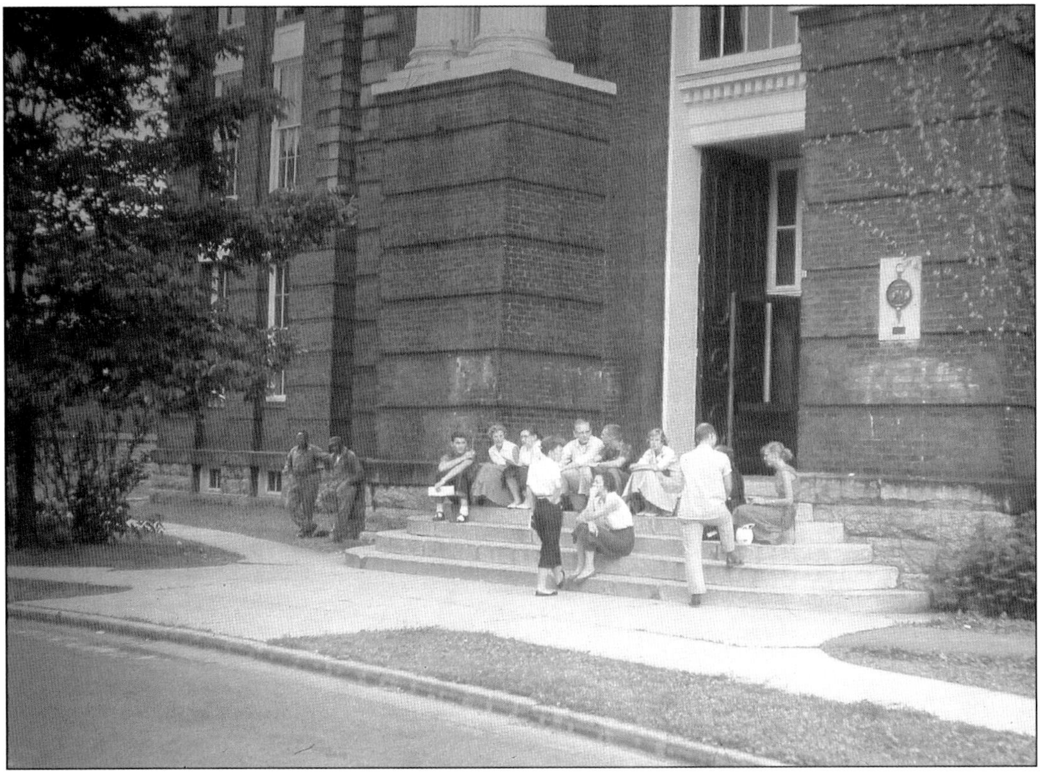

In this photograph from the mid-1950s, Centre College students wait for the bus in front of Old Main. On the steps are Emily Surgenor (sitting, second from left), Jo Frances Gates (sitting, fourth from right), and Joy Bartz (sitting, right). (Courtesy of Guy Ingram.)

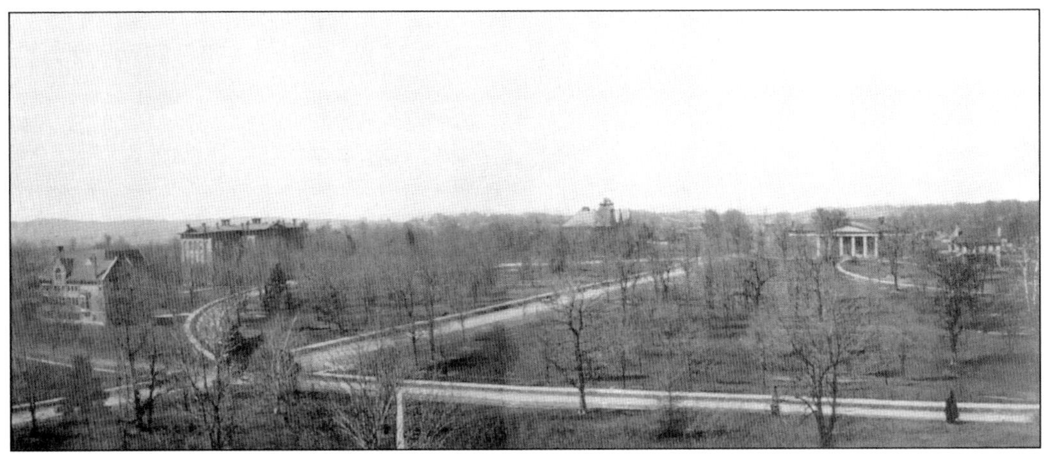

This panorama, likely taken from the steeple of the First Presbyterian Church on the corner of Main and Fifth Streets, shows Centre College's campus in 1903. Visible from left to right are Old Boyle–Humphrey Gymnasium, Old Main, Breckinridge Hall, Old Centre, and Hillcrest House. (Courtesy of Centre College Special Collections.)

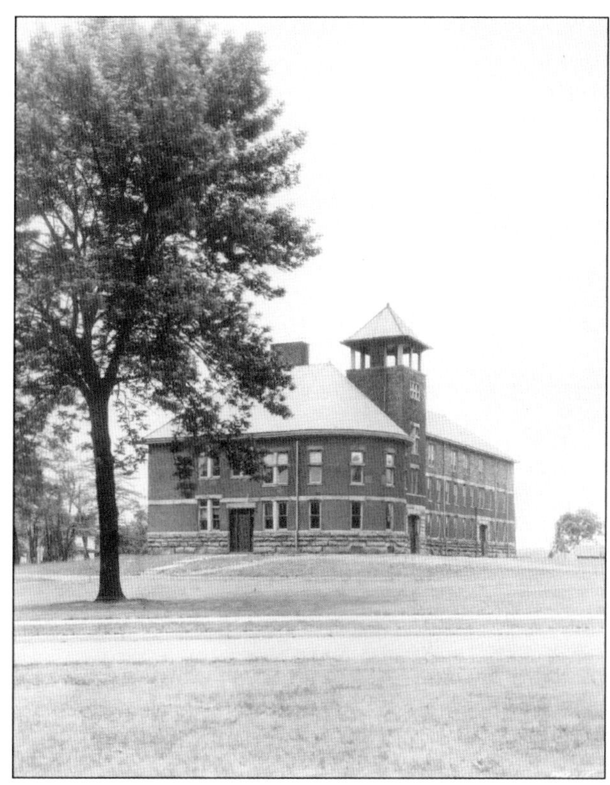

Breckinridge Hall, as seen in the late 1890s (right) and again in 1930 (below), initially served as a dormitory for students of the Danville Theological Seminary. Named for Dr. Robert J. Breckinridge, the building housed seminary students until the school merged with the Louisville Presbyterian Seminary in 1901. Since that day, it has served as a residence hall for Centre College students. Robert McMullen, Centre president from 1944 to 1946, recalled his days as a student living in Breckinridge Hall, with no central heating or bathrooms, just fireplaces and washstands with bowls and pitchers. (Both courtesy of Centre College Special Collections.)

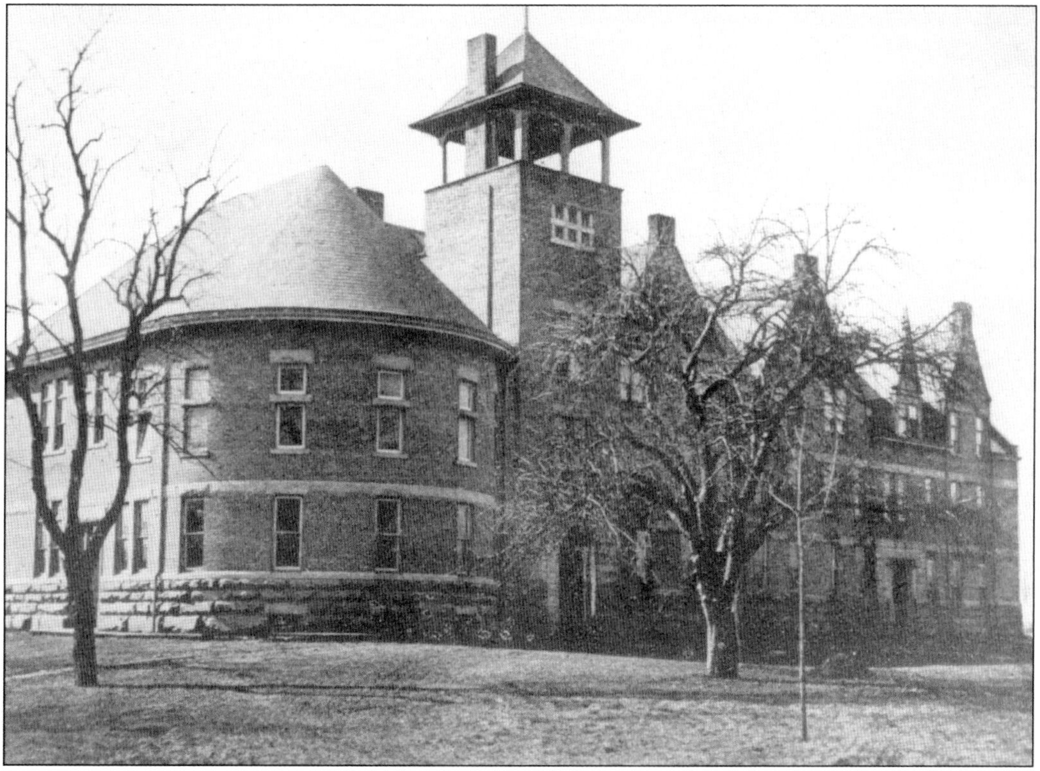

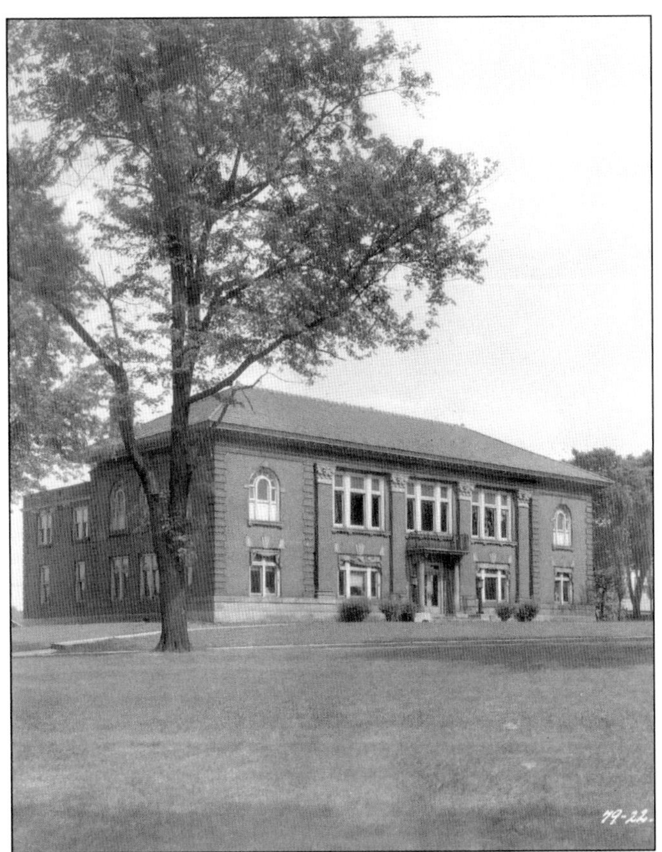


Andrew Carnegie, billionaire businessman and philanthropist, spent much of his wealth on providing communities around the country with educational facilities, the most famous perhaps being his Carnegie libraries. In 1905, Carnegie approached Centre College with an offer of $30,000 to build a library, on the grounds that Centre would match that gift with $30,000 of its own. The necessary funds were raised by 1912, and in 1914, the Carnegie Library (seen at left in 1915) opened to the public. Replacing the old Sayre Library, Carnegie more than doubled the previous facility's capacity and was in use until the Grace Doherty Library was built in 1966. Since then, the Carnegie building (seen below in 1930) has served as a bookstore, campus post office, admissions offices, and dining hall. (Both courtesy of Centre College Special Collections.)

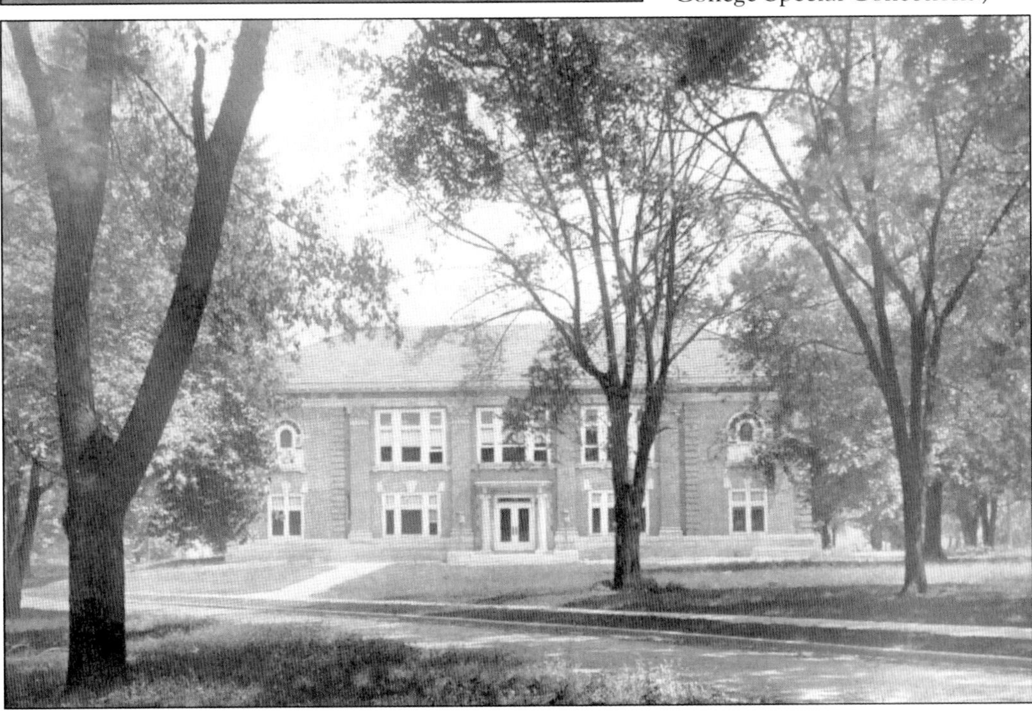

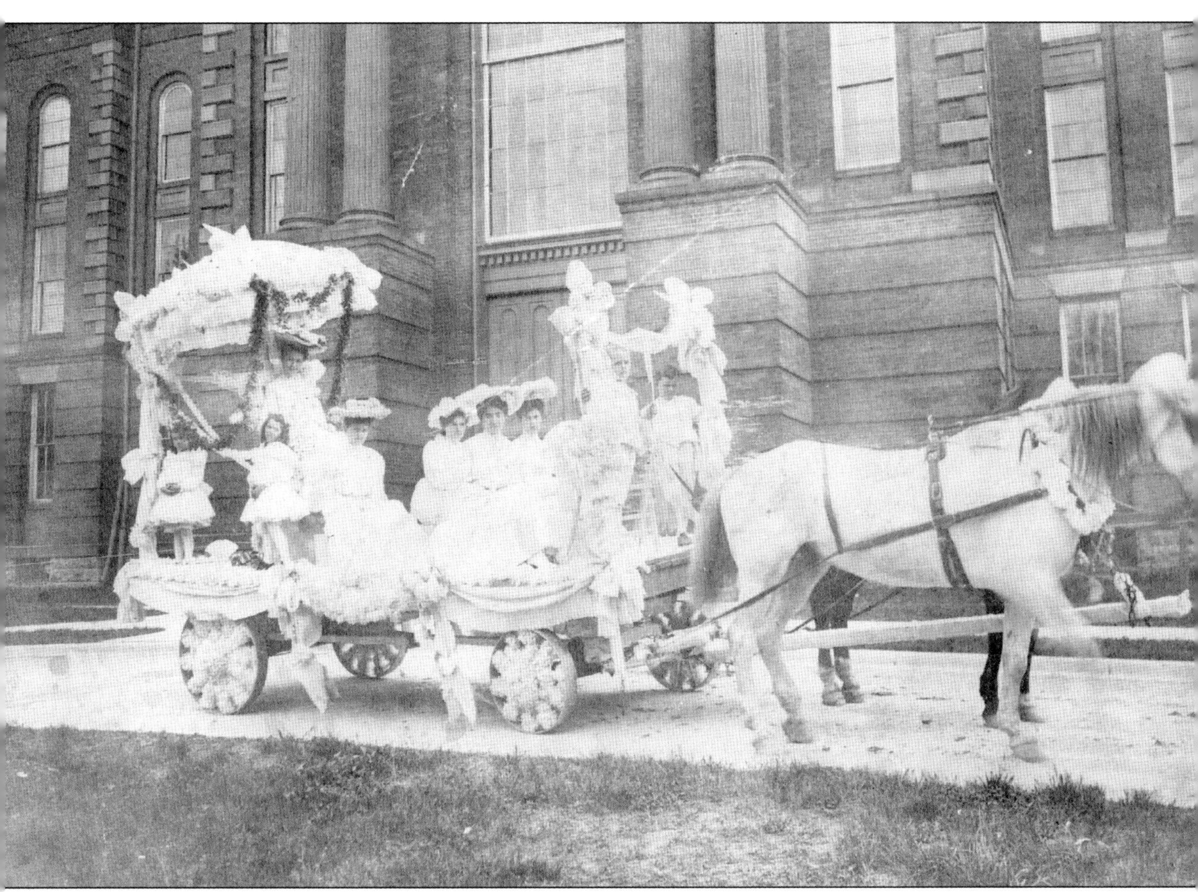

A Centre College tradition that carries on to this day, Carnival was the idea of physical education instructor H.R. Edmunds in 1903. It originated as a social event for the men of the college to mingle with the young ladies of Danville and raise money for the Athletic Association. It rapidly grew into an extravagant party with thousands of attendees. Starting in 1904, the tradition of crowning a king and queen began. Initially, Carnival would be funded entirely by the queen and her family, but this tradition ended in the 1930s, and the college assumed financial responsibility for the event. This photograph, taken in 1904, depicts Centre's Carnival float with Louise Van Winkle as queen. One of the most notable Carnival kings was Alvin "Bo" McMillin in 1921, the year he led Centre's football team to victory over Harvard. (Courtesy of Centre College Special Collections.)

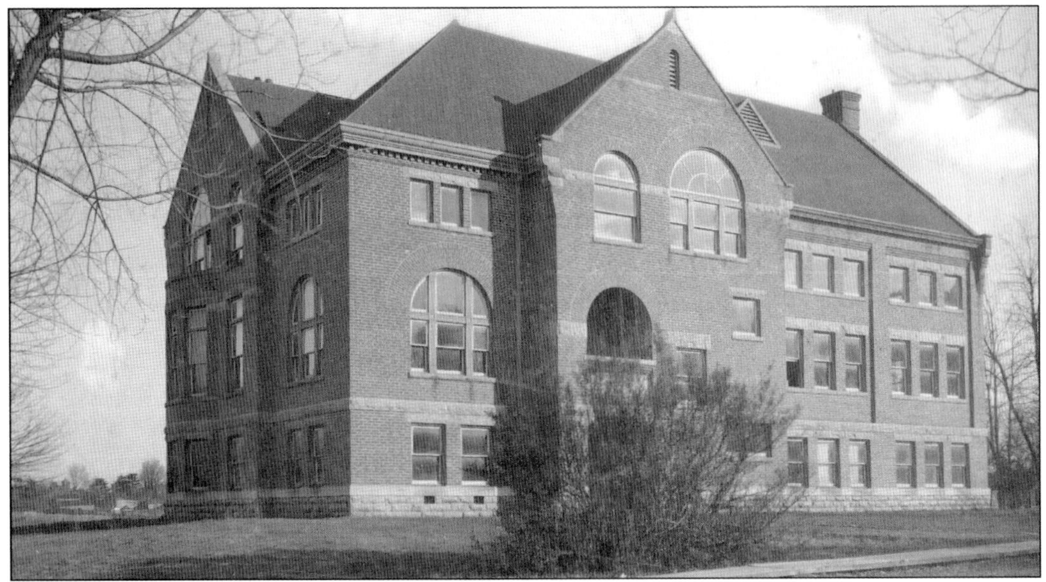

Built in 1892 and named for the donors who funded its construction, longtime college trustee John Boyle and 1866 graduate Alexander D. Humphrey, Old Boyle-Humphrey Gymnasium served as a sports facility until catching fire in 1912. Alumni of the college raised money to replace it in another location, and the remains of Old Boyle-Humphrey Gymnasium were torn down to make room for the new Carnegie library. (Courtesy of Centre College Special Collections.)

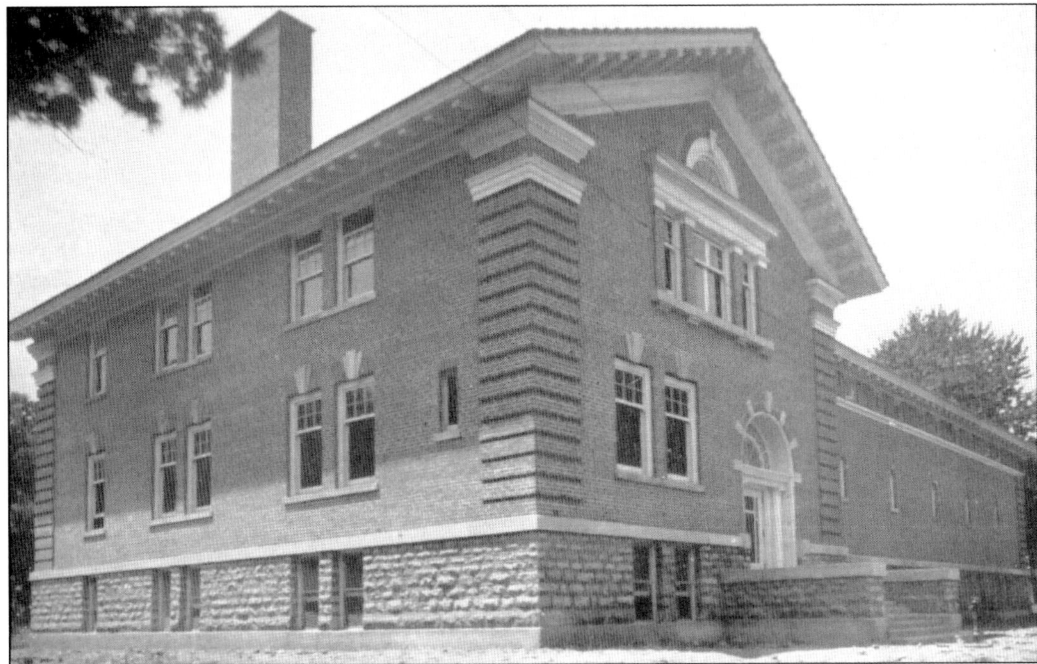

Boyle-Humphrey Alumni Gymnasium, built to replace Old Boyle-Humphrey Gymnasium, was dedicated in June 1914. Only five months after opening, the new gym was gutted by a fire that destroyed the second Sayre Library as well. The gymnasium was rebuilt in 1915 after alumni and students raised money for construction costs and was renamed Sutcliffe Hall in 1961 after major renovations. (Courtesy of Centre College Special Collections.)

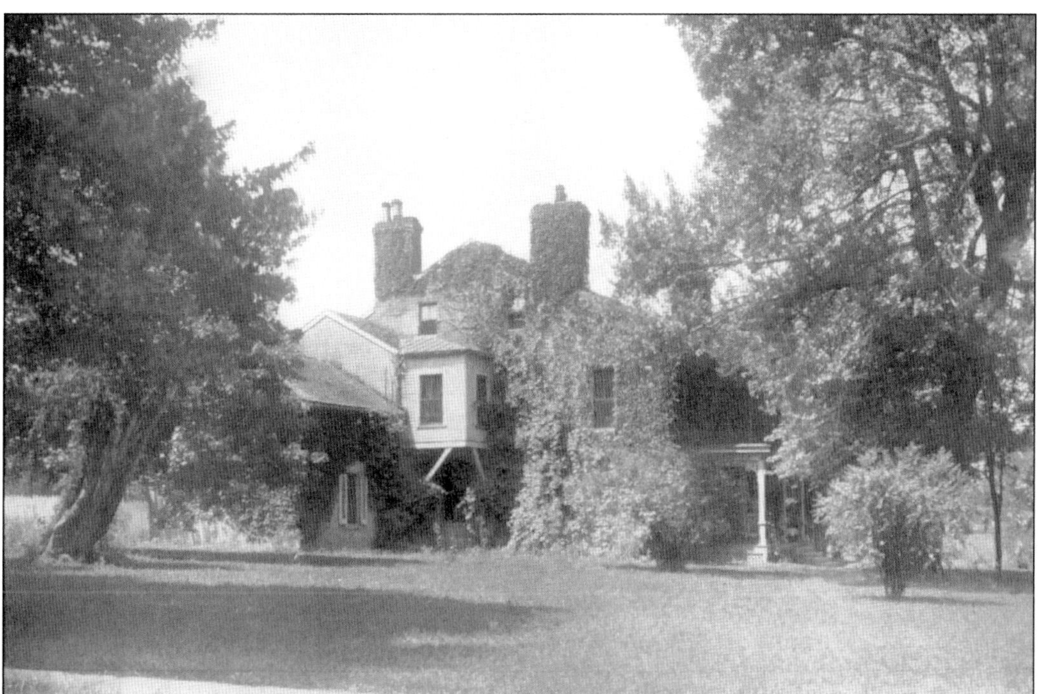

When Centre College opened in 1820, there were no boarding options for students, many of whom lived with Danville families during their schooling. The board of trustees approved the construction of a refectory, which was completed in 1825. The school offered board for $1.50 a week, bedding for $2.50 a session, and candles for 16.66¢ per pound. In 1831, the board of trustees decided to no longer maintain the refectory and began renting it to college president John C. Young as a private home. Hillcrest House, as it came to be known, served as the Centre College president's house from then until 1937. Pictured in 1915 (above) and in 1930 (right), Hillcrest was eventually demolished in 1969, having long since been replaced by Craik House as the president's home. (Both courtesy of Centre College Special Collections.)

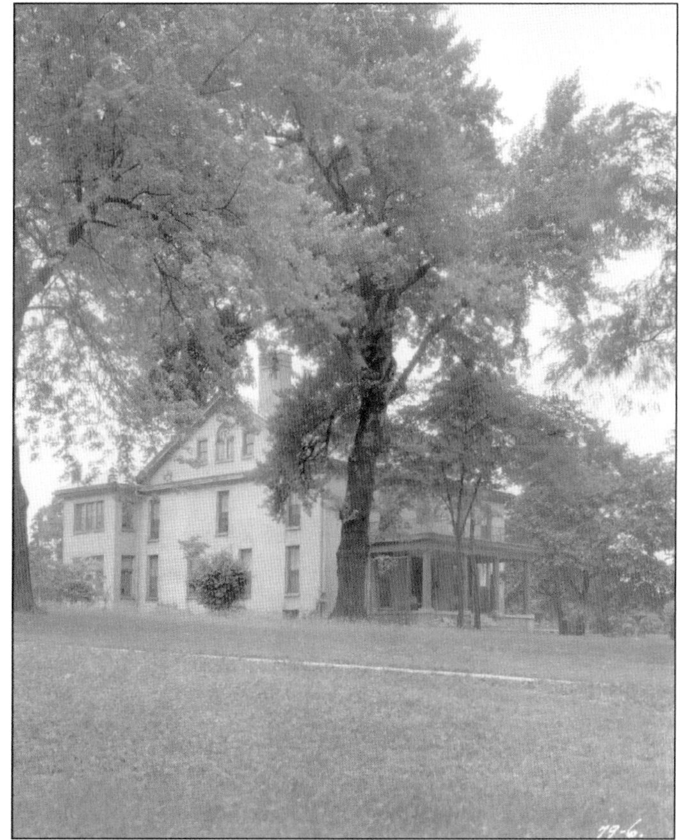

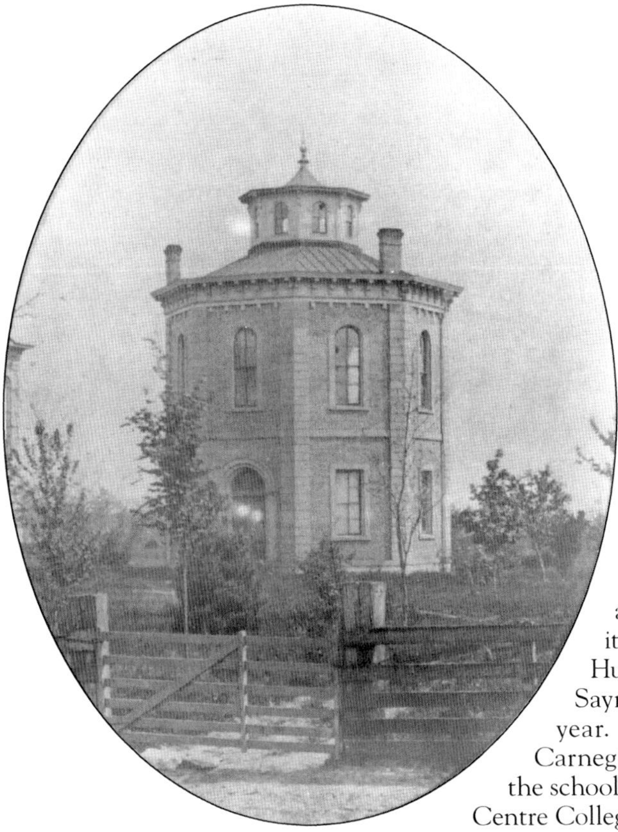

Using a $5,000 donation from David A. Sayre, the first Sayre Library, pictured at left in 1879, was built in 1862 at the location where Breckinridge Hall currently stands. When the second Sayre Library was completed in 1893, the first building was torn down. The second facility, pictured below, served as the campus library until 1913, when it was incorporated into the new Boyle-Humphrey Gymnasium. Both the gym and Sayre Library burned down the following year. Sayre Library was replaced by the Carnegie Library, which more than doubled the school's capacity for books. (Both courtesy of Centre College Special Collections.)

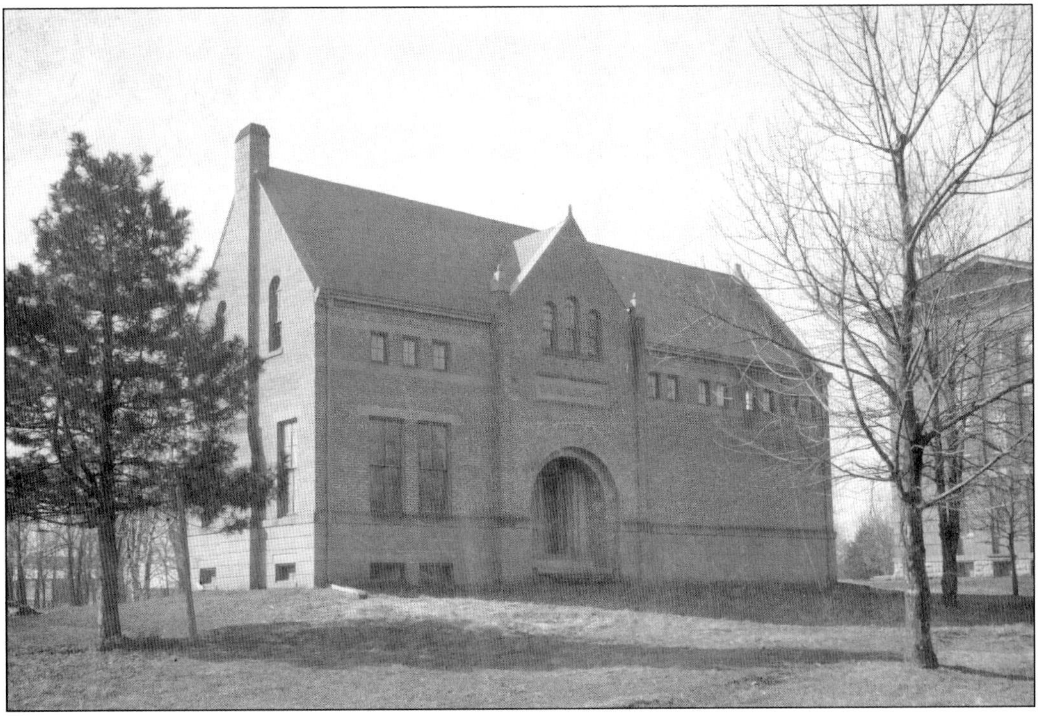

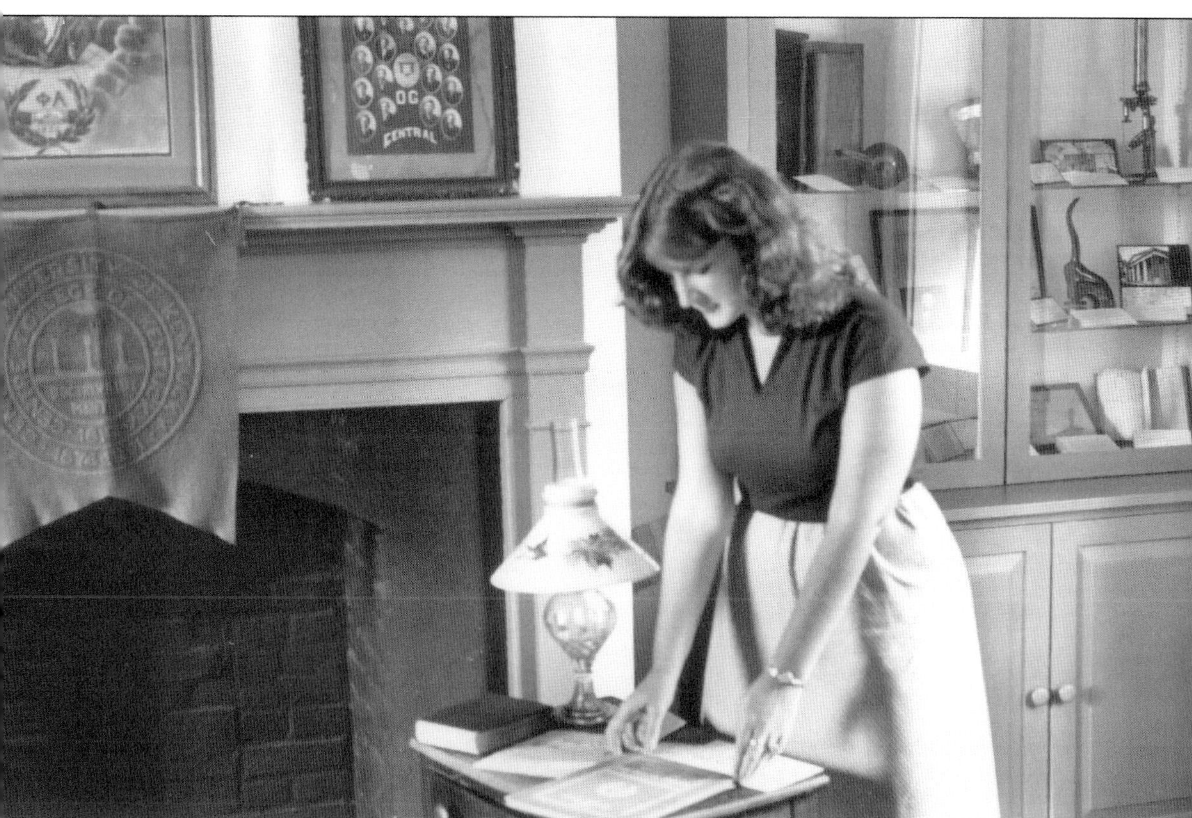


In 1901, Centre College and Central University in Richmond were consolidated under the name Central University of Kentucky for financial and enrollment reasons. Centre College served as the undergraduate school for the university, which also consisted of the Danville College of Law, the Kentucky Theological Seminary, the Hospital College of Medicine, the Louisville College of Dentistry, and three preparatory schools, located in Jackson, Danville, and Elizabethtown. Over the next decade and a half, the various schools ended their affiliations with the university, until only Centre College remained. In 1918, the school's charter was amended, and the state legislature renamed it Centre College of Kentucky. In this image, an unidentified woman studies a book in front of a Central University of Kentucky banner and various photographs and objects from Centre College. (Courtesy of Centre College Special Collections.)

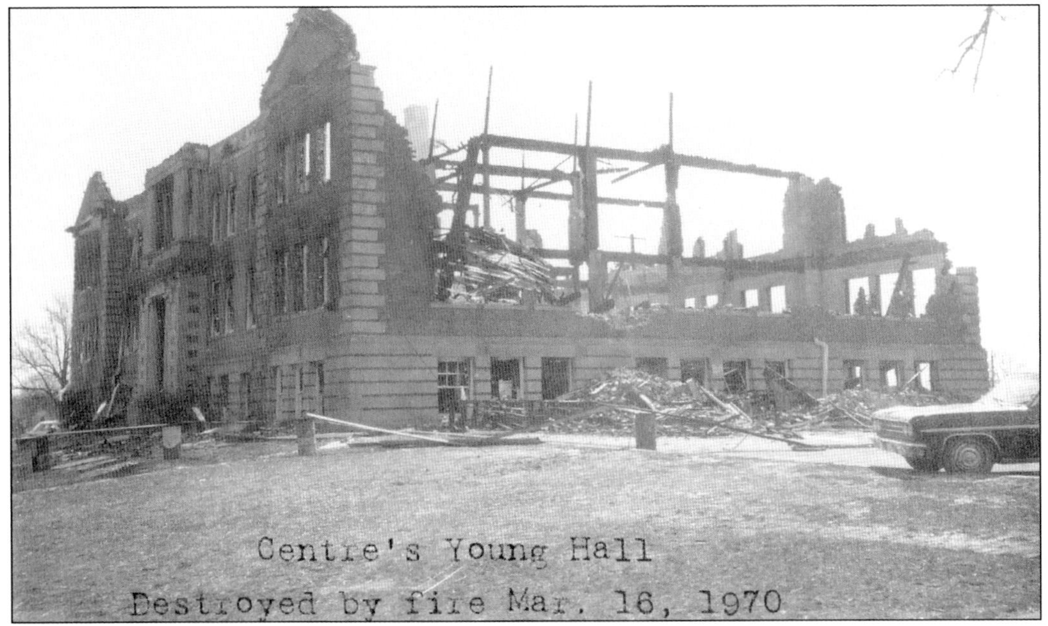


Young Memorial Science Hall, named for John C. Young and William C. Young, father and son who both served as Centre College presidents, was built in 1909. Known as Old Young, it served as Centre's science building until the new Young Hall was built in 1970. Only days before it was scheduled for demolition, Old Young was destroyed by fire. (Courtesy of Guy Ingram.)

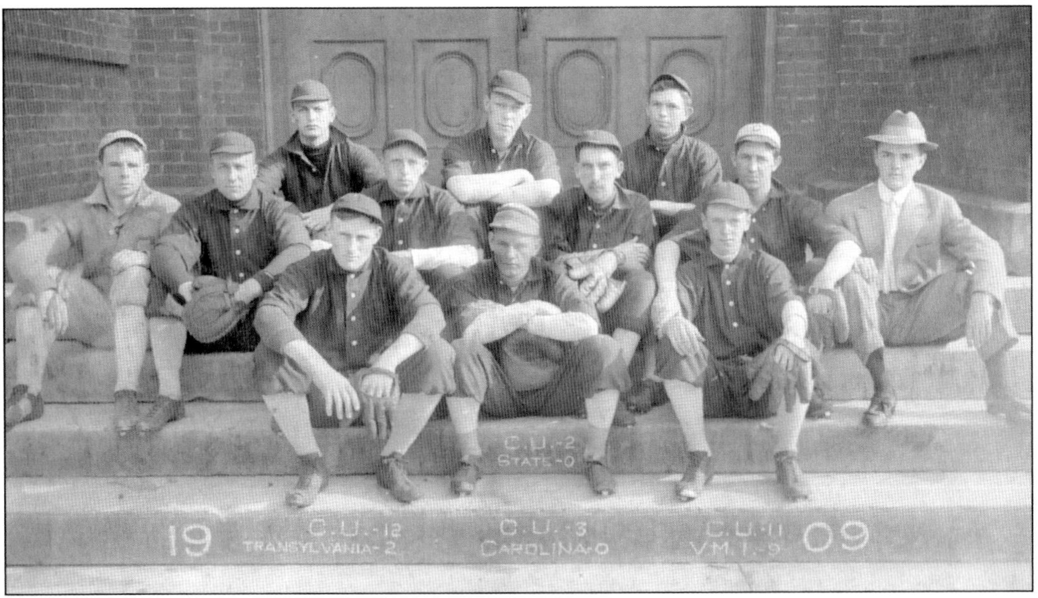


This portrait of Centre College's 1909 baseball team and coach was taken on the steps of Old Main, where players celebrated their state championship wins and a season record of 13 wins and four losses. They are, from left to right, Coach Johnson, followed by players Cave, Prichard, Diederich, Duffy, Seelbach, Devant, Fred Vinson, Arnold, Hawkins, Harper, Webber, and team manager Hager. Vinson, one of Centre College's many prolific alumni, served as a member of the US House of Representatives, secretary of treasury under President Truman, and as the 13th chief justice of the US Supreme Court. (Courtesy of Centre College Special Collections.)

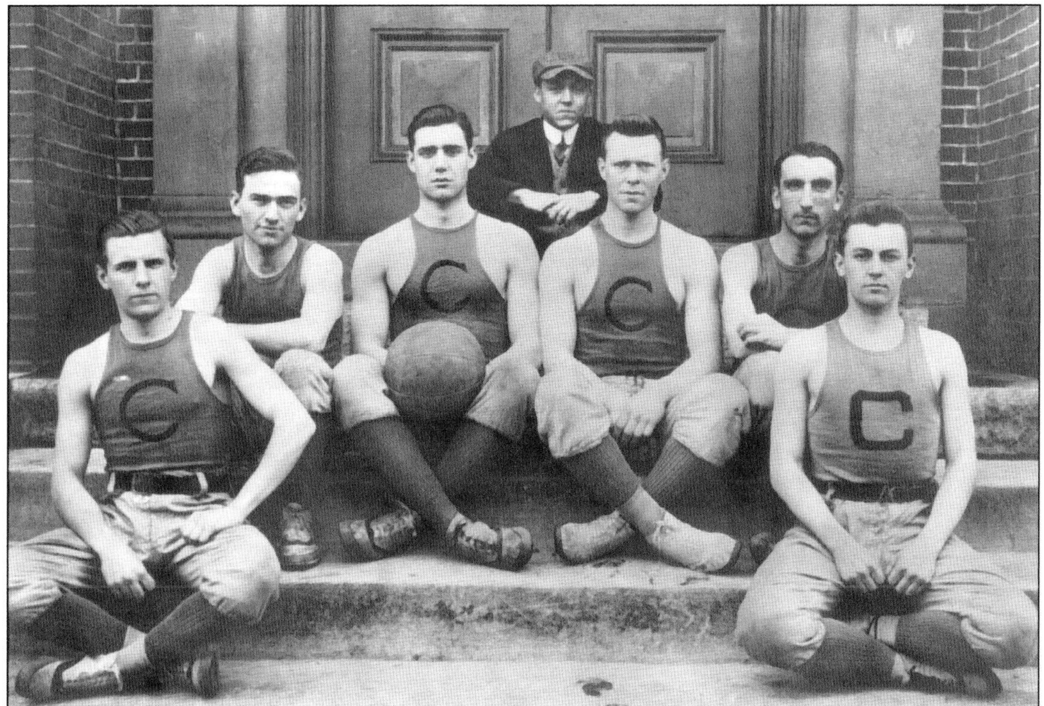

This 1911 portrait of the Centre College basketball team features, from left to right, Dosker, Hornbeak, team captain William Seelbach, assistant manager Breathitt, junior manager Louis Seelbach, Fred Vinson, and Flack. Fred Vinson's portrait, lovingly referred to as "Dead Fred," accompanies students to basketball games, and has not missed a Centre College home football game since the tradition started after Vinson's death in 1953. (Courtesy of Centre College Special Collections.)

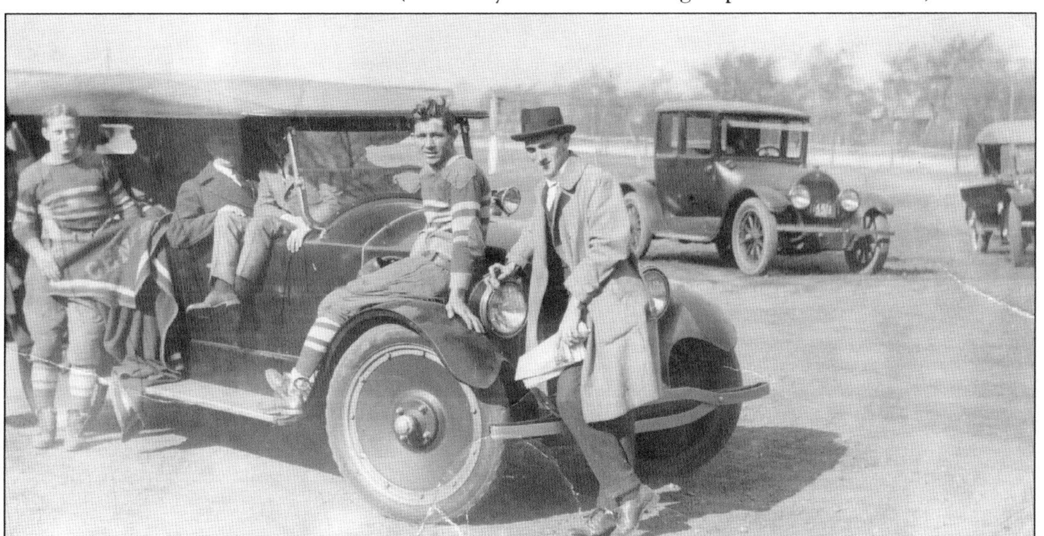

In this photograph, Centre College football players relax outside Harvard Stadium, one day prior to their historic match against the Crimson. Coach Charles Moran sits at the wheel with three players identified in the image—Harry Snoddy holds a Centre College blanket, Alvin "Bo" McMillin sits on the car's fender, and George Joplin leans on the hood. The Centre College Praying Colonels won the October 29, 1921, game 6-0. (Courtesy of Centre College Special Collections.)

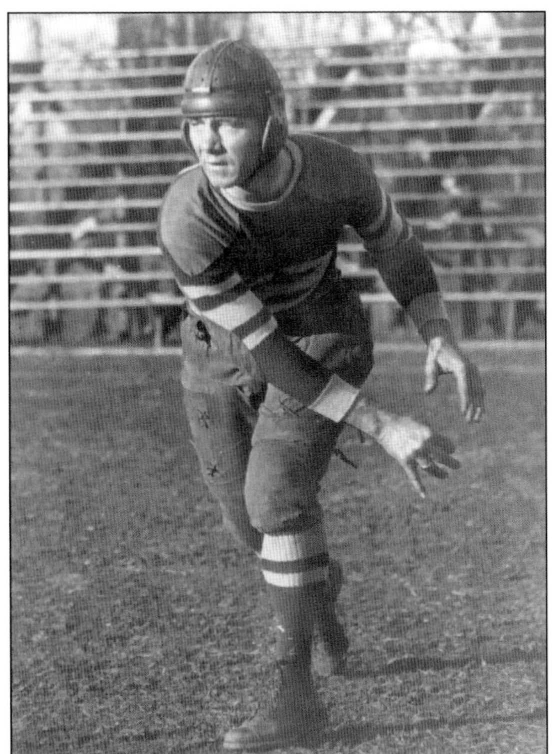

Alvin "Bo" McMillin began playing football at Centre College in 1917, only to have his college career interrupted by a short stint in the Navy in the final year of World War I. McMillin returned to Centre College to play football from 1919 through 1921, the year in which he scored the lone touchdown against Harvard University in what was known as "football's upset of the century." He was inducted into the College Football Hall of Fame in 1951. (Courtesy of Centre College Special Collections.)

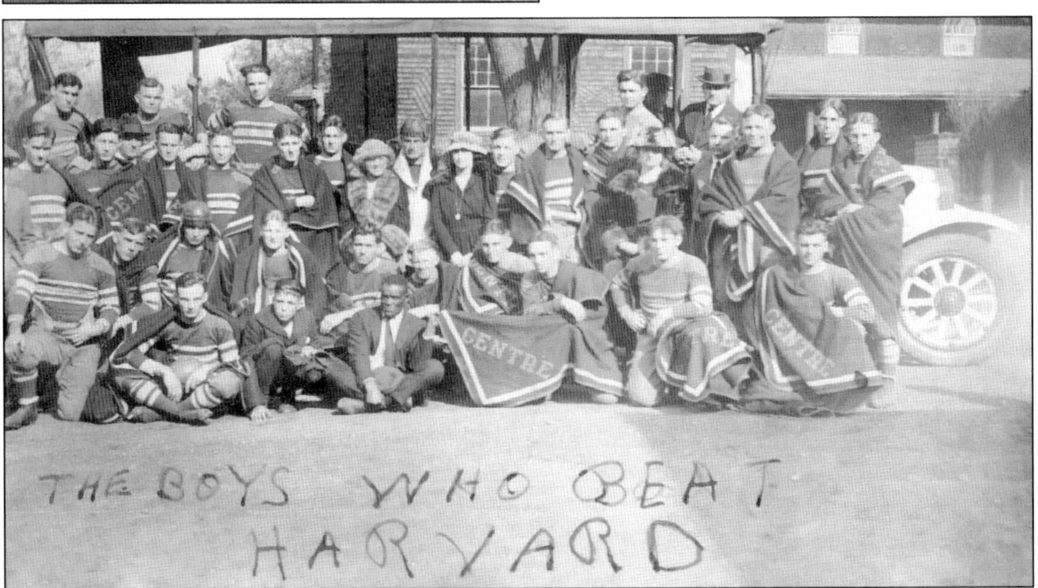


This photograph of Centre College football players and fans was taken after the famous 1921 match in which the Centre Praying Colonels beat the Harvard Crimson 6-0, with a lone touchdown by Bo McMillin. The local newspaper, the *Danville-Advocate*, ran a headline celebrating the win, printing "McMillin, The Hero of the Football World, President of the United States for the Time Being. He Is The Great Effulgent Star," concluding with "God Bless Our Team, each and all of them." If asked what the formula for a winning football team is, Centre alumni and students alike will respond, "C6-H0." (Courtesy of Centre College Special Collections.)

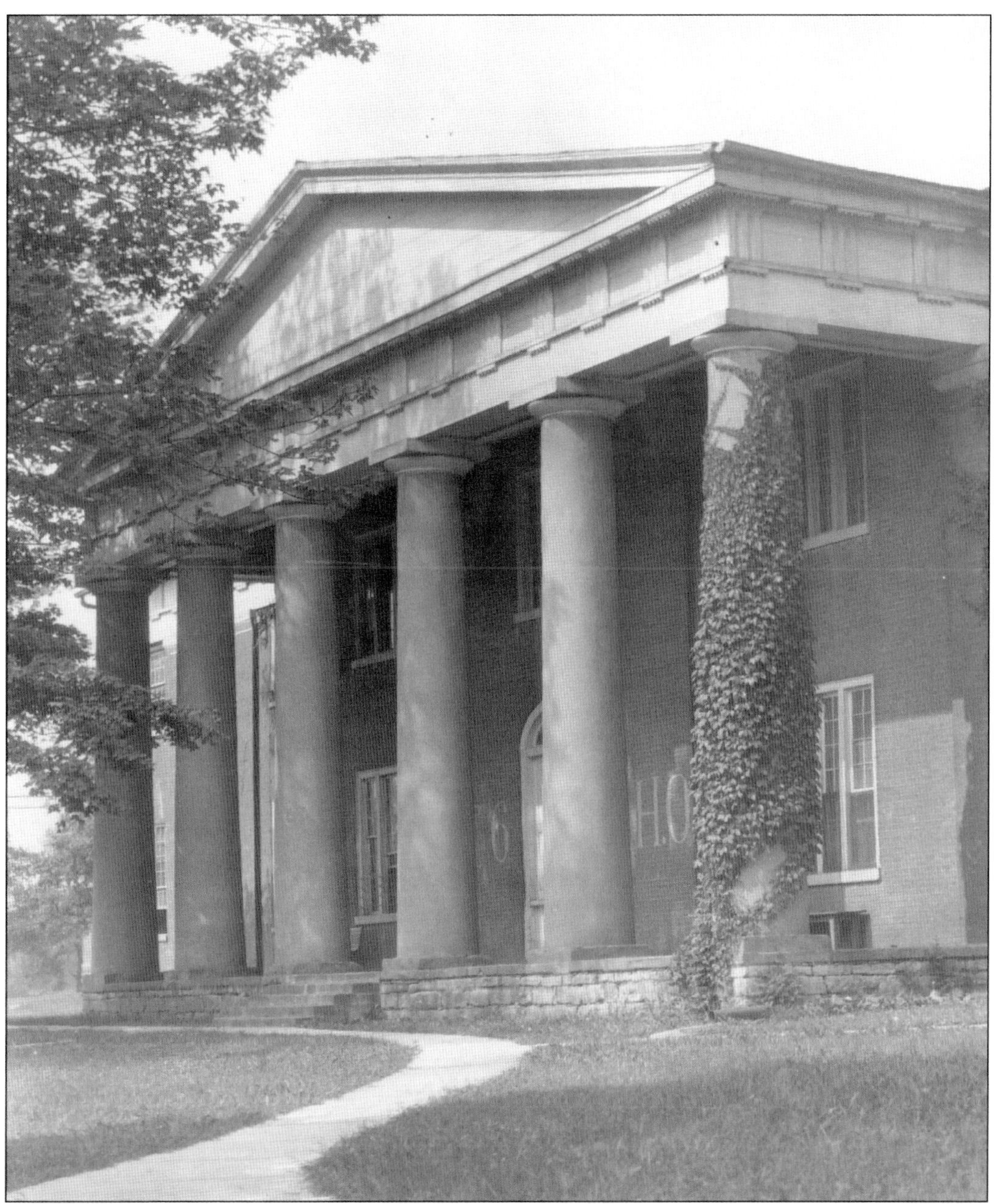


This photograph of Old Centre shows the only graffiti permitted on campus by the school's board of trustees: "C6-H0." This "formula for victory" celebrates the Centre College football team's win against Harvard University in 1921. "C6-H0" remains scattered throughout campus to this day; however, in 1921, the formula was not limited to buildings. Ruby Moss, a woman who witnessed the celebrations, wrote in a letter: "Every window in town received a coat of yellow and white paint in Centre 6 Harvard 0. It was the 'real stuff' too, not whitewash. Two boys painted an old cow that they found grazing on the campus, then rode the poor old thing up town. They got the fire engine out, and every Centre boy that could stick on 'stuck.' The score was painted on lots of the boxcars out at the station, at the end of Main—both ends—just everywhere." (Courtesy of Centre College Special Collections.)

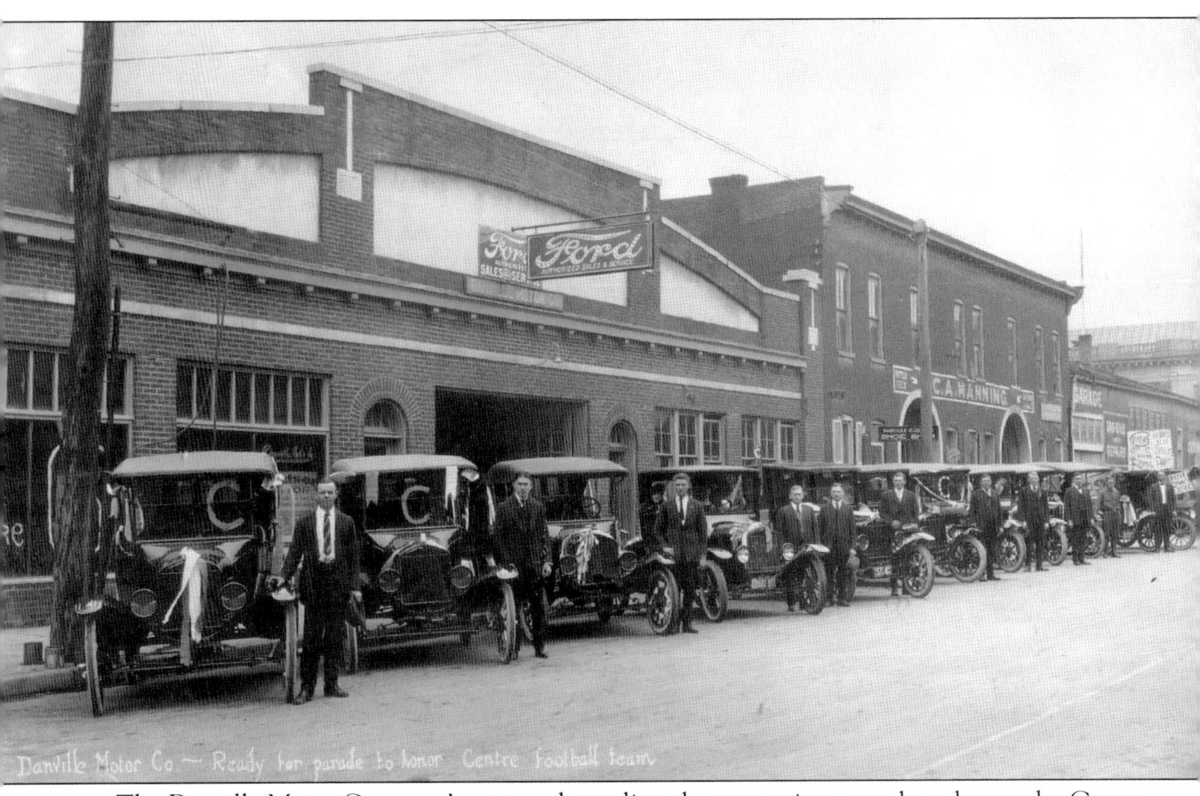


The Danville Motor Company's men and cars line the streets in a parade to honor the Centre College football team's victory over Harvard University in 1921. Ruby Moss, who watched the parade, wrote to a relative, "The team came first on the fire engine, then the Centre Five, then Gov. Morrow and the 'notables,' every Centre boy, K.C.W. girls next, and then all the automobiles. The speeches were made in front of the court house. Wish you could have seen the Centre Five. They had a piano on an open truck, and the two boys that played the saxophones sat on top of the piano. The others in it sat in chairs on the truck, and they played the Centre song as they drove along." (Courtesy of Centre College Special Collections.)

# *Five*

# Kentucky School for the Deaf

Gen. Elias Barbee, a senator whose daughter Lucy was deaf, understood the need for an institution that would cater to deaf children. Working with Judge John Rowan in 1822, Barbee saw the Kentucky Asylum for the Tuition of the Deaf and Dumb established in 1823. The name was later changed to the Kentucky School for the Deaf in 1904. This was the first state-sponsored school of its kind in the country and the first school for the deaf west of the Allegheny Mountains. For two years, the school operated in the Yellow House on Main Street, which has long since been razed. In 1826 and 1836, Kentucky's Great Compromiser, Henry Clay, helped secure two land grants for the school; when they were sold, the Kentucky School for the Deaf used the profits to finance the construction of school facilities. In 1884, the Kentucky School for Negro Deaf was established as a division of the school, which integrated fully in 1963. Initially, three years of learning were offered to students. However, the school currently offers preschool through high school education for its students, many of whom retain their ties to the institution. The school is still in operation today, serving nearly 200 faculty and students. Its oldest surviving building, Jacobs Hall, was built in 1857 and today holds a museum and archives, teaching the public about the Kentucky School for the Deaf's fascinating history.

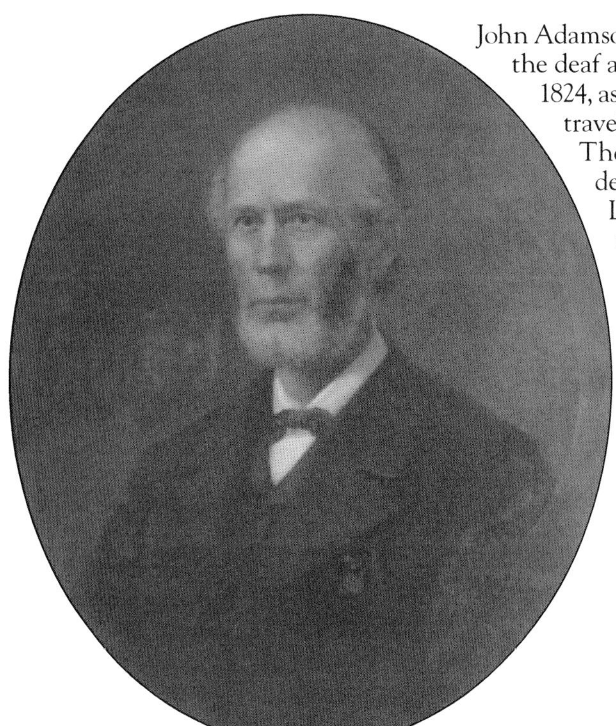

John Adamson Jacobs was the first trained teacher of the deaf at the Kentucky School for the Deaf. In 1824, as a 17-year-old Centre College student, he traveled to Hartford, Connecticut, to study. Thomas Gallaudet, a leading American deaf educator, assigned him to work with Laurent Clerc, a deaf Frenchman. Jacobs then returned to Danville and served as teacher, principal, and superintendent of the Kentucky School for the Deaf. Under his leadership, the school enrolled over 400 students by the Civil War and expanded its campus to accommodate an ever-increasing enrollment. (Courtesy of the Kentucky School for the Deaf.)

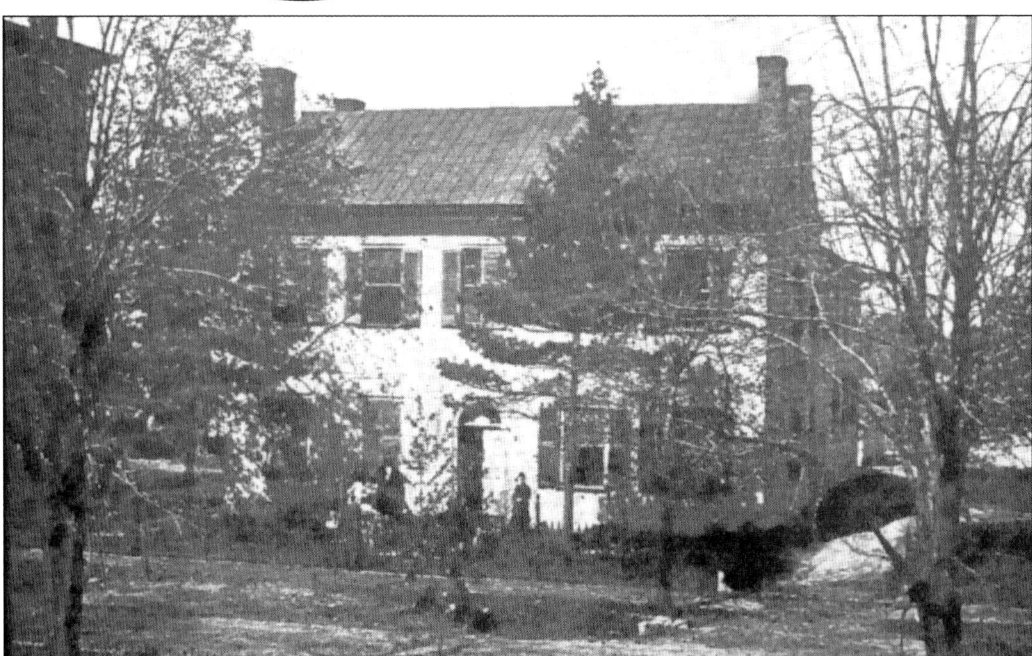

In 1826, the small school moved from the Yellow House on Main Street to its permanent location on Second Street. The Centre College Board of Trustees purchased the Tompkins House, a two-story brick dwelling with eight rooms, two halls, and an attic, and ten acres of land for $5,000. The Tompkins House provided a home for the officers and female students; male students lived in a small two-room cottage nearby. (Courtesy of the Kentucky School for the Deaf.)

John Blount was the first deaf teacher at the Kentucky School for the Deaf, appointed by John Jacobs Senior in 1847. The night after the Battle of Perryville in October 1862, he took the older male students to the battlefield to help bury the dead. (Courtesy of the Kentucky School for the Deaf.)

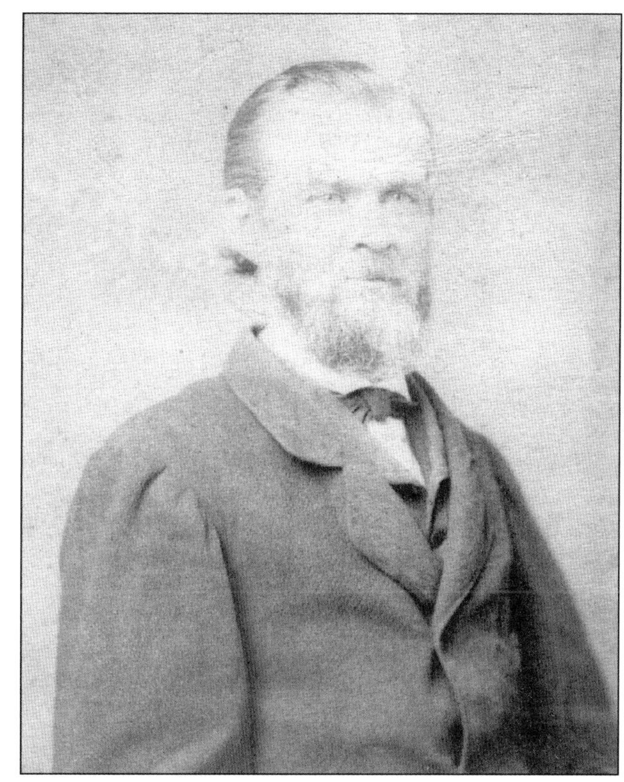

Warrick Hall, established by the Commonwealth of Kentucky as a separate school for African American deaf students, was administered by the Kentucky School for the Deaf. Warrick Hall, an antebellum mansion, was purchased and used for classrooms and a dormitory until Washington Hall was built in 1952, at which point Warrick was razed. The first African American student at the school, 25-year-old Owen Alexander of Owenton, Kentucky, was admitted in 1885. (Courtesy of the Kentucky School for the Deaf.)

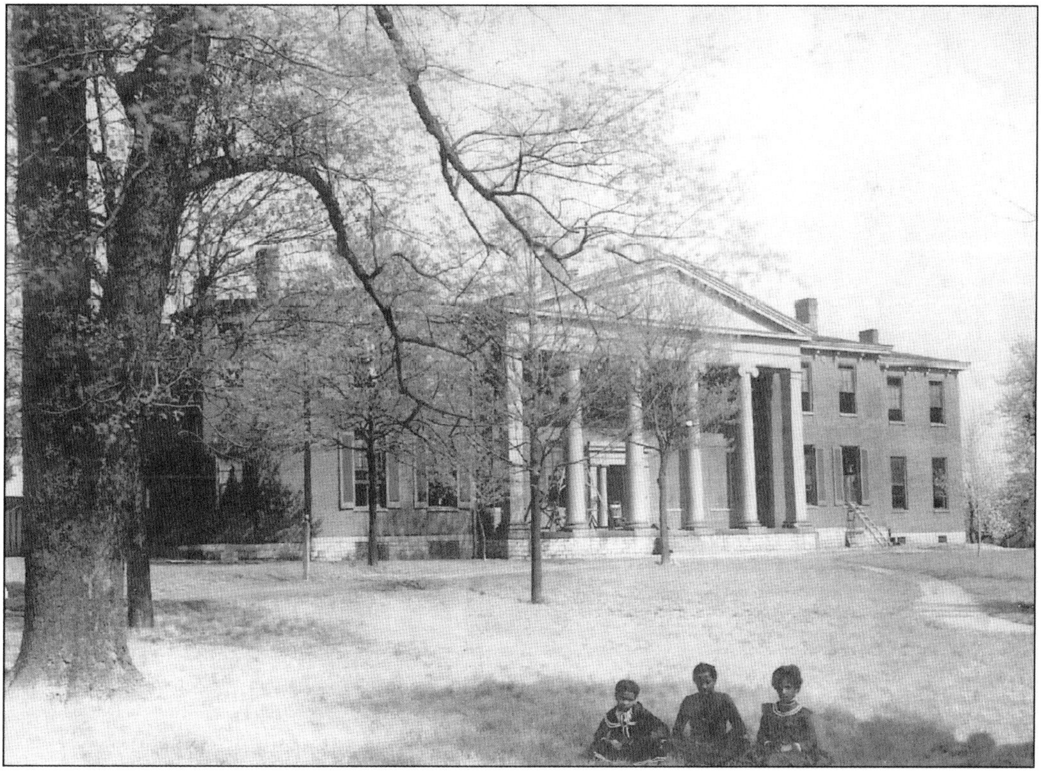

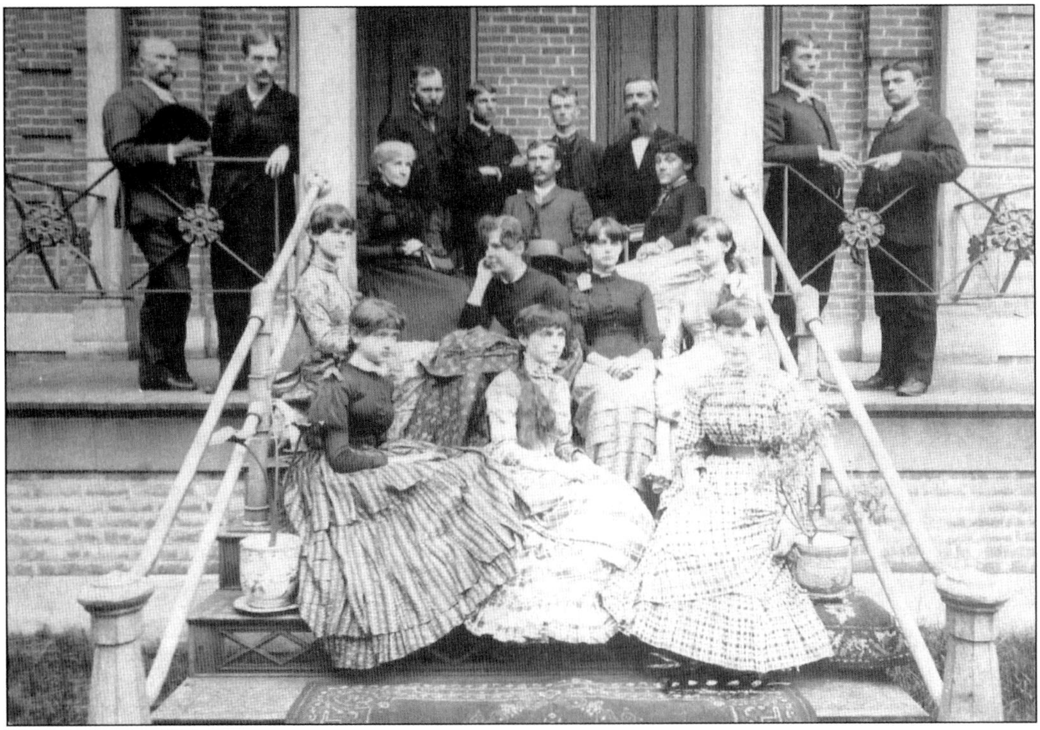

The students in the graduating class of 1886 pose with their teachers on the front steps of the Main Building (above). The Main Building was comprised of Jacobs Hall, built in 1857, Kerr Hall, built in 1882, and Dudley Hall, built in 1882. In the late-19th-century view of the Main Building below, the two-story enclosed passageways are visible between the halls; they allowed students to travel easily to dormitories, classrooms, the dining room, and the chapel. The photograph was taken from the school's park, across Second Street. (Both courtesy of the Kentucky School for the Deaf.)

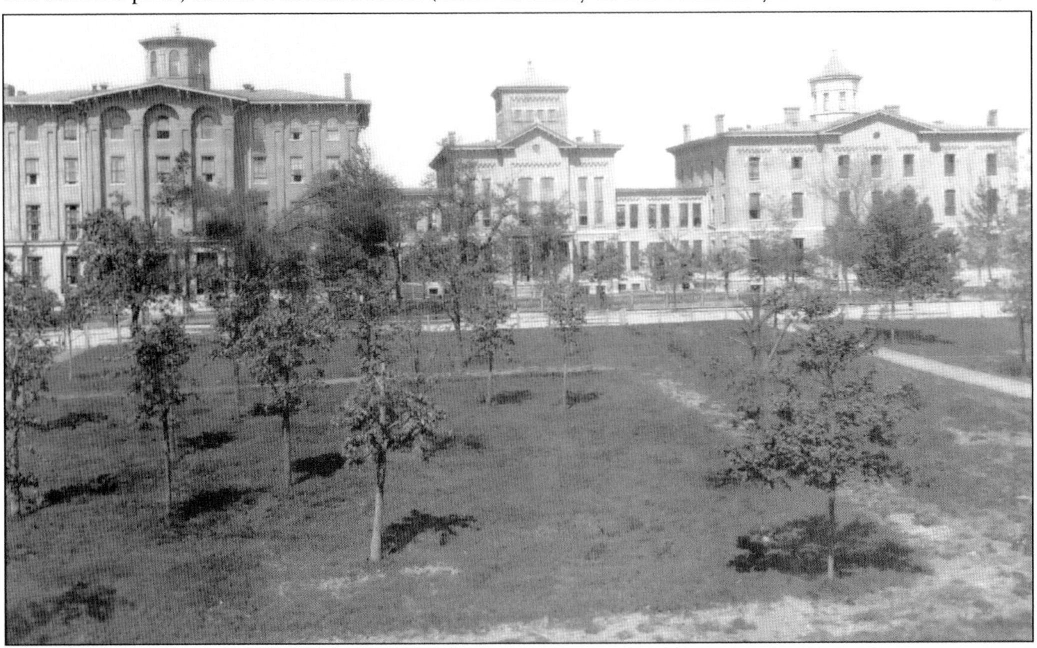

William K. Argo was born in nearby Garrard County in 1858 to Robert and Martha Hobbs Argo, both of whom were deaf. William graduated from Centre College in 1879 and started a teaching position at the Kentucky School for the Deaf that same year. In 1884, he was selected to be the sixth superintendent of the school and served until 1894. (Courtesy of Centre College Special Collections.)

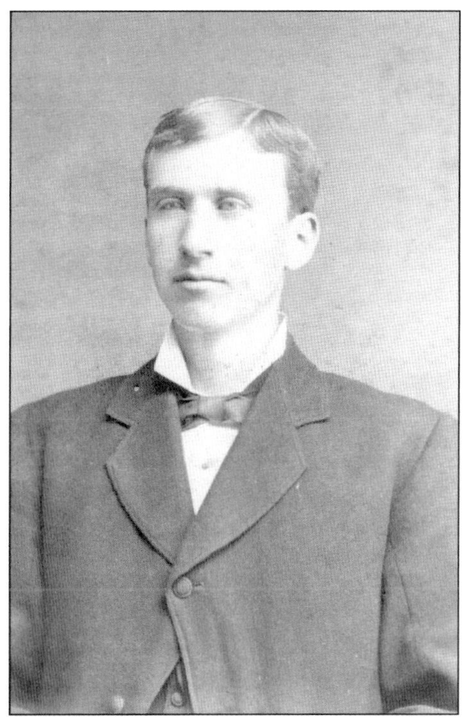

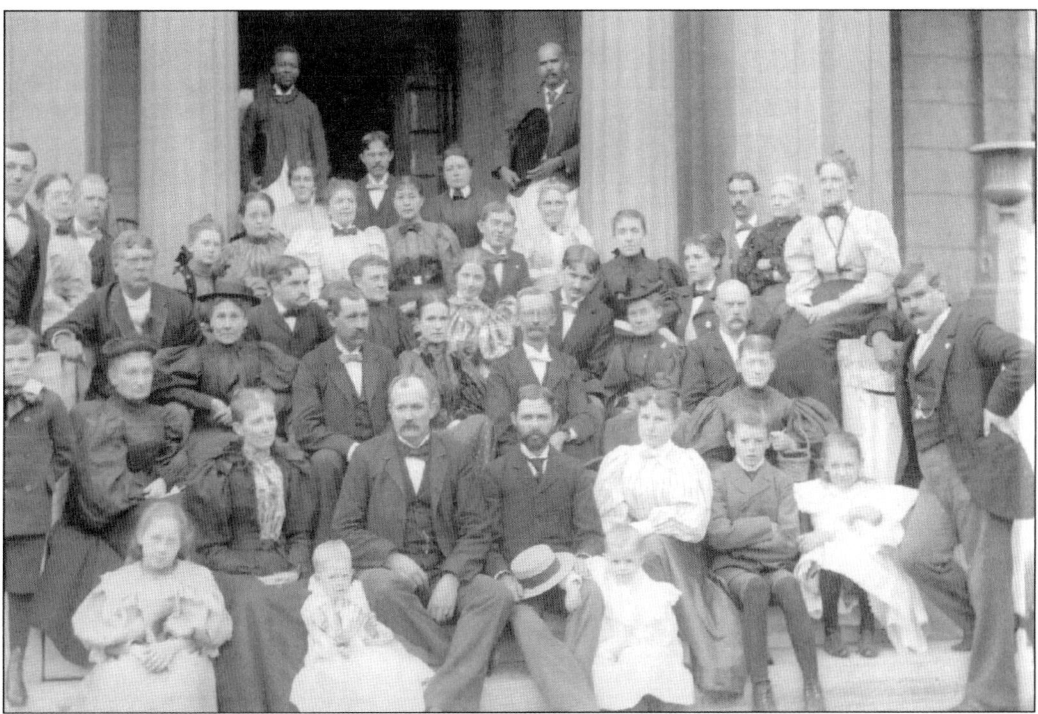

In this 1891 photograph, unidentified Kentucky School for the Deaf officers pose with their family members on the porch of Jacobs Hall. Named for John Adamson Jacobs, the building was erected in 1857 and still stands today, serving as the museum and archives of the school. (Courtesy of the Kentucky School for the Deaf.)

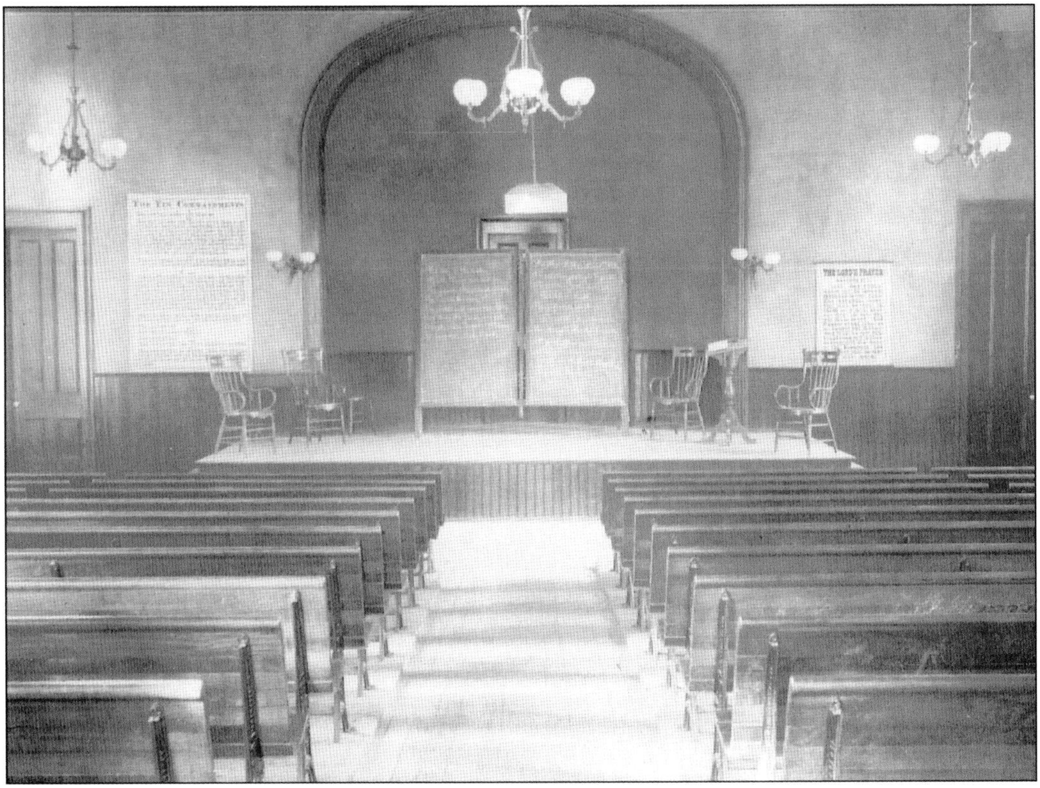

The Old Chapel (above) was built in 1852, and Kentucky School for the Deaf students would meet there every day for nondenominational services and lessons taught by the superintendent, teachers, and occasional guest lecturers. With larger enrollments and an aging Old Chapel, services and classes were moved to the second floor of Kerr Hall. The photograph below shows the staircases in Kerr Hall leading to the chapel. Old Chapel was eventually razed to make way for an ever-growing campus. (Both courtesy of the Kentucky School for the Deaf.)

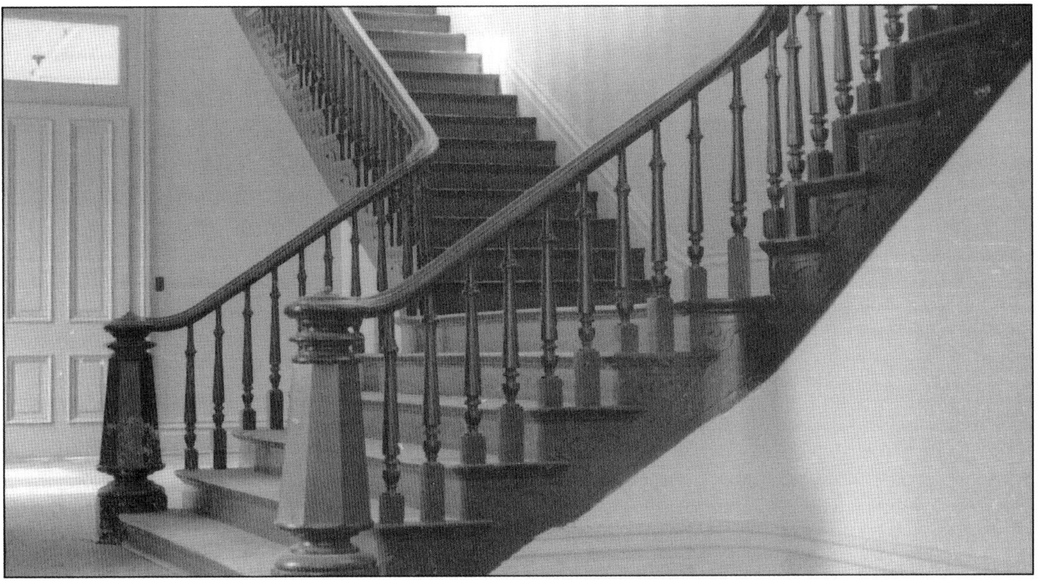

Four fire escapes were added to campus buildings, two each at Jacobs and Dudley Halls in 1895. George M. McClure, editor of the school's paper *The Kentucky Standard*, wrote, "We have fire drills frequently, training each pupil what to do in case of fire. The smallest tot can descend as safely and about as quickly as the strongest man. Tests have shown that over a hundred people can descend from our buildings in one minute." (Courtesy of the Kentucky School for the Deaf.)

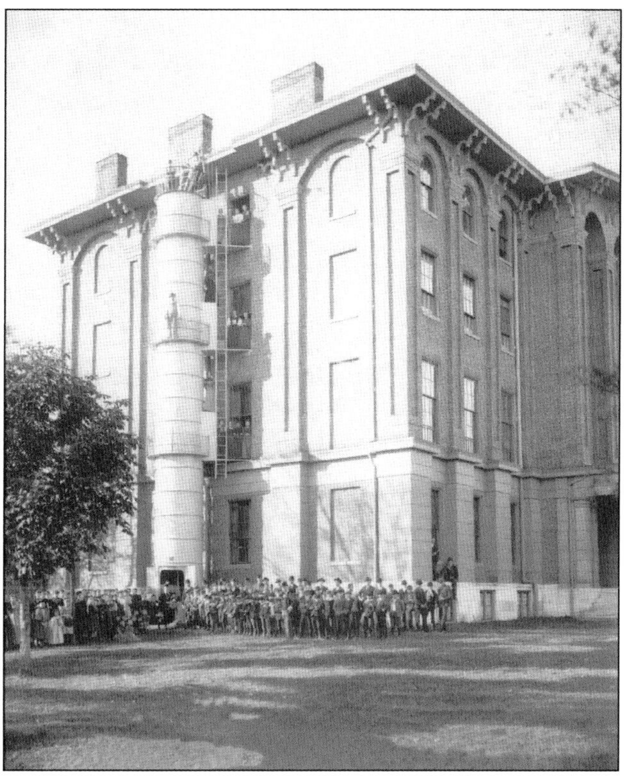

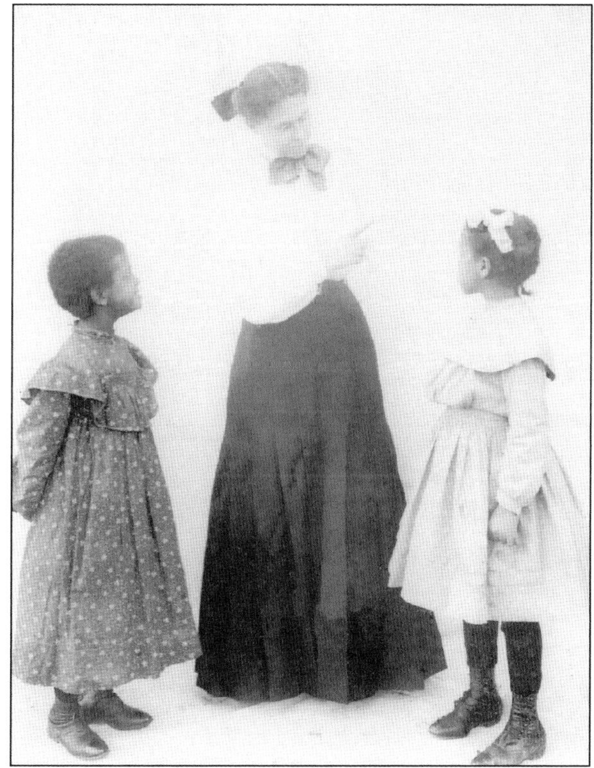

Elizabeth "Lizzie" Keenon Blount poses in this undated photograph with two of her students. A Kentucky School for the Deaf graduate from Mercer County, Lizzie Keenon taught at the Colored School from 1904 to 1907. She married William Blount, a fellow teacher and son of John Blount, the school's first deaf teacher. (Courtesy of the Kentucky School for the Deaf.)

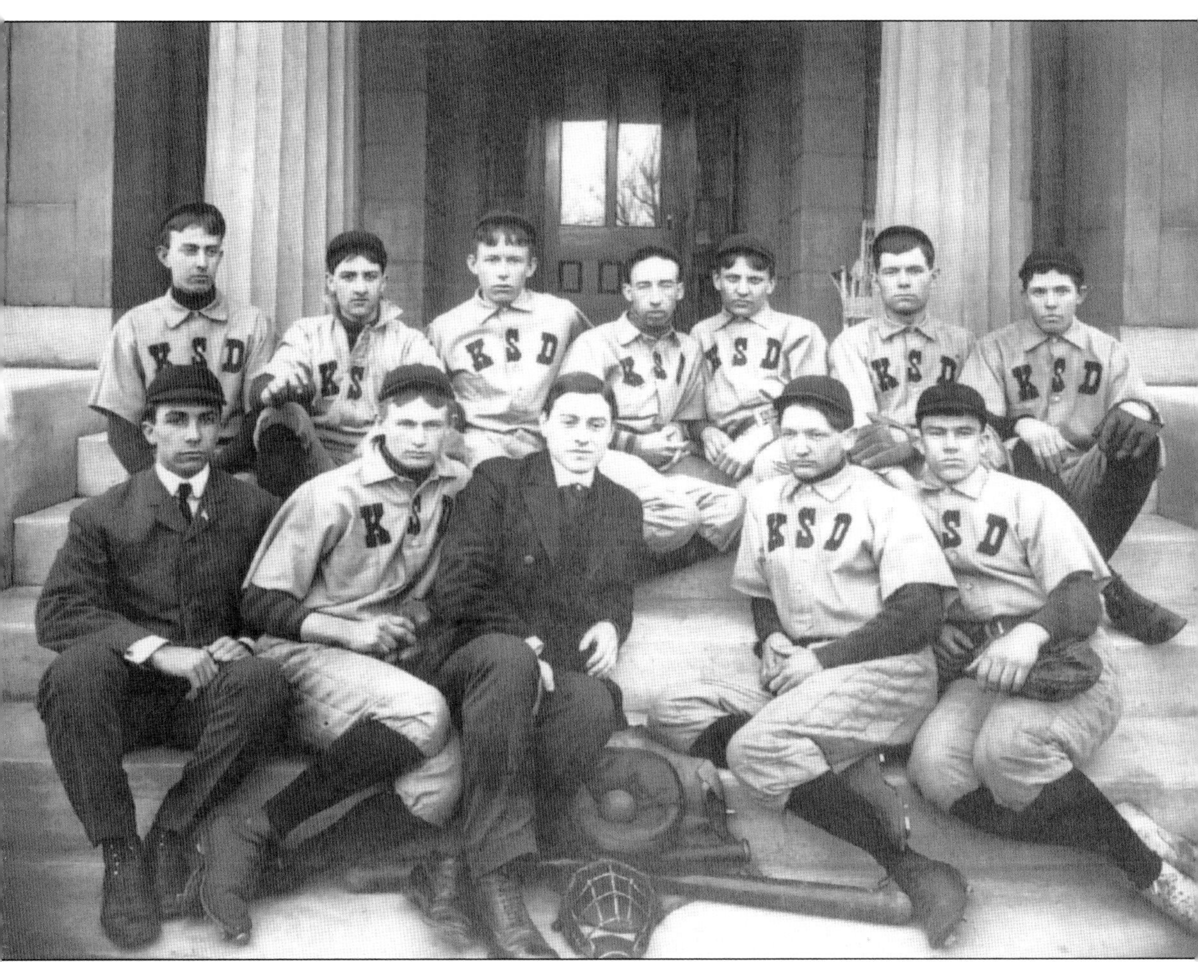


The 1901 Kentucky School for the Deaf baseball team, managed by Max Marcosson (center in suit), poses for this photograph. The students organized games with local teams such as Hogsett Academy, Centre College, and Berea College. Their star player was William E. Hoy, who could neither hear nor speak and who later played center field for several major league teams including the Washington Senators, the Cincinnati Reds, the Chicago White Sox, and the Louisville Colonels. It is said that Hoy was the father of baseball sign language, responsible for developing signs in the sport. Umpires used to call out balls and strikes, but, being deaf, Hoy was unable to hear them. He then asked the third base coach to raise his right arm for a strike and his left arm for a ball. Later, a coach signaled strikes and balls to him in the outfield, and eventually the umpires would use these same signs. (Courtesy of the Kentucky School for the Deaf.)

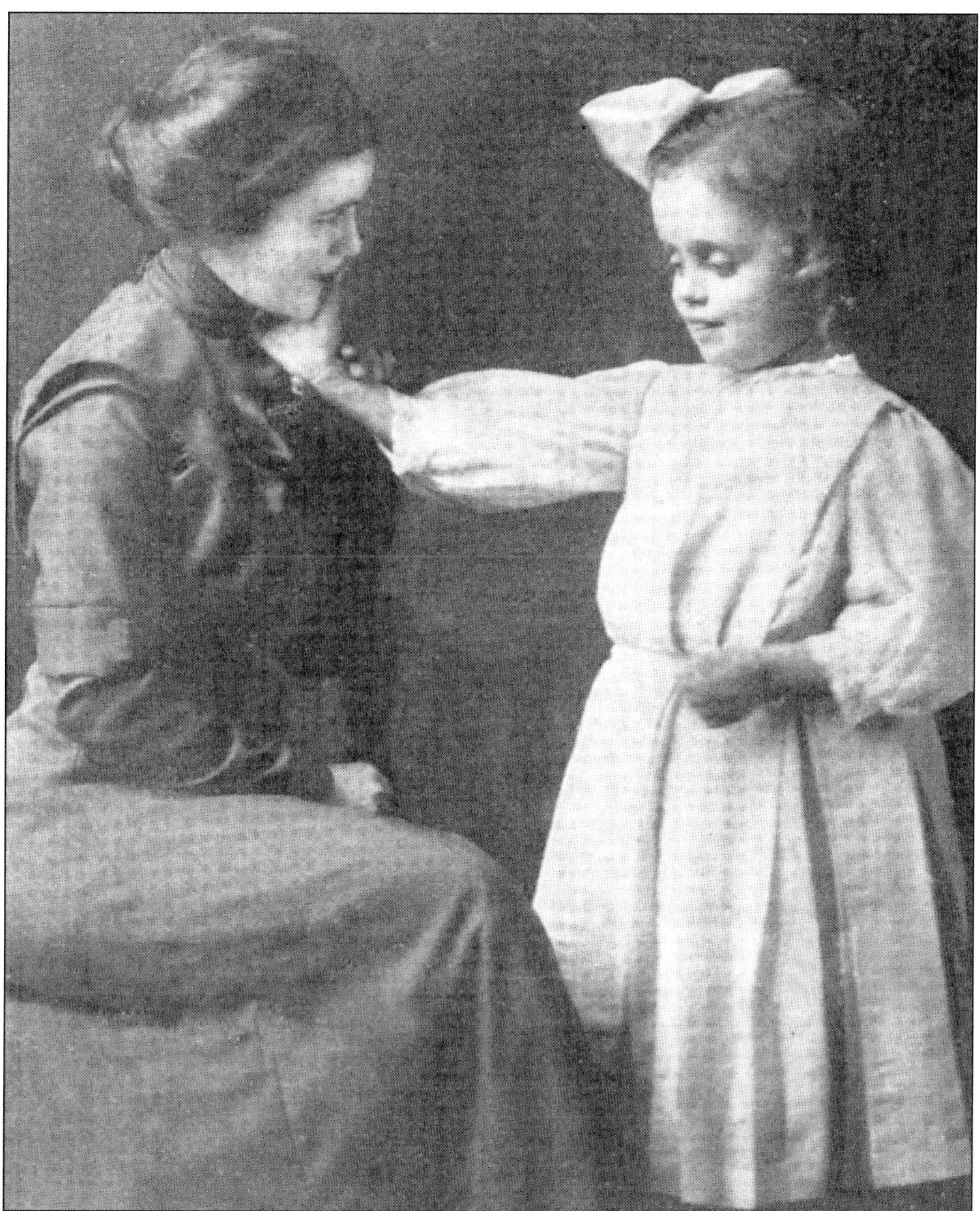

In this 1911 photograph, teacher Sophia Alcorn and student Oma Simpson, who was both deaf and blind, demonstrate how Alcorn taught Oma to read speech and eventually to speak. She put Oma's thumb on her lips, her first finger on her cheek, her second finger on the jawbone, and the fourth and little finger on her throat. Kentuckians fondly referred to Oma Simpson as "our own Helen Keller." Oma moved to New York in 1920 and did not continue her education, passing away in 1927. A Lincoln County native, Sophia Alcorn taught at the Kentucky School for the Deaf from 1909 until 1920. She left the school for the South Dakota School for the Deaf in 1920. She taught Tad Chapman there and developed the Tadoma method for teaching students who were deaf and blind. (Courtesy of the Kentucky School for the Deaf.)

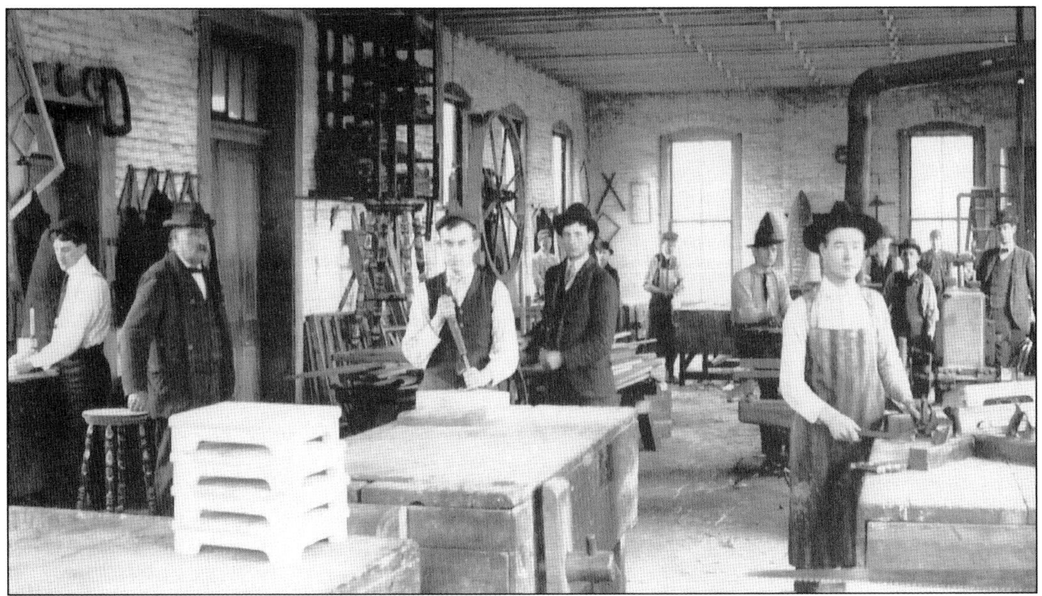

The early-20th-century photograph above depicts the shoemaking department, supervised by David Wilson (left, in bowler hat). The Kentucky School for the Deaf offered vocational classes for students in addition to shoemaking, including print work, agriculture, and livestock handling. The printing office (below) began operations in 1874, when the school's newspaper, *The Kentucky Deaf-Mute,* was first published. In 1896, the newspaper changed its name to *The Kentucky Standard*, continuing publication until 2004. The students also printed specialized instructional books for Kentucky School for the Deaf teachers such as Mary Woolslayer. James Beauchamp (seated at desk) was in charge of the printing office when this photograph was taken in the 1950s. (Both courtesy of the Kentucky School for the Deaf.)

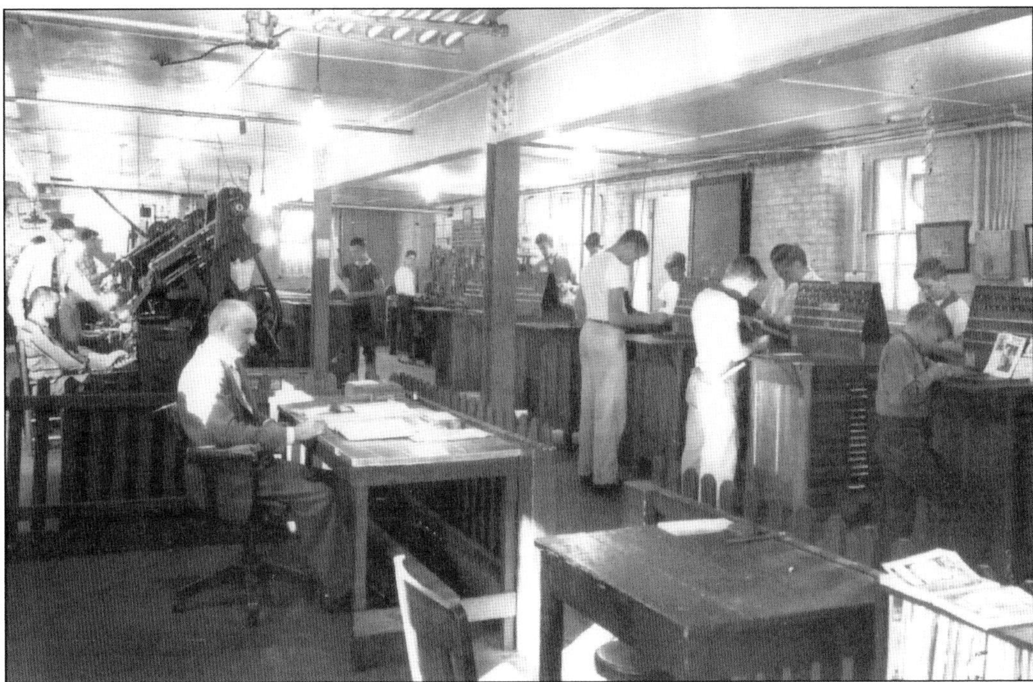

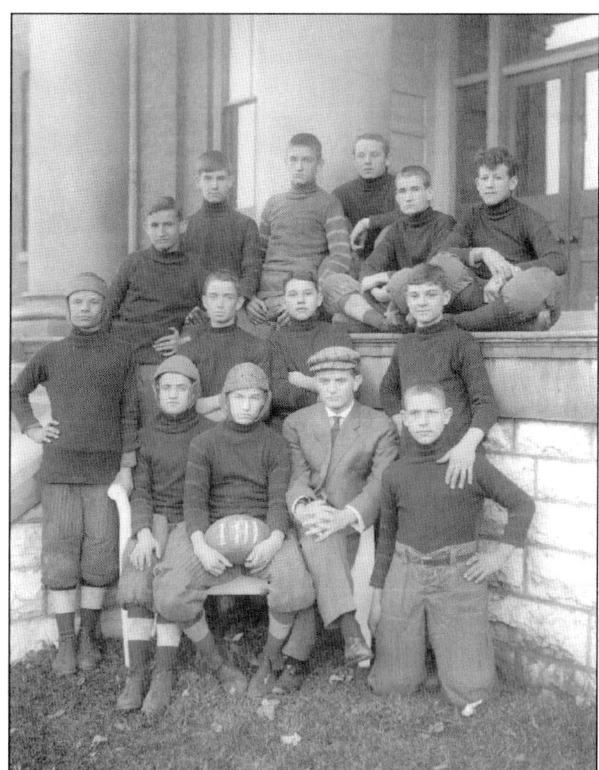

Sports were an important part of school life for many students at the Kentucky School for the Deaf. The 1911 football team (right) poses with coach Otto Meunier (center, wearing cap). According to *The Kentucky Standard*, the young boys on the football team enjoyed many rough scrimmages as they mastered the rules of the sport. The 1932 basketball team (below), comprised of older students, poses in height order from left to right with coach C.B. Hoffmeyer (right). (Both courtesy of the Kentucky School for the Deaf.)

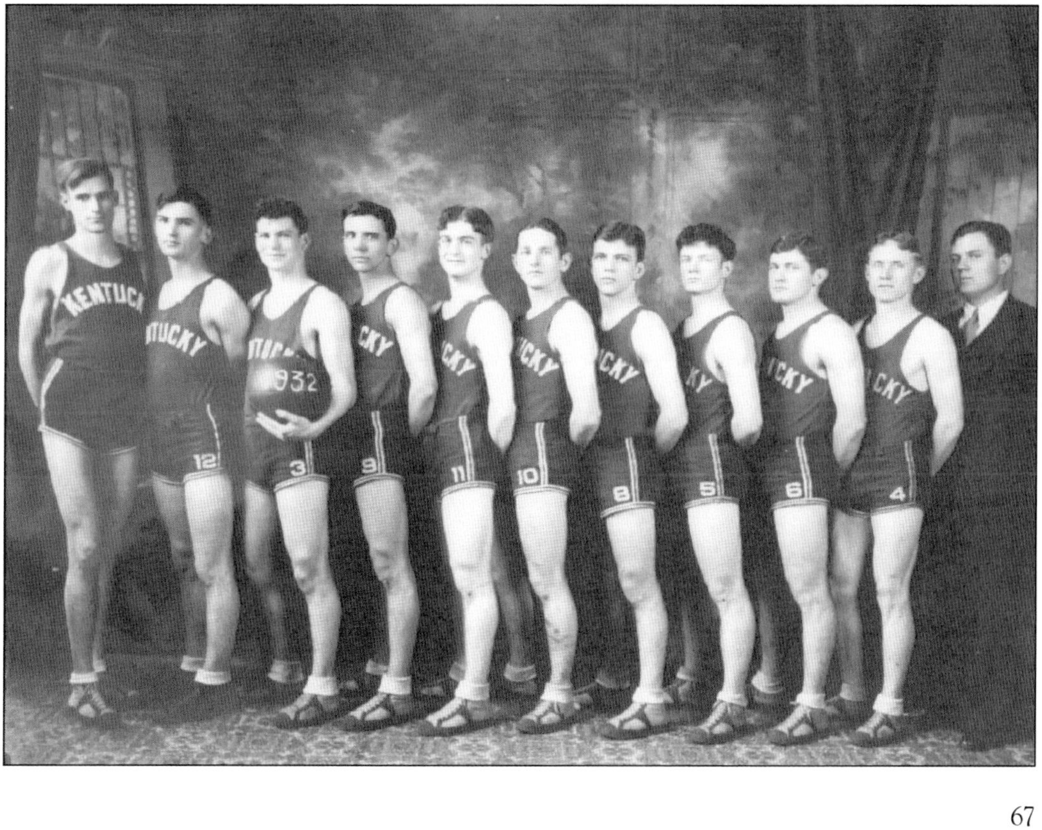

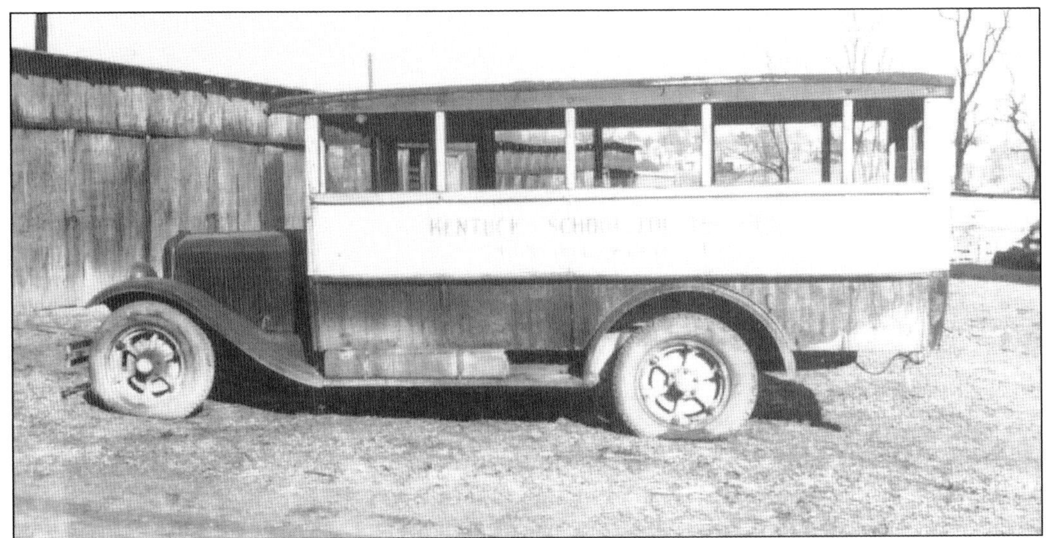

In 1929, Col. E.R. Bradley donated $1,545.30 to the Kentucky School for the Deaf, which bought a Dodge Six school bus for outings and educational trips. The bus was custom-built for the school, featuring inward-facing seats so students could communicate via sign language while traveling. (Courtesy of the Kentucky School for the Deaf.)

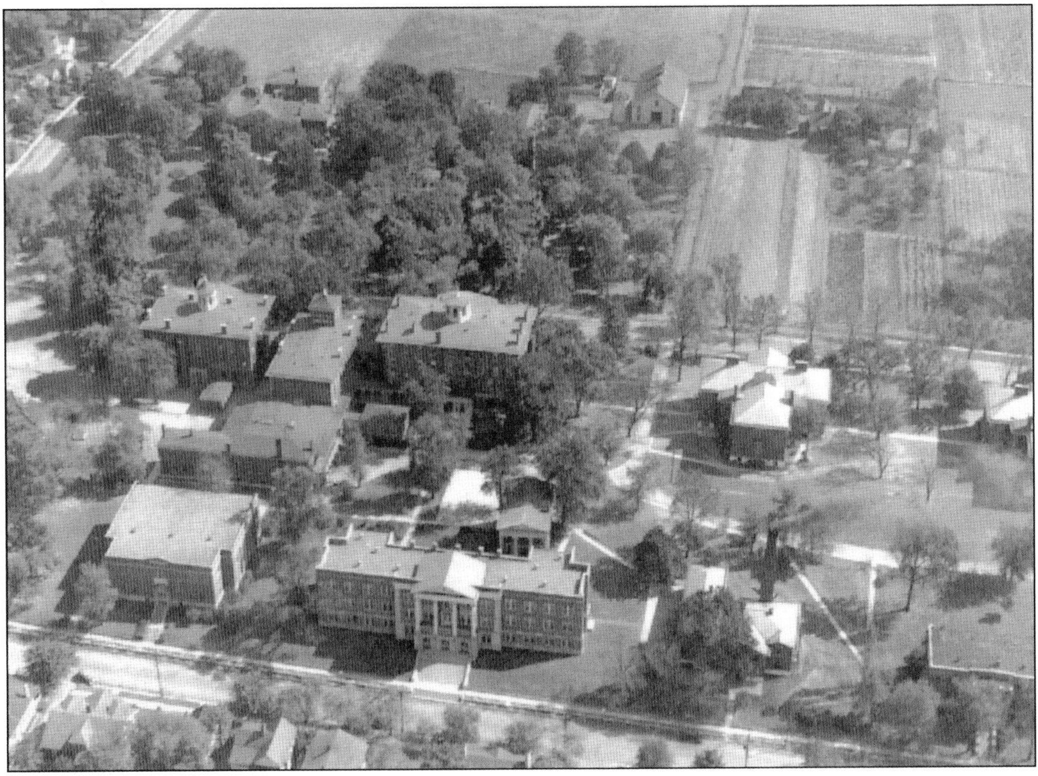

This 1939 aerial view shows the whole Kentucky School for the Deaf campus. The three buildings in the center-left with cupolas are, from left to right, Dudley, Kerr, and Jacobs Halls. To their right are Gallaudet and Clerc Halls. The school's farms are visible in the upper portion of the photograph. (Courtesy of the Kentucky School for the Deaf.)

Girls in the graduating class of 1948 peer over the fourth floor atrium opening at their dormitory, Jacobs Hall. The atrium was built in typical architectural style for deaf facilities, with open sightlines allowing students to communicate freely between the levels using sign language. (Courtesy of the Kentucky School for the Deaf.)

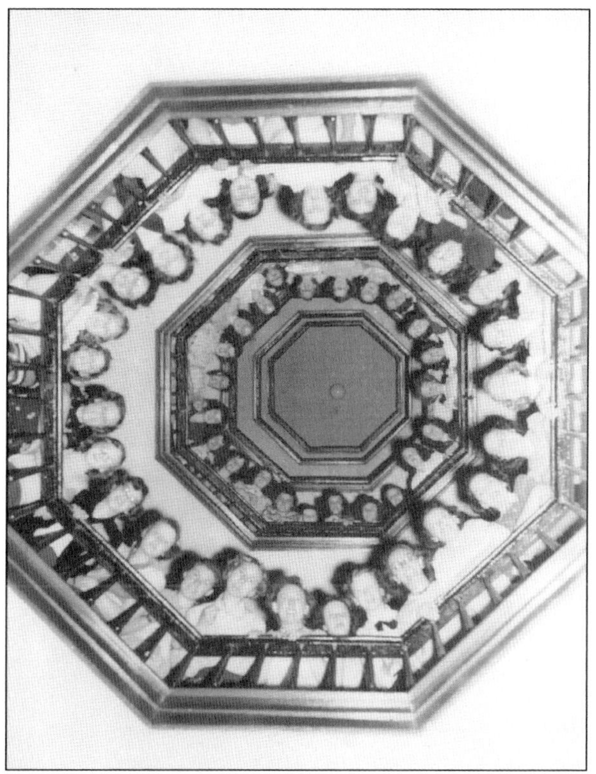

Supervisor Warren Livingston stands with African American students in front of Washington Hall in 1952, when the new building opened. By Kentucky law, integration at the Kentucky School for the Deaf occurred in stages: vocational training in 1954, all classes in 1959, and, in 1963, full integration in dormitories and dining halls. Working from 1980 to 1990, Susie Sweat-Bates was the first African American to teach daily speech classes in a classroom setting at the school. (Courtesy of the Kentucky School for the Deaf.)

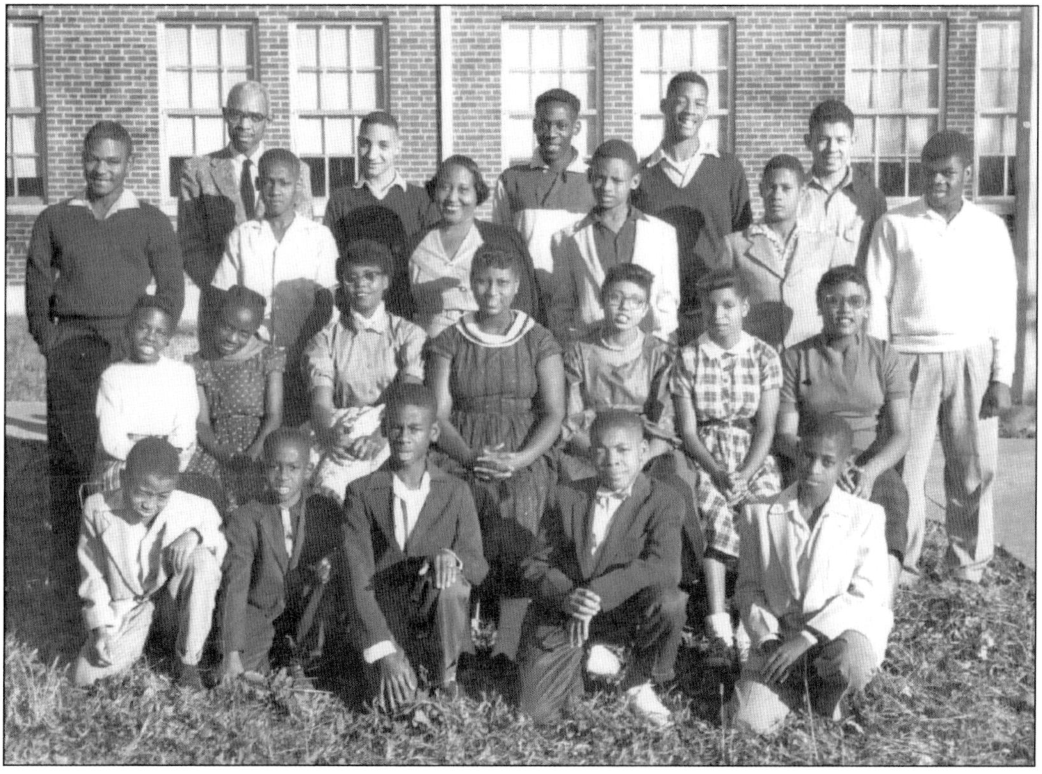

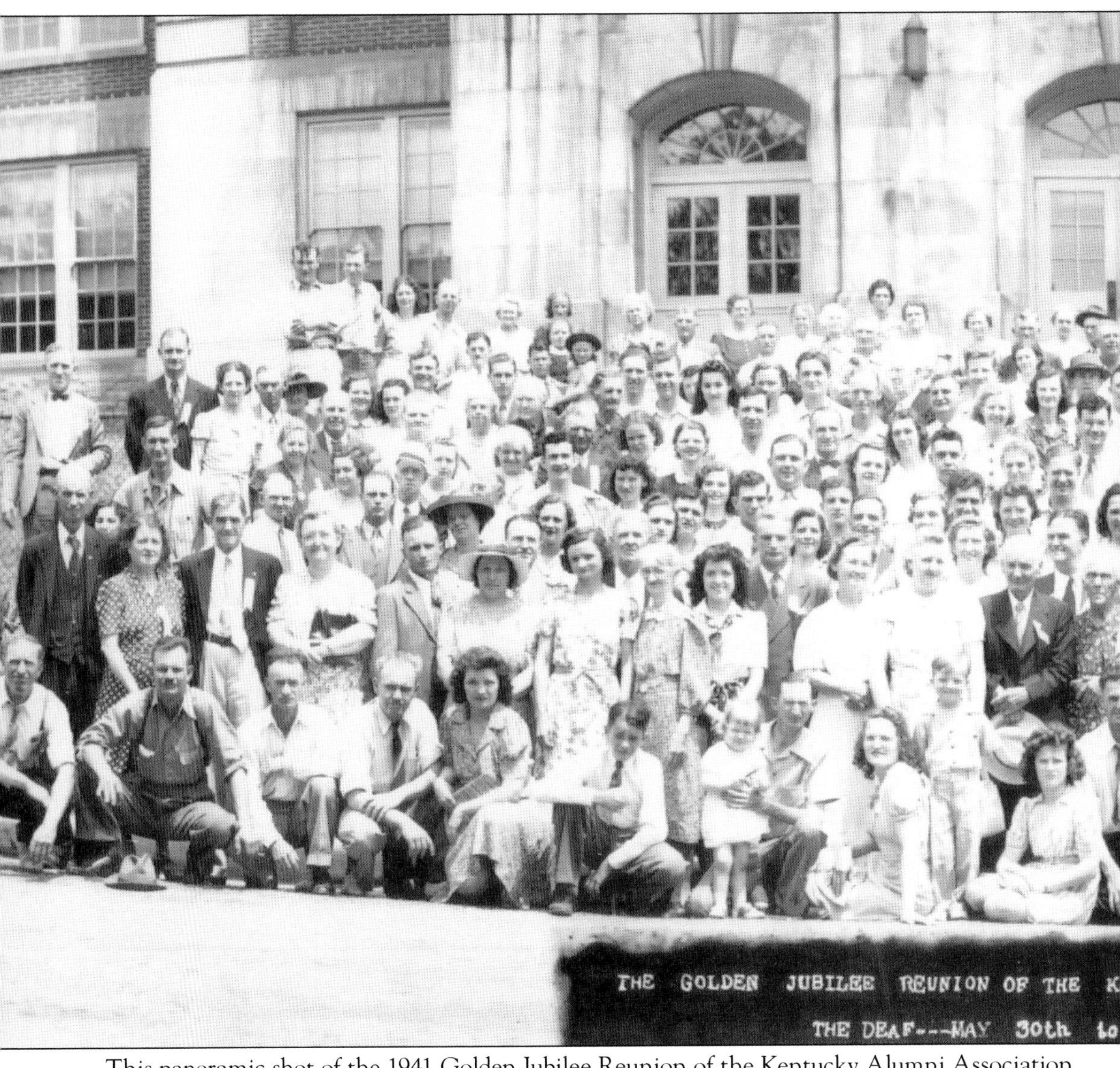


This panoramic shot of the 1941 Golden Jubilee Reunion of the Kentucky Alumni Association of the Kentucky School for the Deaf was taken in front of Lee Hall on Third Street. The first reunion was held in 1891; among those present at the 1891 reunion was Evelyn Sherrill, one of the first three pupils who entered the school in 1823. Attendees organized the Kentucky Alumni Association following the 1891 reunion. The Kentucky School for the Deaf has very close ties

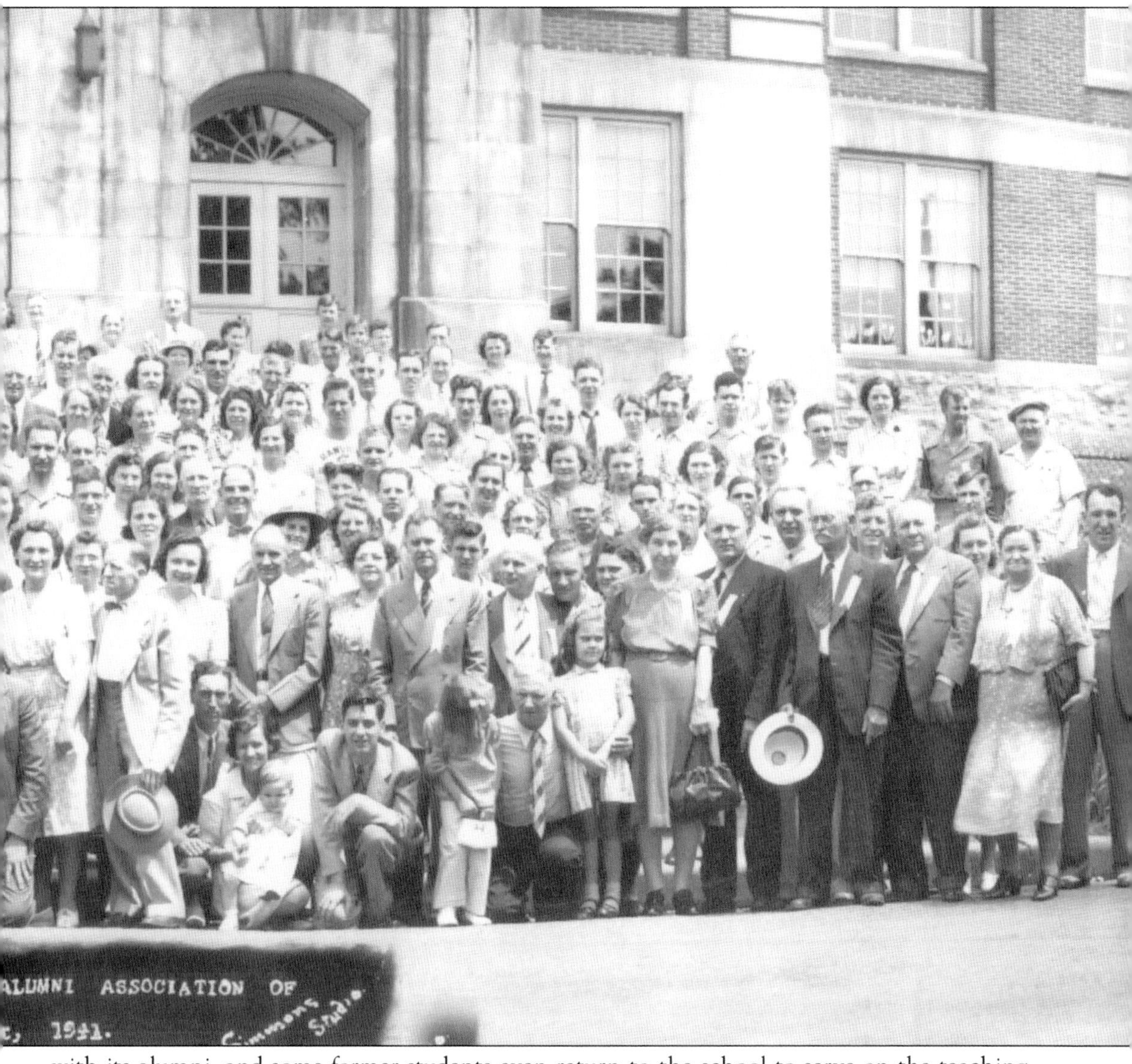


with its alumni, and some former students even return to the school to serve on the teaching staff, such as John Blount, the school's first deaf teacher. Every year, homecoming events draw many current students and alumni, who have fond memories of their time spent at the Danville campus. (Courtesy of the Kentucky School for the Deaf.)

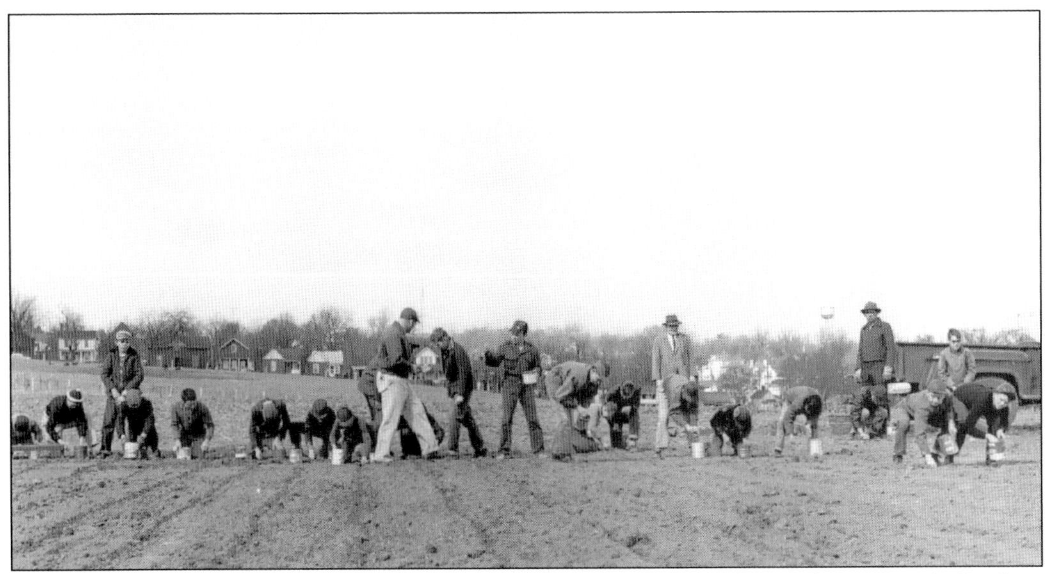

Every spring, farm manager Mr. Rankin would put out a call for student volunteers to help plant crops, turning them into fun events, like his "Onion Planting Parties." In the 1959 photograph above, Rankin (standing at right in cap) oversees some of the intermediate students working the land. When it was time to harvest, Rankin would call students back to the fields, as seen in the undated photograph of students picking beans below. Having farms on campus allowed the Kentucky School for the Deaf to provide training for students as well as put food on the dining tables. (Both courtesy of the Kentucky School for the Deaf.)

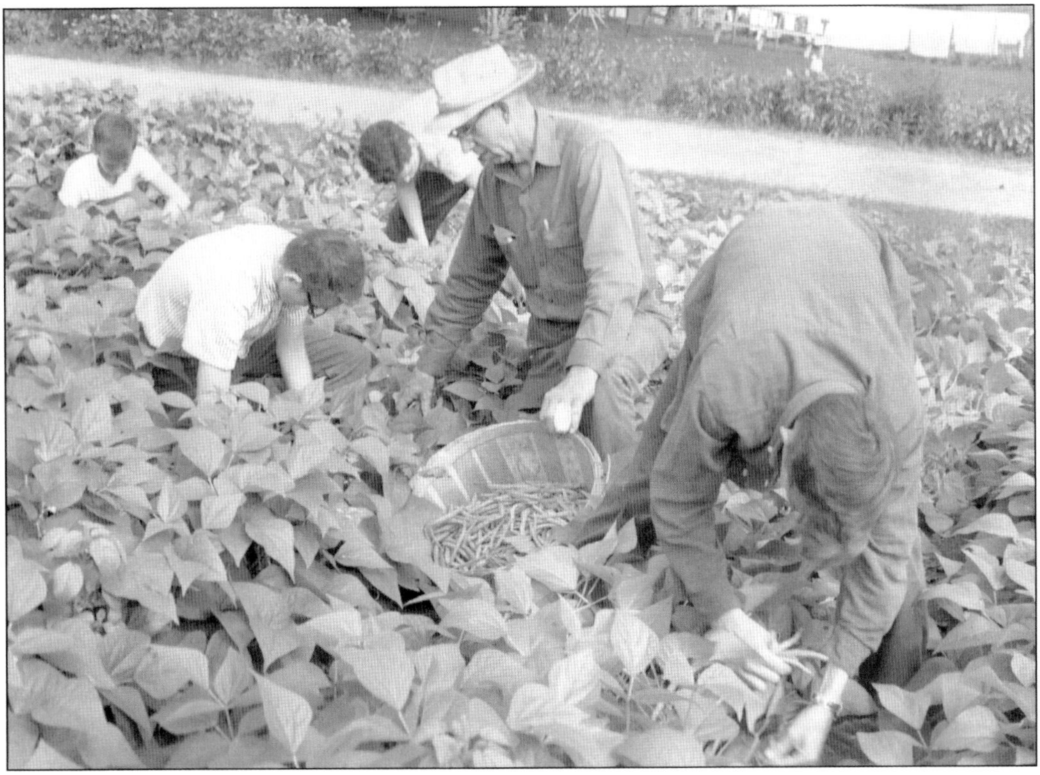

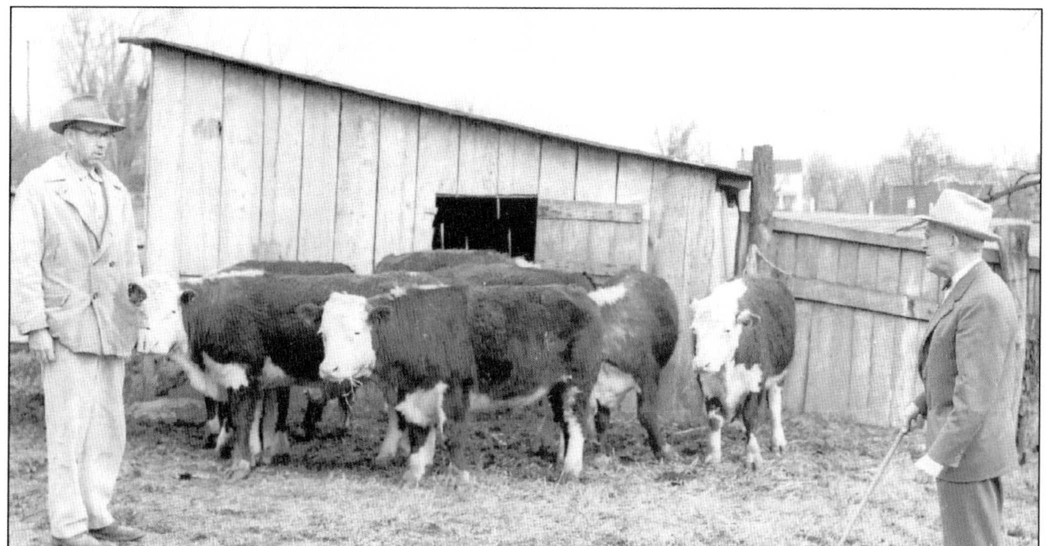

Although the Kentucky School for the Deaf had a dairy herd at the beginning of the 20th century, the first herd of beef cattle came to the school farm in 1957 and provided fresh beef and additional vocational training for the students. Mr. Rankin (right), farm manager, discusses the beef cattle operations with an unidentified dairyman. (Courtesy of the Kentucky School for the Deaf.)

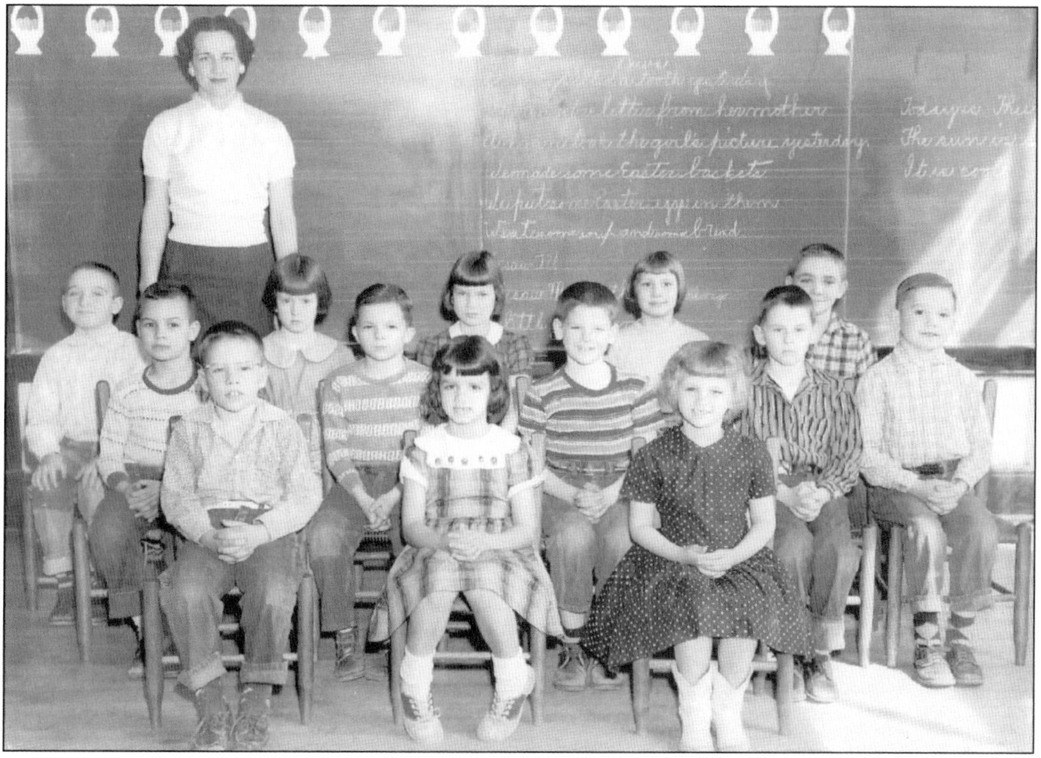

In this 1957 photograph, primary students pause in the middle of their language lesson to pose with their teacher, Agnes White. The Kentucky School for the Deaf initially offered only three years of schooling for its students, but it expanded to include preschool through high school classes when the need for such was realized. (Courtesy of the Kentucky School for the Deaf.)

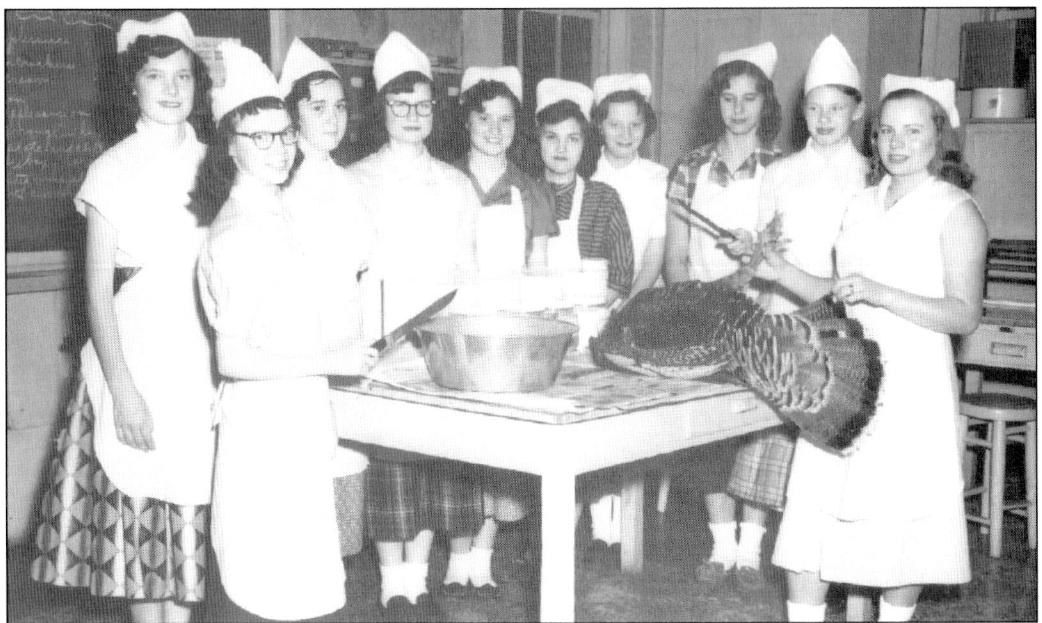

Holiday celebrations were an important tradition at the Kentucky School for the Deaf, particularly for out-of-state students who could not easily return home to spend time with their families. In the 1957 photograph above, older female students prepare a turkey dinner for Thanksgiving from scratch in their home economics class. Posing with their presents in front of the school's Christmas tree as older students mingle in the background, younger students are surprised by a visit from Santa Claus in a 1958 photograph (below). (Both courtesy of the Kentucky School for the Deaf.)

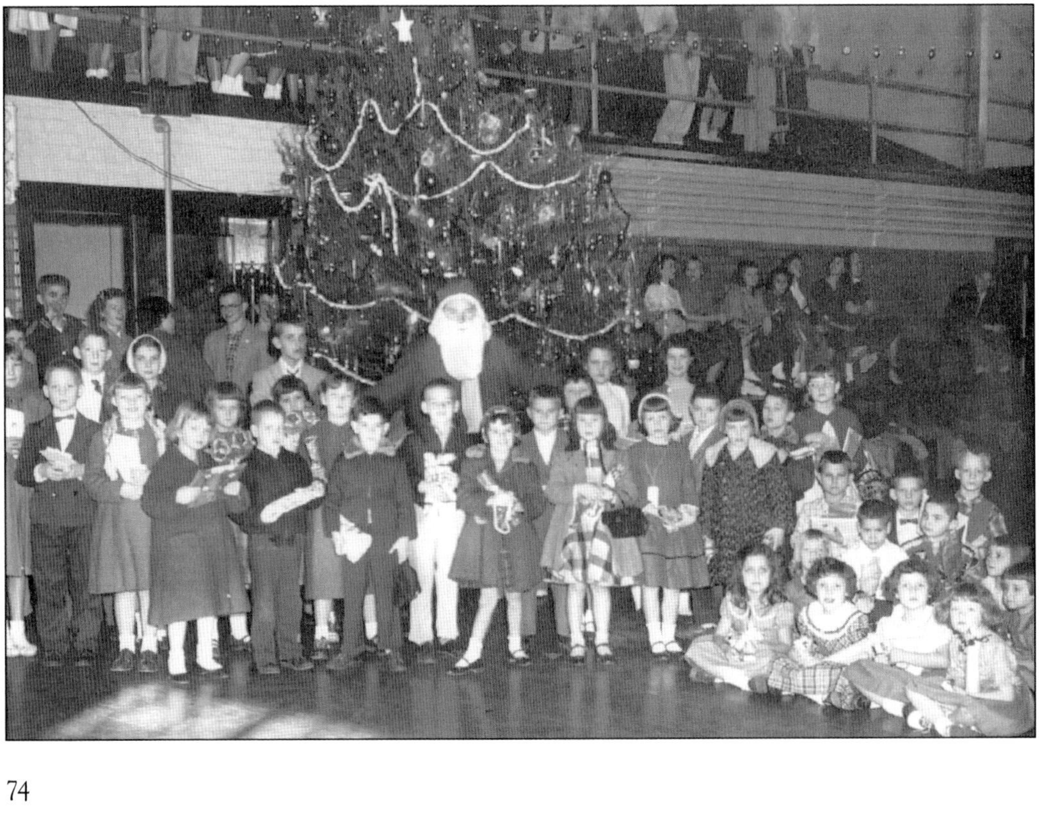

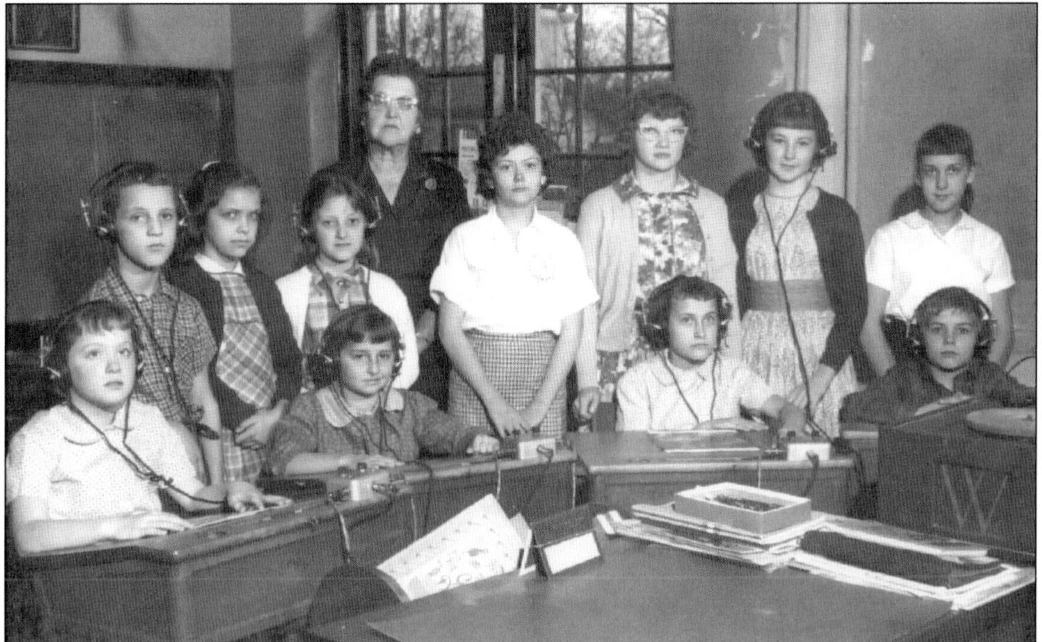

Not all students at the Kentucky School for the Deaf were entirely deaf; by the 1960s, the school had been using group hearing aids for several years. In this 1962 photograph, teacher Josephine Nunnelly and her class demonstrate how they use a Warren Group Hearing Aid. (Courtesy of the Kentucky School for the Deaf.)

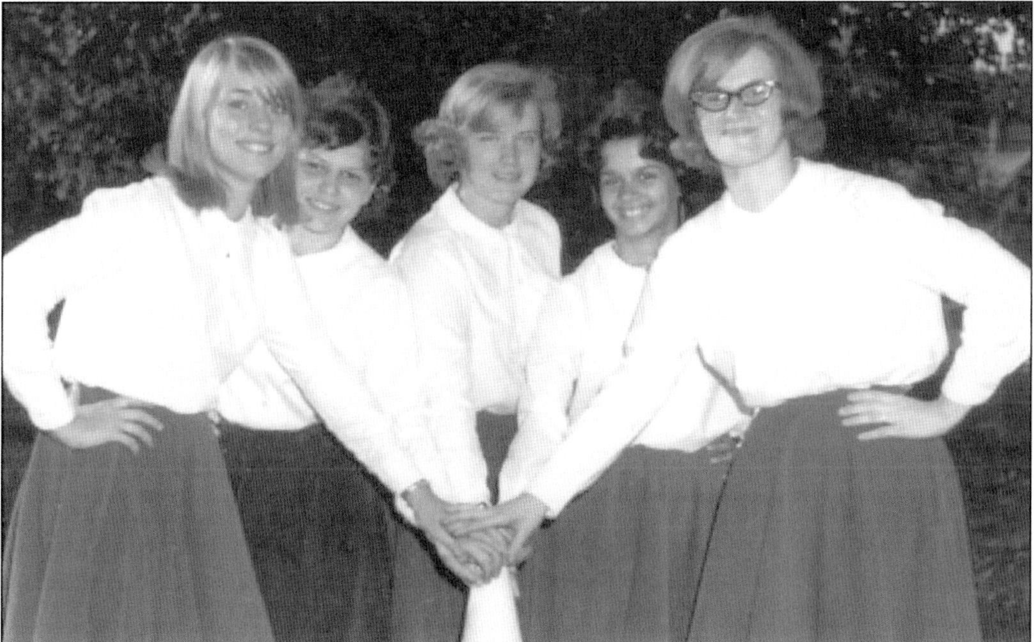

No sporting event at the school was complete without the Kentucky School for the Deaf cheerleading squad. In this 1965 photograph, pictured from left to right are cheerleaders Olivia Whitt, Mary McCarthy, Pamela Feck, Shirley Fritz, and Geraldine Jones. (Courtesy of the Kentucky School for the Deaf.)

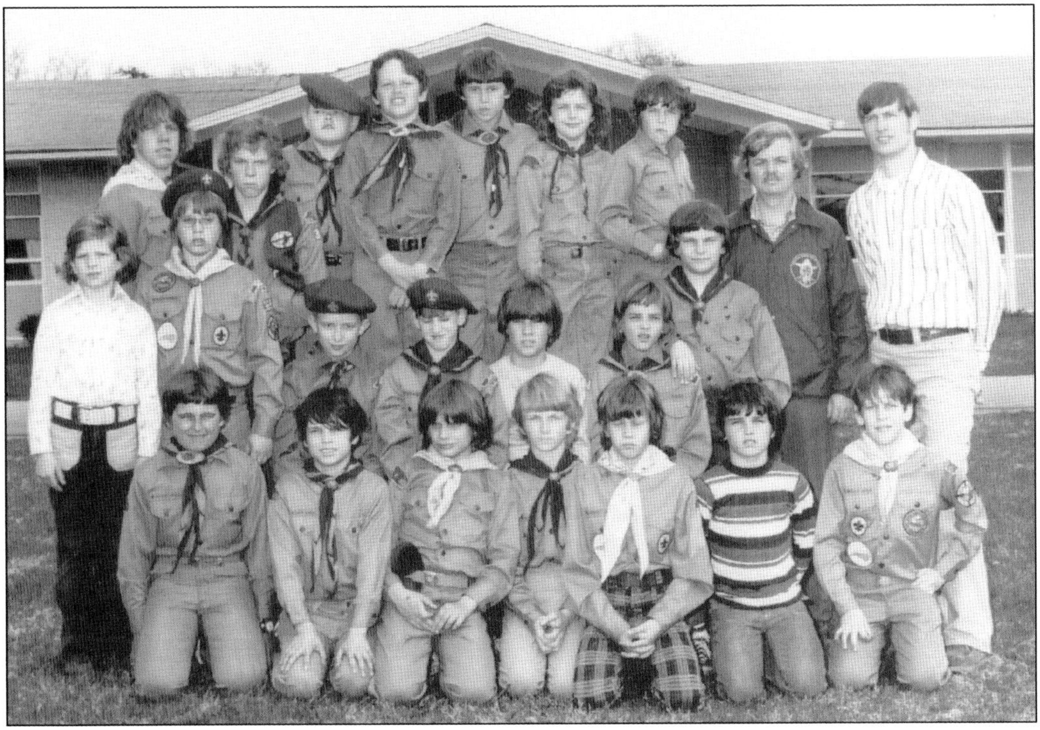

In 1968, Boy Scout executive Robert Broome, Scoutmaster John Gentry, and Kentucky School for the Deaf superintendent Jack Brady worked together to organize the first Boy Scout troop that the school had seen in 54 years. The Scouts met weekly in Rogers Hall on campus. (Courtesy of the Kentucky School for the Deaf.)

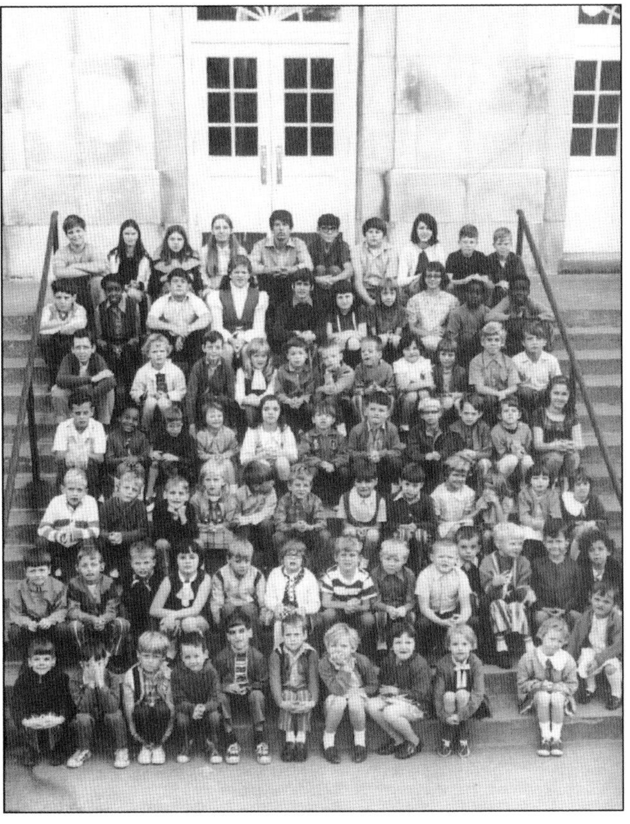

The Kentucky School for the Deaf saw its largest group of new students—80 in total—enrolled in 1971. In 1963 and 1964, a wave of rubella, or German measles, swept through the country. This caused a rise in the birthrate of deaf and multihandicapped children, resulting in the largest student populations in the school's history in the 1970s. (Courtesy of the Kentucky School for the Deaf.)

# *Six*

# Kentucky College for Women

In 1854, the Kentucky Legislature granted a charter for the Henderson Female Institute. Fundraising began, and in 1859, a four-story brick building was erected, opening to the public in 1860 under the name Caldwell Female Institute. The Civil War years were difficult for the new school, and it struggled to retain students and remain solvent throughout the conflict. It did, however, recover substantially after the war and came under the control of the Second Presbyterian Church in 1874. In 1876, the same year it changed its name to Caldwell Female College, the school was destroyed in a devastating fire. It closed for four years, reopening in 1881 after buying the property of the old Danville Classical and Military Institute. The school consolidated with Bell Seminary in 1885 and renamed itself Caldwell College two years later, ushering in an era of prosperity and growth. In 1913, the institution made its final name change to Kentucky College for Women, and opened as a department of Centre College 13 years later. The Kentucky College for Women closed its doors in 1962 after consolidating its campus with Centre College.

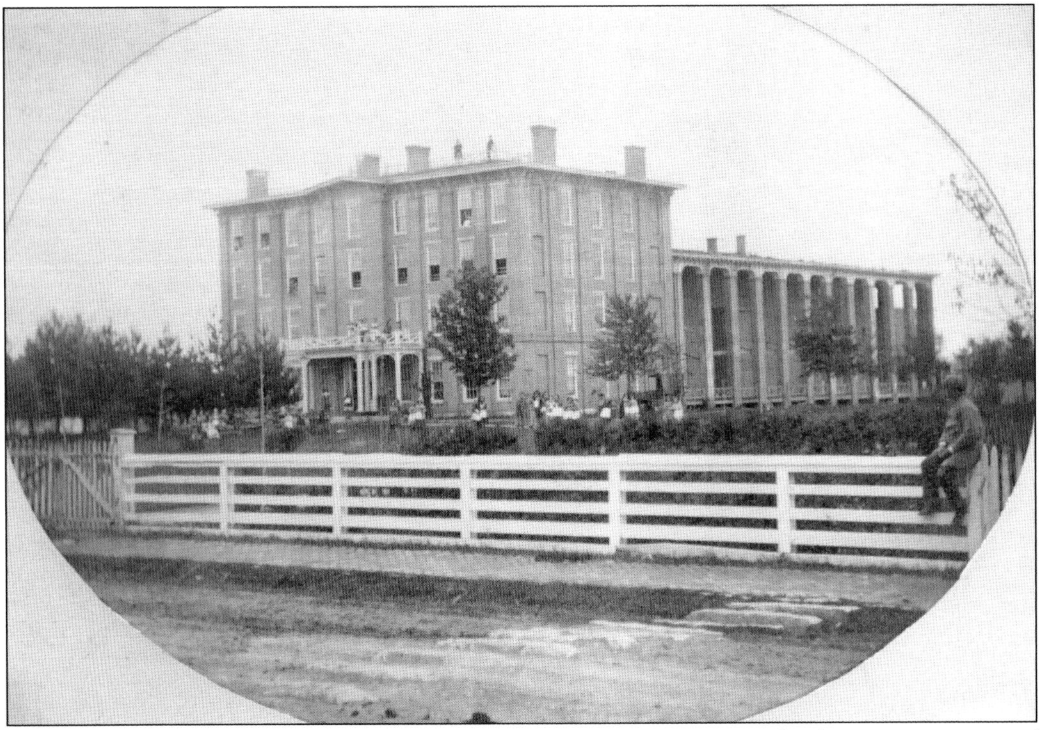

Granted a charter by the Kentucky state legislature in 1854 to provide the young women of Kentucky "educational advantages similar to those afforded young men in the historic Centre College," the Caldwell Female Institute opened to students in 1860. The school, pictured here in 1870, changed its name to Caldwell Female College in 1876, the same year a devastating fire destroyed the campus's only building. (Courtesy of Centre College Special Collections.)

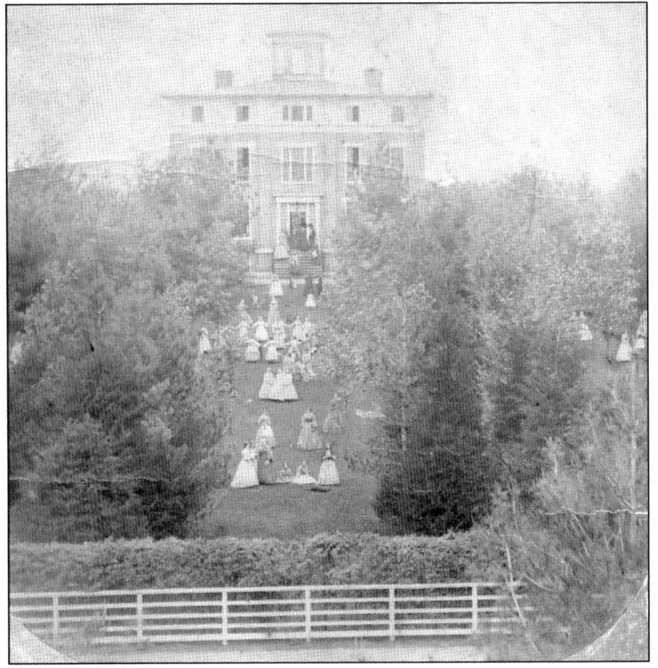

Chartered in 1860, the Danville Female Academy operated under the First Baptist Church of Danville. The academy's trustees purchased the land and home of Dr. Thomas W. Jackson and turned them into a campus and school building. Pictured here around 1865, the school eventually merged with the Caldwell Institute in 1869, and the campus was later used by the Danville Classical and Military Institute. (Courtesy of Centre College Special Collections.)

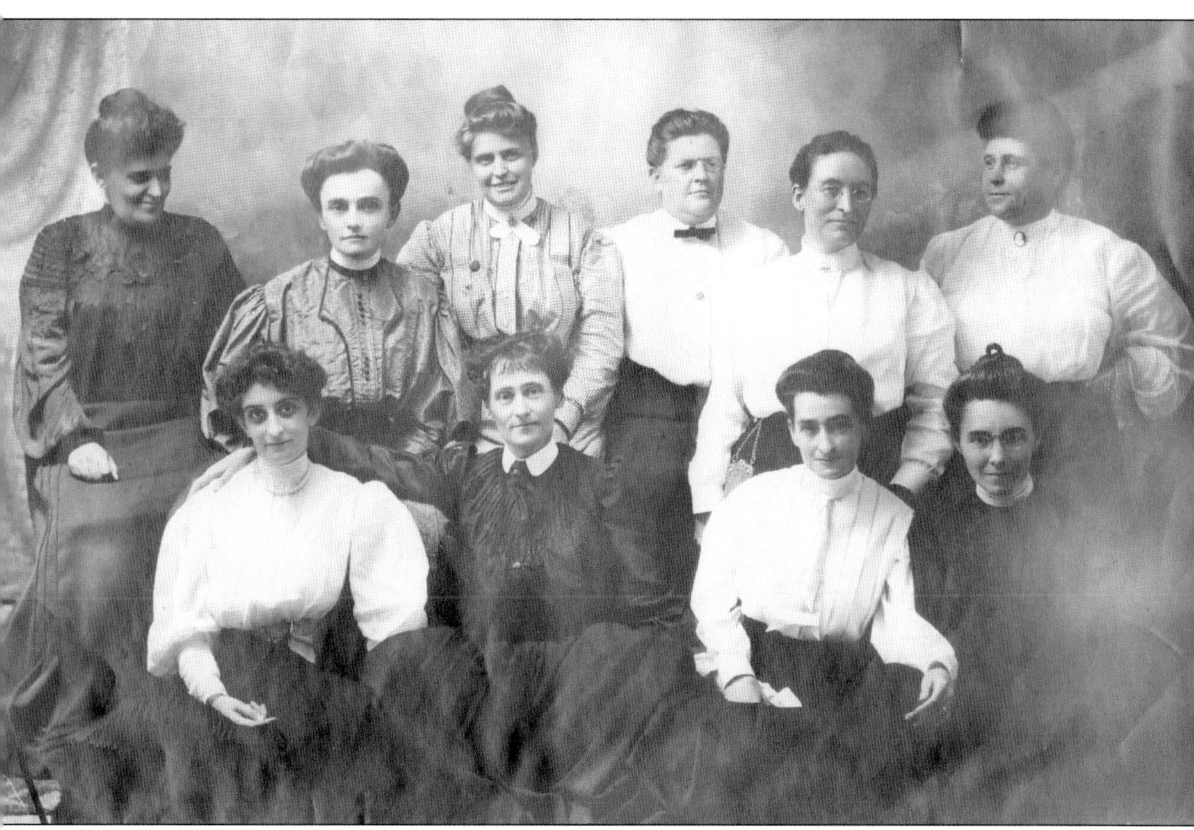

Bell Seminary for Young Ladies, located on Lexington Avenue where the Lexington Avenue Baptist Church currently stands, was described in an 1880 catalog as being situated "within large pleasant grounds in one of the most agreeable parts of town." The seminary opened its doors in 1876, and for the next ten years, the school offered primary and preparatory classes for both boys and girls as well as collegiate courses for young women. In 1886, Bell Seminary merged into Caldwell College. Pictured in this undated photograph are, from left to right, (sitting) Sadie Cook Perry, Mattie Duke Tarlton, Clara Lee McGorty Bryce, and Phoenie Salter Chestnut; (standing) Nan McDowell, Sophia Bright Logan, Josie Smith Robertson, Ella Barker, Mollie Johnson Lee, and Lauren Baker Allen. (Courtesy of Centre College Special Collections.)

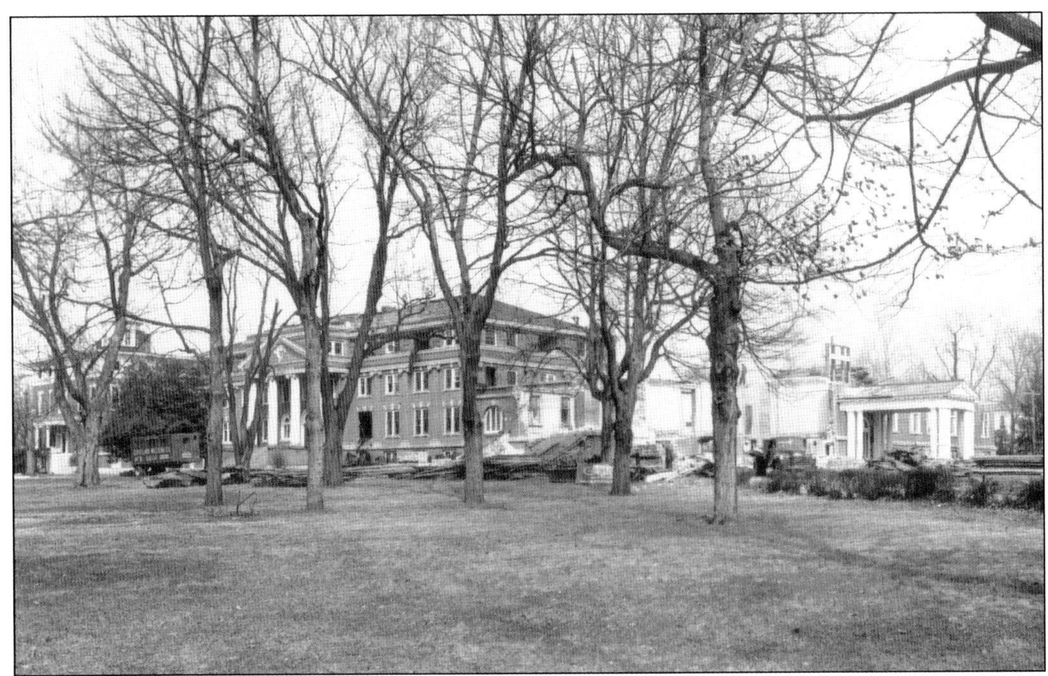

Caldwell Female College dropped the word *Female* from its name in the late 1880s, then renamed itself Kentucky College for Women in 1913, remaining so until merging with Centre College in 1962. This view of the campus shows West Hall (left), Morgan Hall (center), and the nearly-razed East Hall (right). (Courtesy of Centre College Special Collections.)

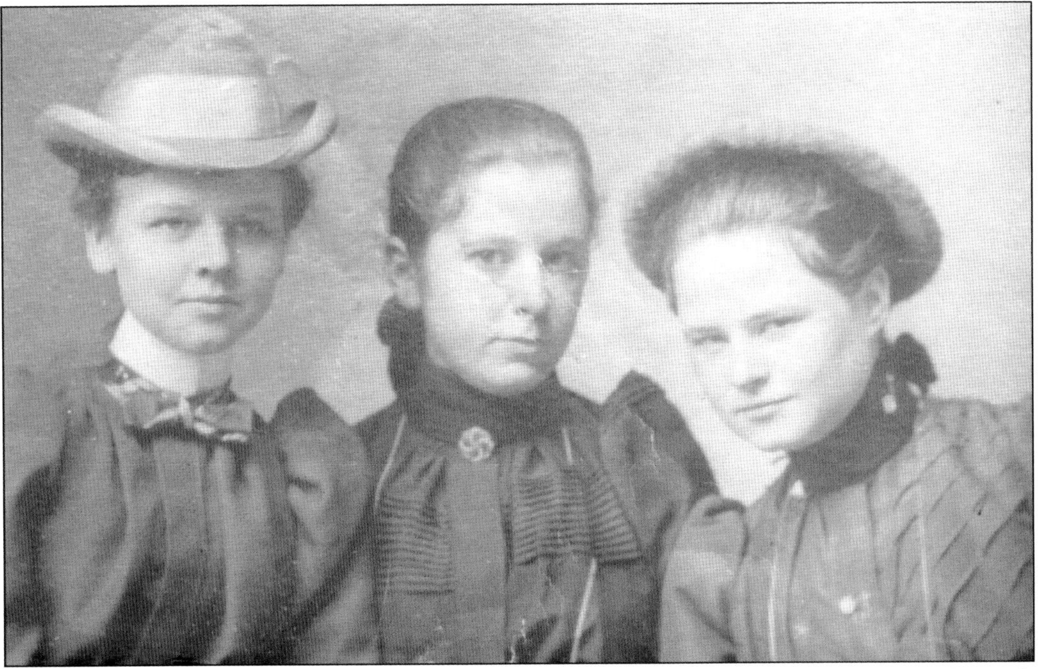

This portrait of three Caldwell College students was taken around 1900, during an era of growth and success at the institution. Pictured from left to right are Louise Bohon, Emily Letcher, and Josie Mae MacGoodwin. (Courtesy of Centre College Special Collections.)

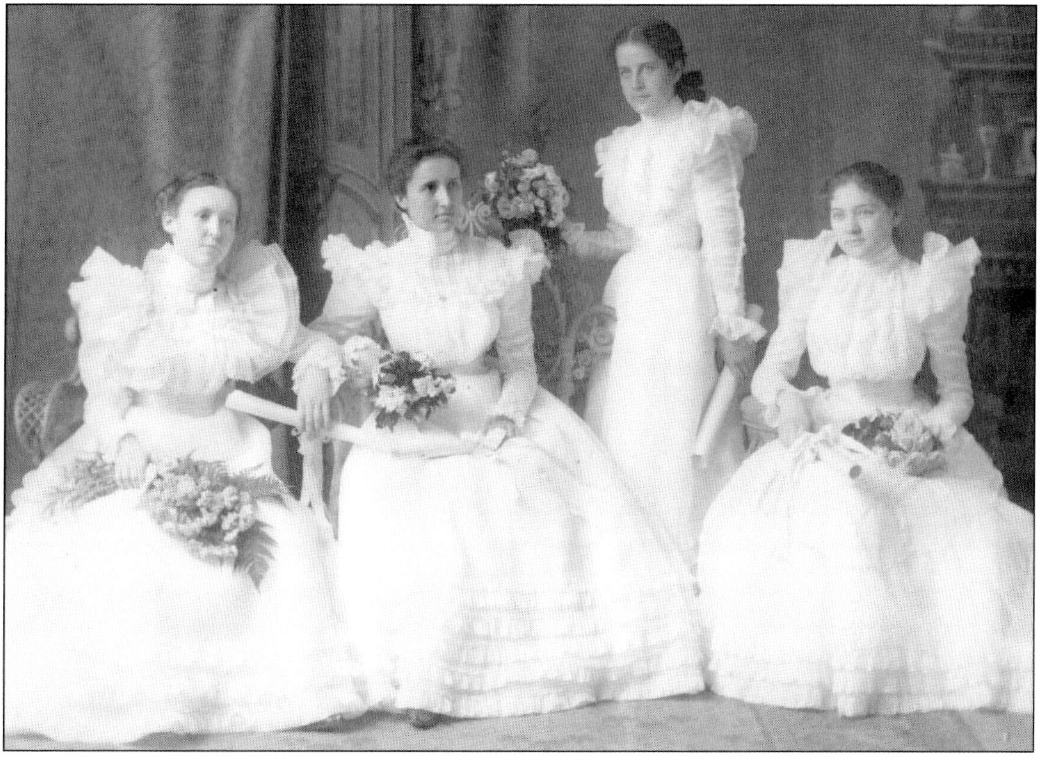

The studio portrait above shows the Caldwell College class of 1898. Dressed in their fine white gowns, from left to right, are Eva Jones, Margaret Sallie, "Willie" Sallie, and Marie Spears. Six more Caldwell College students, adopting a silly pose in the 1901 photograph below, are identified as Josie Mae MacGoodwin Bailey, Amanda Rodes, Louise Bohon Johnson, Margaret Rodes Moore, Emily Letcher, and Cyrena Dunn May. Dr. John C. Ely was president of the college when these girls attended, and the curriculum offered for students included elementary and college preparatory work. (Both courtesy of Centre College Special Collections.)

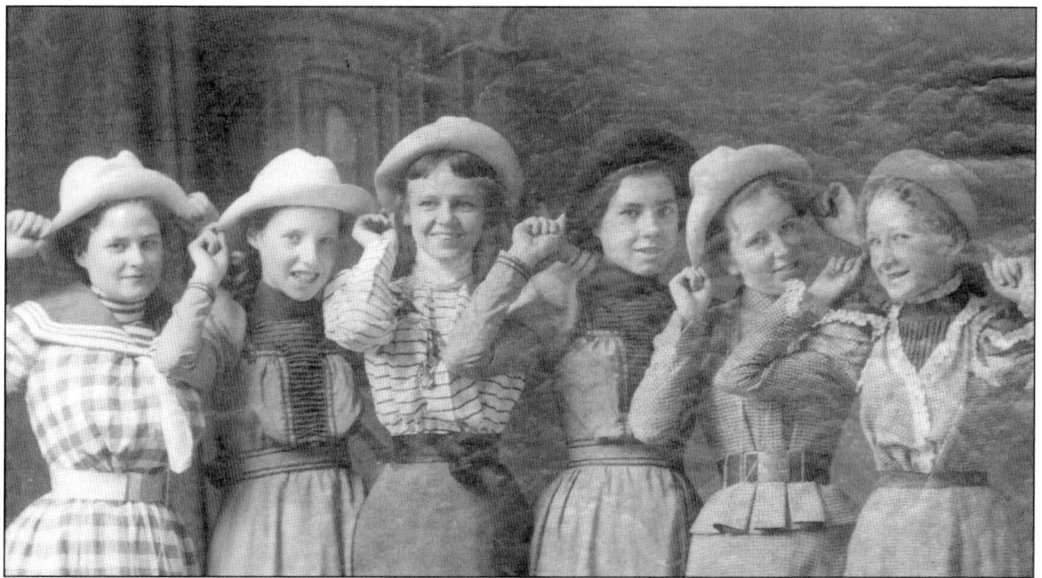

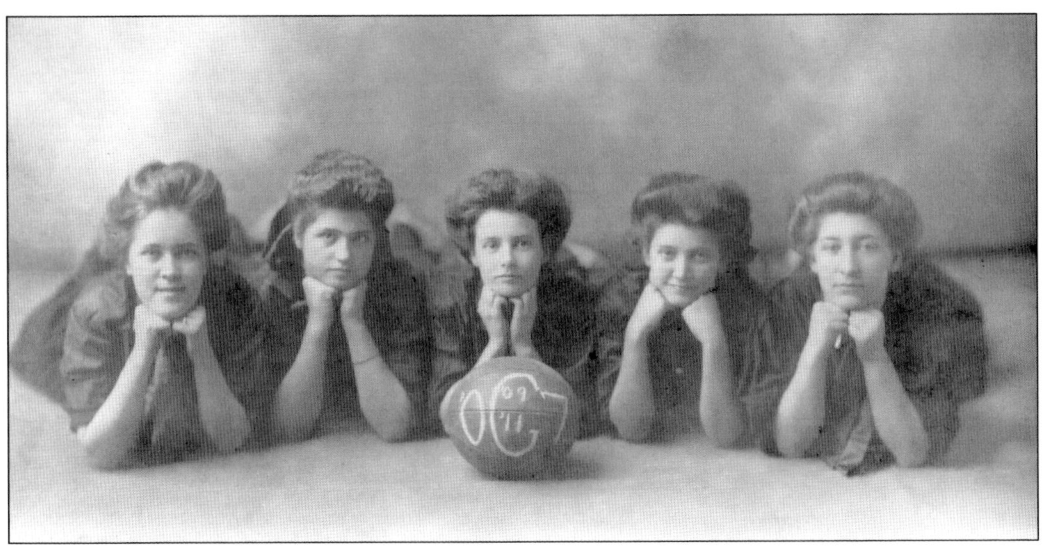

In addition to their scholarly pursuits, young ladies of Caldwell College would often get involved in intramural sports for exercise and socializing. The photograph from the 1907 season above shows the basketball team, named the Wahpanoochis. Players from left to right are Grace Dyer, Mary Ashby Cheek, team captain Lucie Waller, Mary Brown, and Bessie Goss. The unidentified members of the 1910–1911 interclass basketball team (below) pose in a similar shot, holding a basketball with a logo and school year. (Both courtesy of Centre College Special Collections.)

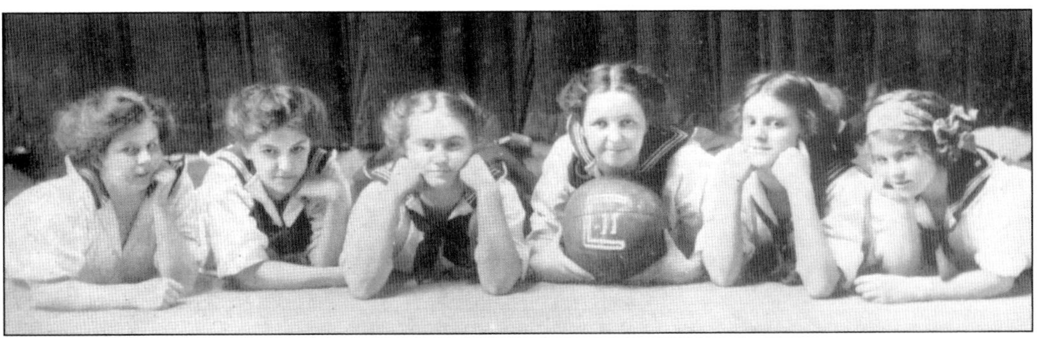

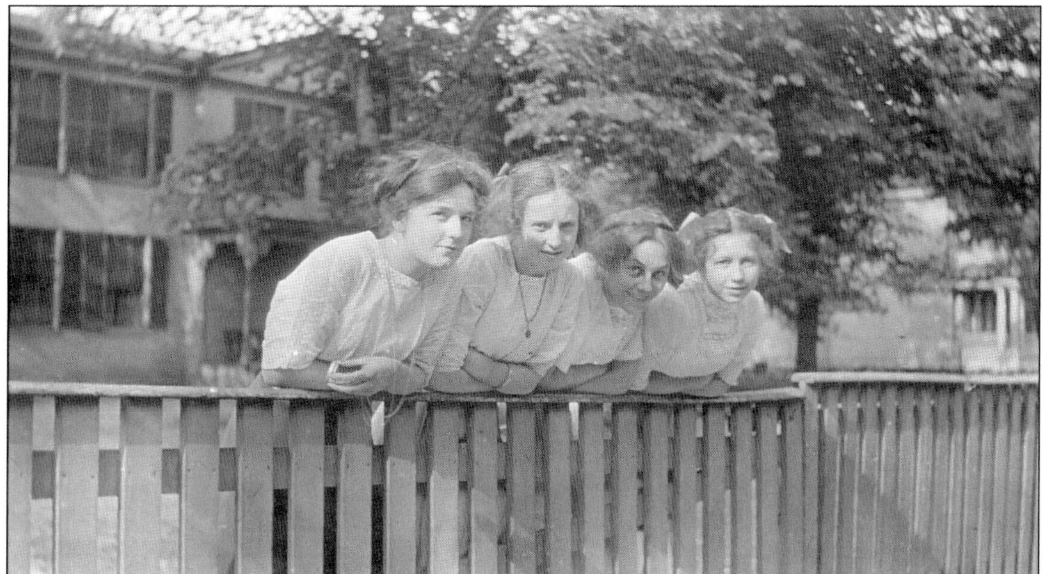

Four Caldwell College students lean on a fence in this photograph from around 1912, one year prior to the school amending its charter and changing its name to the Kentucky College for Women. From left to right are Martha A. Butt, Katherine Letcher, Frances Allen, and Jane Letcher. (Courtesy of Centre College Special Collections.)

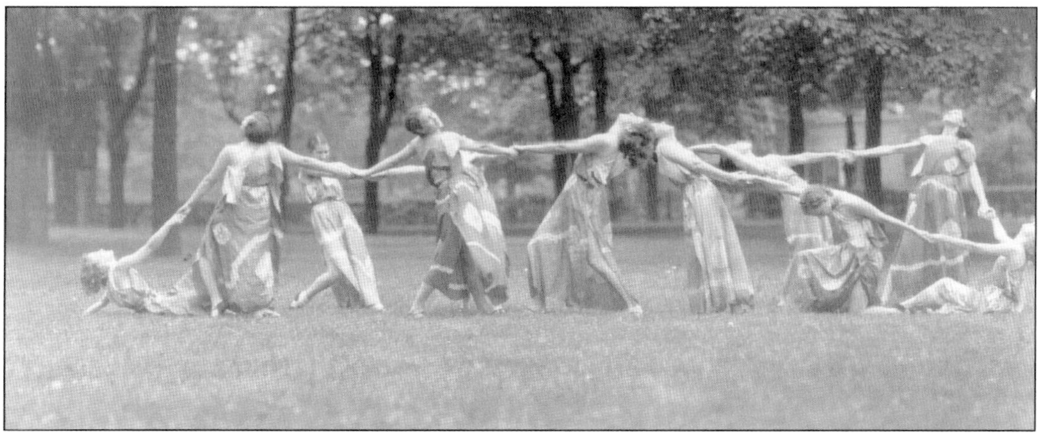

Unidentified students from the Kentucky College for Women pose in a dance formation in this photograph from the 1920s. Around the time this image was taken, the school was prospering as never before, and it had even begun offering standard college courses that led to a bachelor of arts degree. (Courtesy of Centre College Special Collections.)

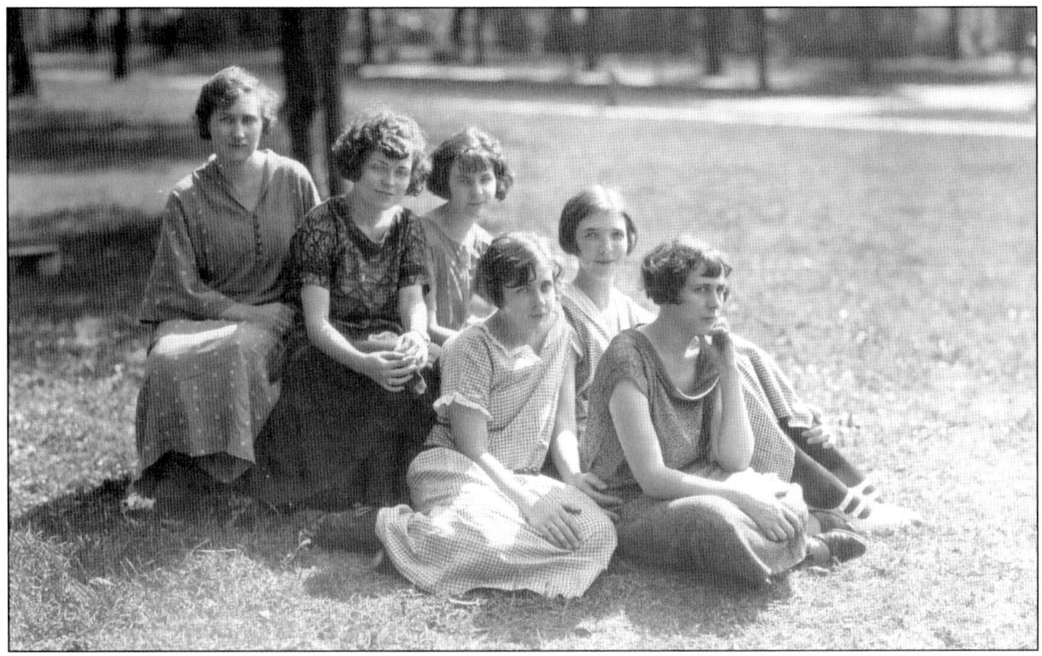

This photograph, taken around 1925, shows six unidentified students from the Kentucky College for Women. The last year that the school was an independent institution was 1925; in 1926, the Kentucky College for Women opened as a department of Centre College, and the two schools consolidated in 1930. (Courtesy of Centre College Special Collections.)

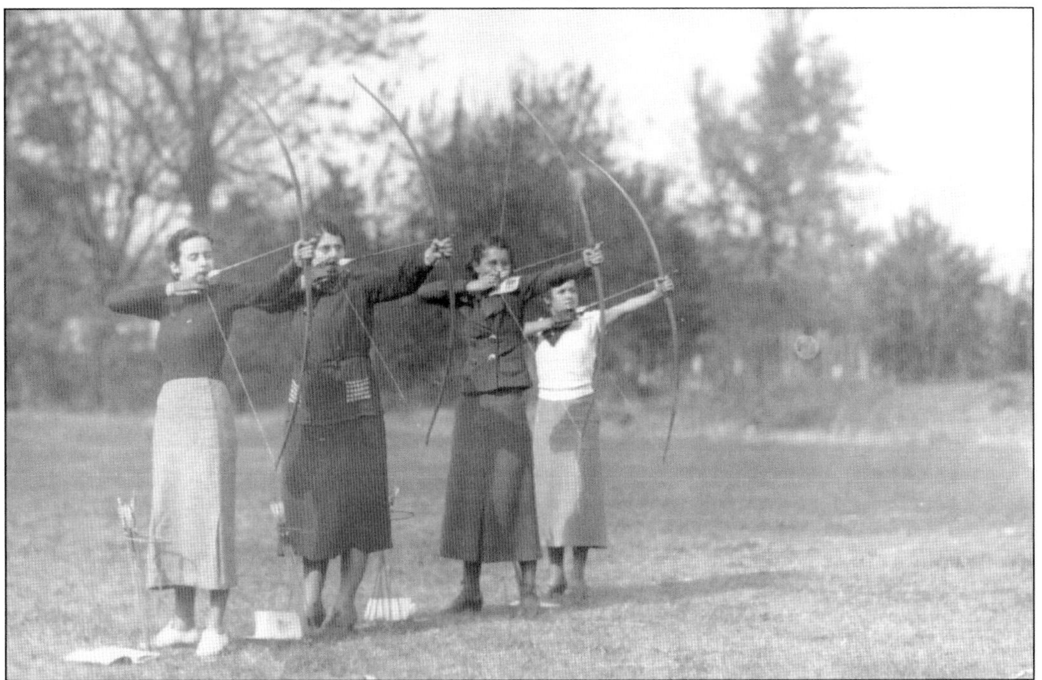

Four Kentucky College for Women archers pose with their bows at the ready in this 1935 photograph. From left to right are Margaret Hamlett, unidentified, Dorothy Lancaster, and Nancy Campbell. (Courtesy of Centre College Special Collections.)

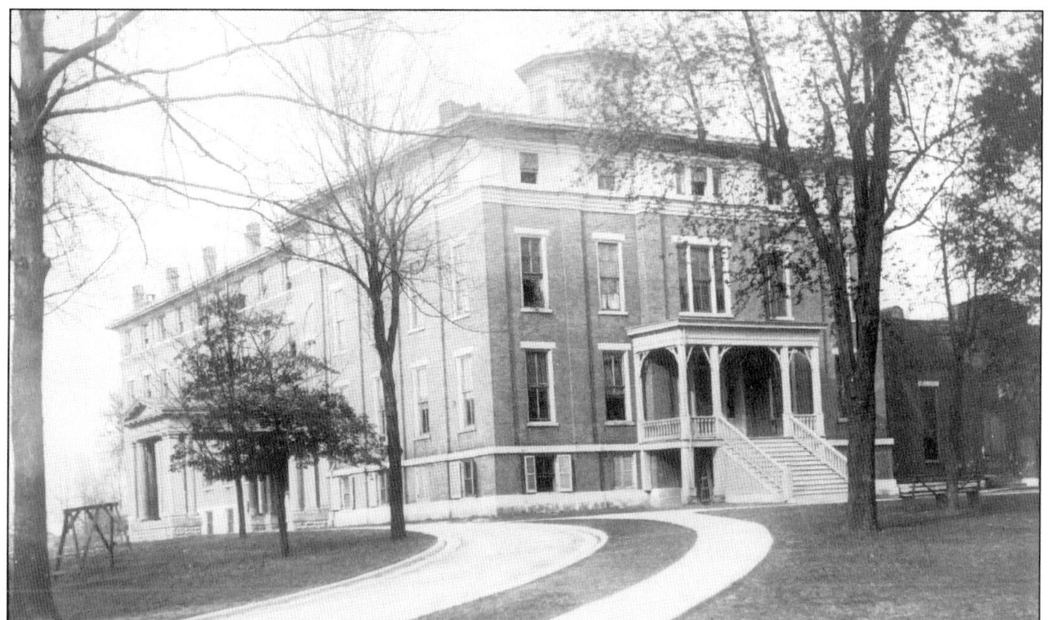

East Hall was built on the Kentucky College for Women campus in 1916, housing dormitories and the school's dining hall. Pictured here in 1961, the building was razed a year later to make room for the new Danville High School. (Courtesy of Centre College Special Collections.)

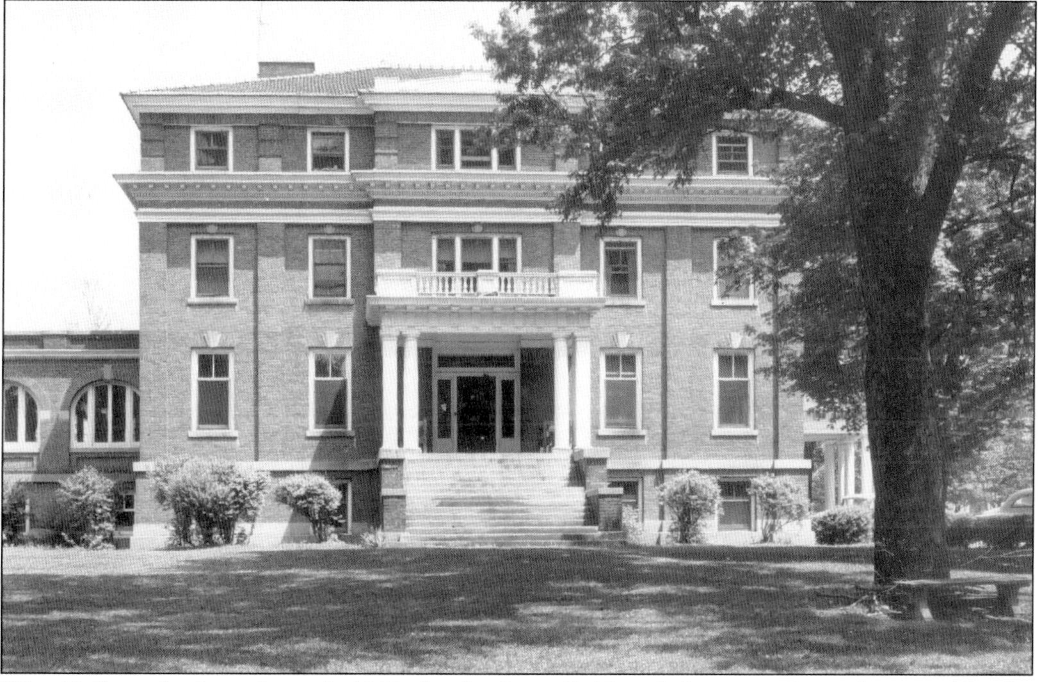

West Hall was built in the early 1860s for the Danville Female Institute. It was later used by the Danville Classical and Military Institute, then purchased by the Caldwell Female College in 1880, four years after the school's only building burned down. West Hall served as a dormitory and housed the school's chapel and musical studios until it was razed in 1962 to make room for the new high school. (Courtesy of Centre College Special Collections.)

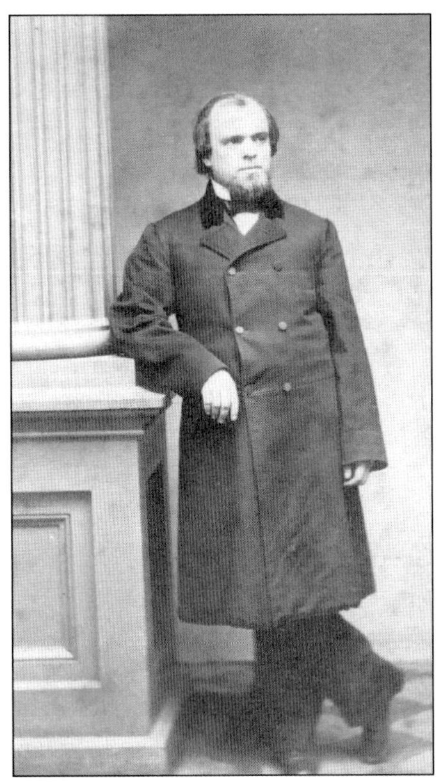

Augustine Hart succeeded Prof. A.E. Sloane as president of Caldwell Female Institute in 1864. He guided the school through two turbulent Civil War years. In an 1864 letter to his mother, Hart shared that the teachers at Caldwell "are a regular Yankee community," most having come from northern states. However, they would never talk about Union victories with their students, as "Many of our girls are of course daughters of rabid secessionists." Hart resigned in 1865. He was replaced by Rev. L.G. Barbour, who led the school into prominence after the state began its postwar recovery. (Courtesy of Centre College Special Collections.)

On January 25, 1962, unidentified students of the Kentucky College for Women leave their school building for the final time. The Kentucky College for Women, which underwent numerous name changes for the 102 years it was open, had become a department of Centre College in 1926 before consolidating into one institution. The women's college closed its doors in 1962, and the campus was sold to the Danville school system. Most of its buildings were demolished to make room for a new city high school. (Courtesy of Centre College Special Collections.)

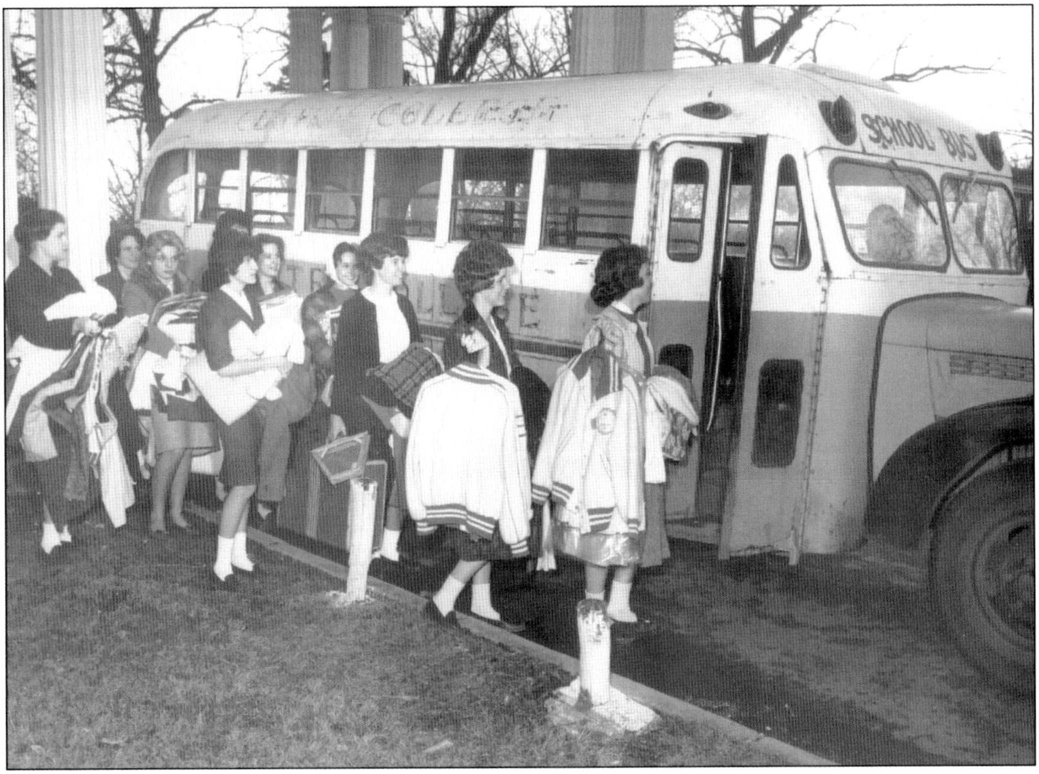

# *Seven*

# Main Street Danville

A Main Street is more than just a thoroughfare through the middle of a town; it holds the collective memory of a community, providing a shared space where locals go to learn about their history, enjoy familiar businesses and restaurants, and explore the culture a town has to offer. Danville's Main Street is no different; it was named a Great American Main Street Award Winning Community by the National Trust for Historic Preservation, and a portion of it has been in the National Register of Historic Places since 1986. Many longtime Danville residents often talk fondly about their favorite memories of Main Street: which drug store had the best soda fountain, what parades they attended, which bench in front of the courthouse offered the best view of the happenings in town, and more. Since its creation in 1986 by Carol Senn and Centre College professor Clarence Wyatt, the Heart of Danville program has been promoting economic development, beautification, historic preservation, and community involvement in the Main Street area of Danville. More than 200 years of history mingle with fresh, new businesses on Main Street, making Danville the unique town it is today.

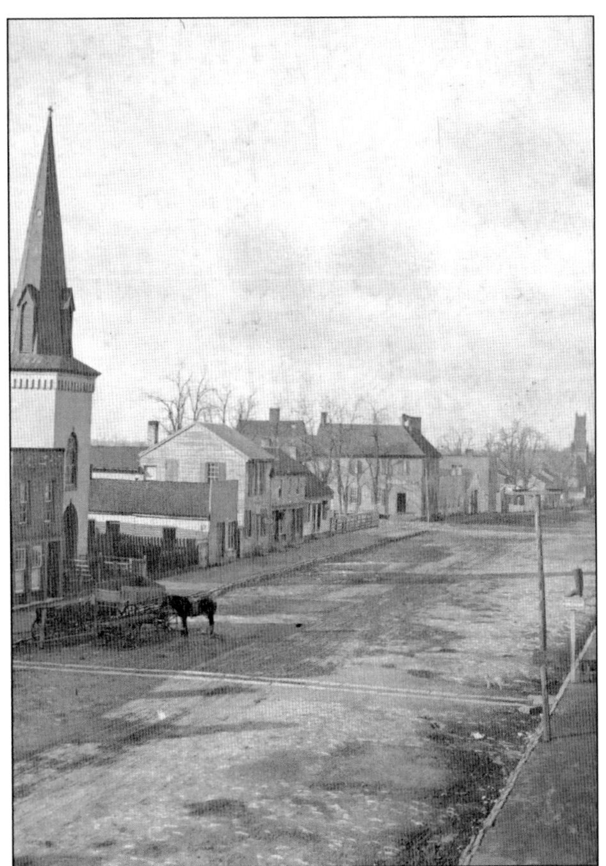

Thought to be two of the earliest photographs taken of Danville, these 1875 views of Main Street feature buildings that are still in use today. The south side of Main Street (left) features the Trinity Episcopal Church on the left; the First Presbyterian Church's steeple is visible at center right. Also seen in the photograph is the Yellow House, the first building of the Kentucky School for the Deaf. The north side of Main Street (below) includes a row of businesses, with the cupola of the Boyle County Courthouse visible above their roofs. (Both courtesy of Centre College Special Collections.)

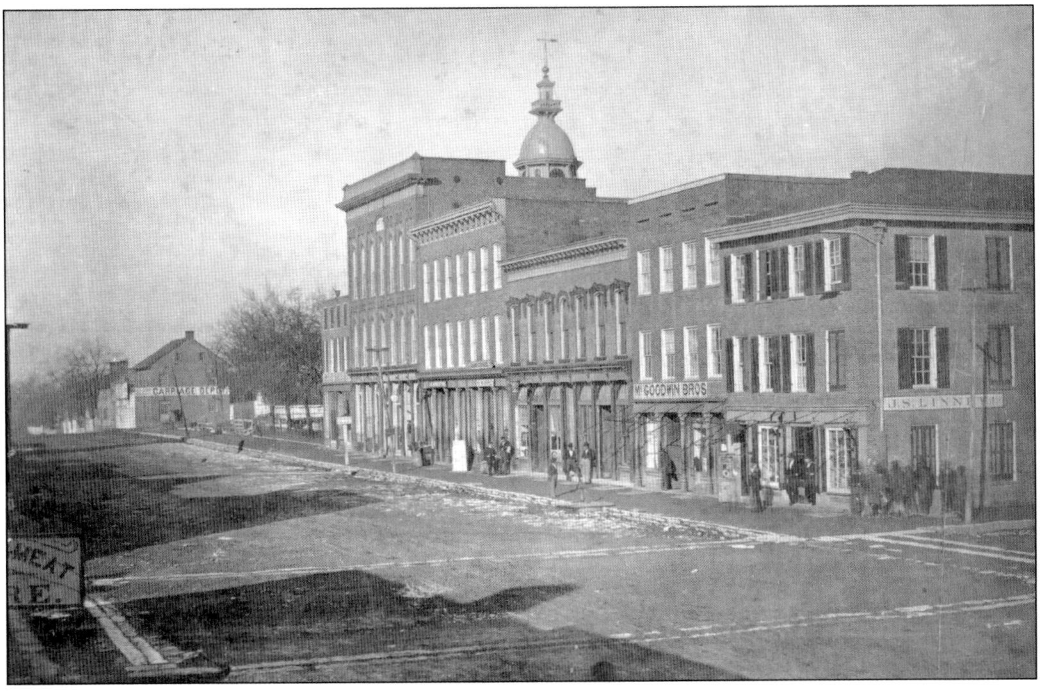

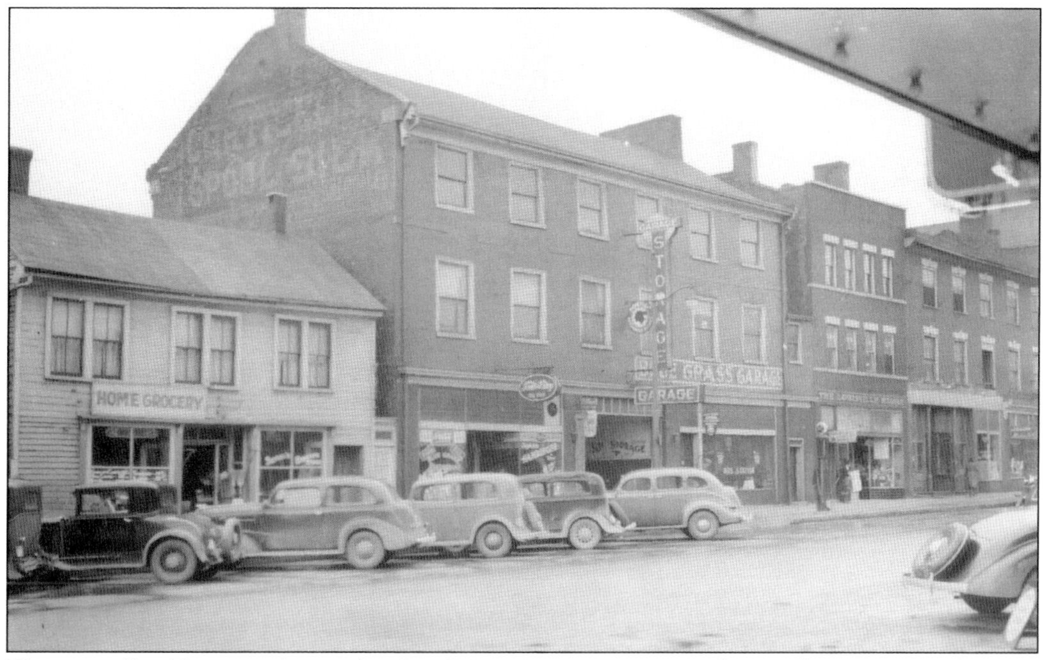


This row of buildings on the south side of Main Street was a part of Danville's commercial center from the late 18th century up through the present day. The mid-1930s west-facing photograph above shows Ayer's Silversmith Shop (on the left), which was constructed around 1790 and still stands today. To the right is the McIlvoy House, built around 1806. The east-facing photograph below depicts the McIlvoy House, which served as Daniel McIlvoy's home, the town post office, a bank, and the Bluegrass Garage before being razed. (Above, courtesy of Centre College Special Collections; below, courtesy of NPS Historic American Buildings Survey.)

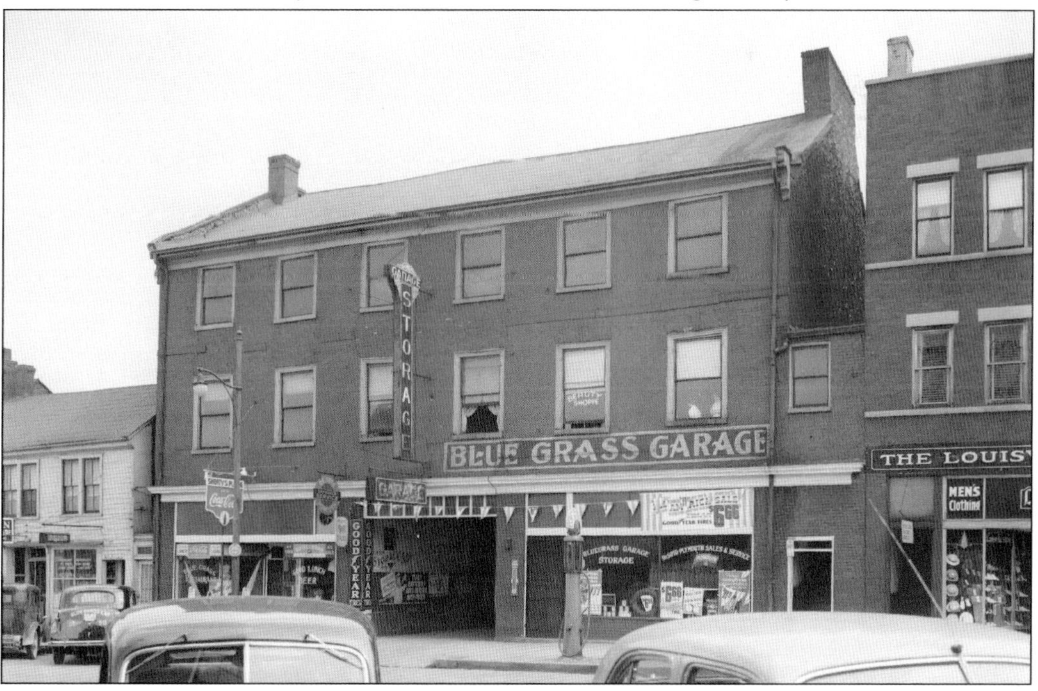

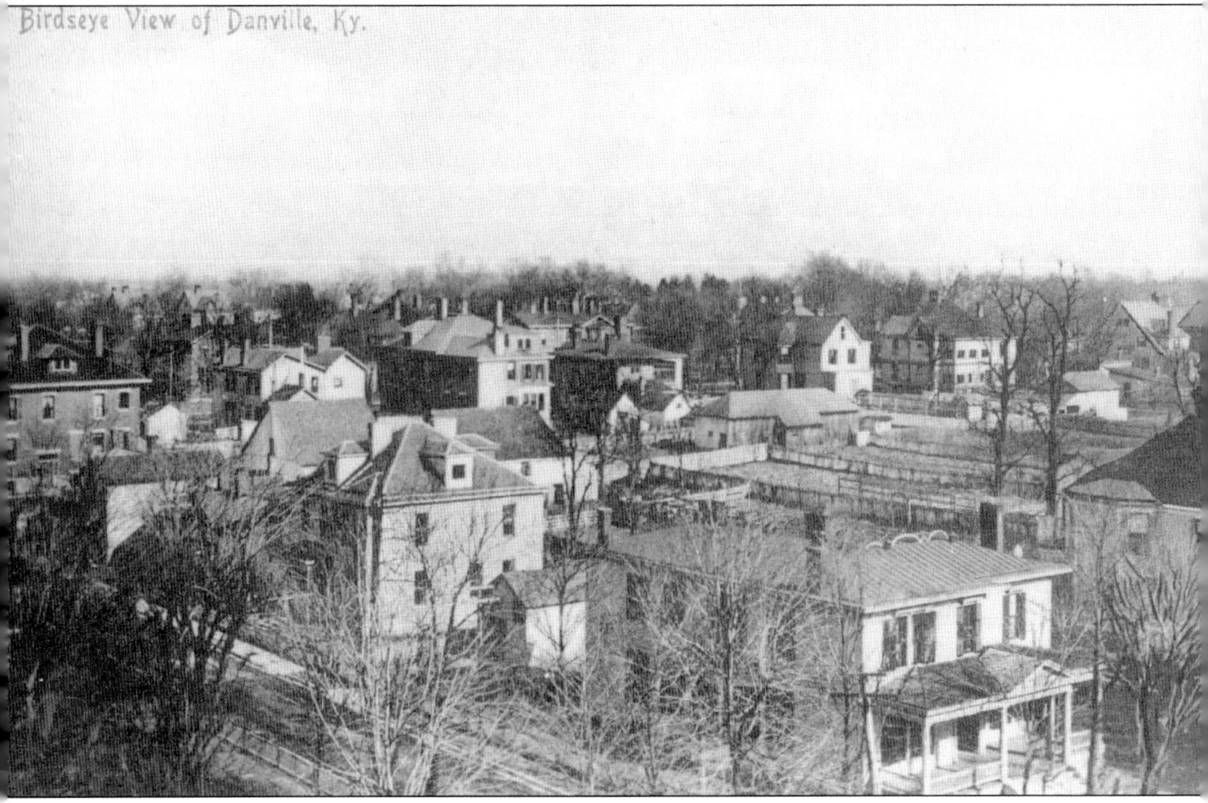

Birdseye View of Danville, Ky.

This bird's-eye view of Danville, taken in 1910 from the steeple of the First Presbyterian Church on the corner of Main and Fifth Streets, shows Main Street and the downtown area. In the distance, the Second Presbyterian Church steeple (center), the Boyle County Courthouse cupola (right center), and the Trinity Episcopal Church steeple (right) are all visible, peeking over the

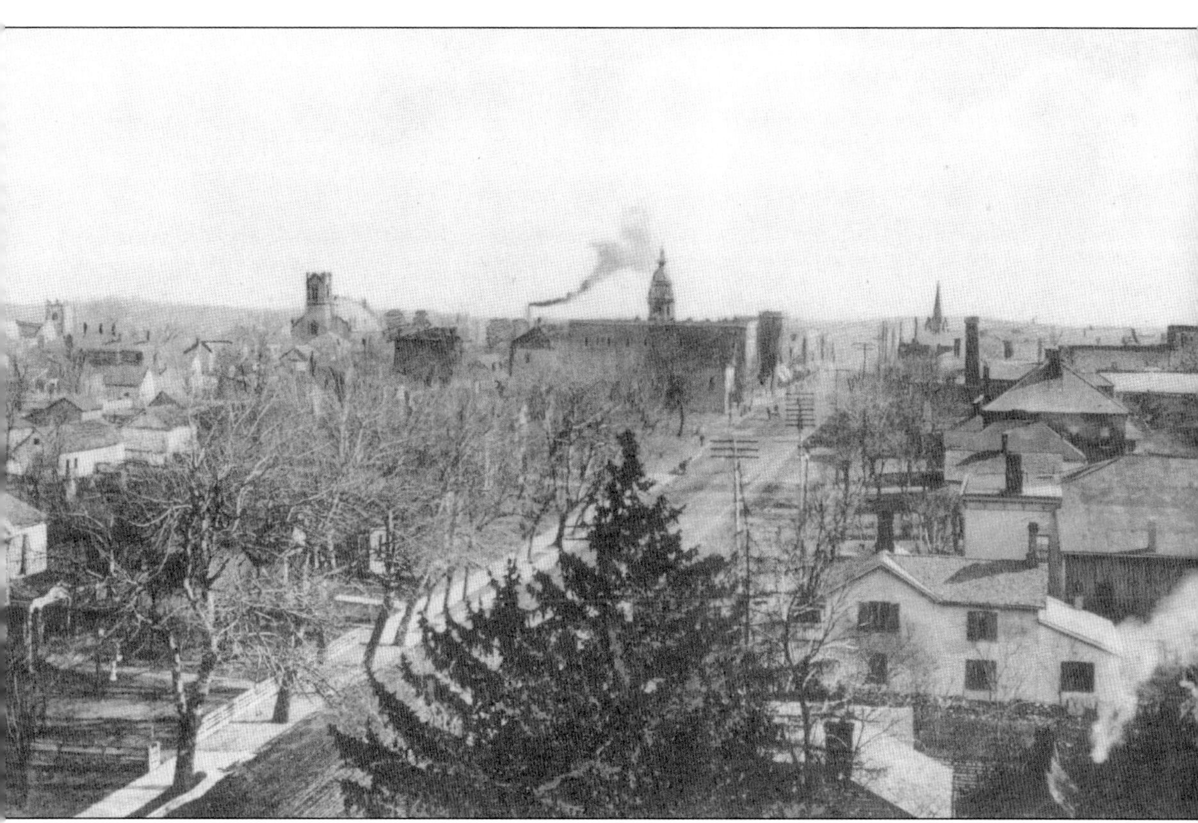

rooftops of various businesses and residences. Most of the buildings lining Main Street are still used today, and many of the houses on secondary streets are still inhabited. (Courtesy of Centre College Special Collections.)

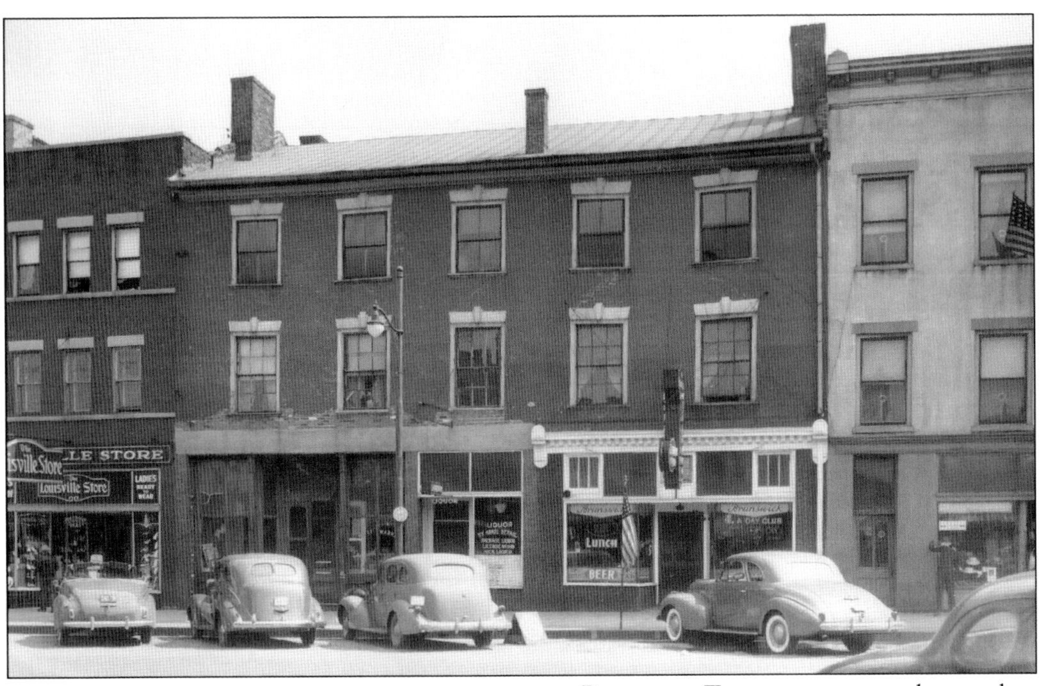


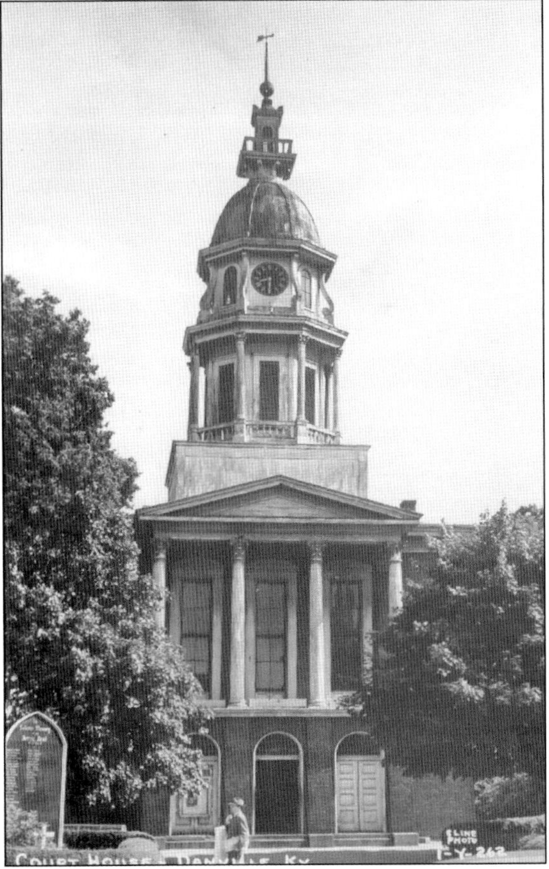

Davenport Tavern, constructed around 1808 by Richard Davenport, is seen here in 1940 serving as a modern business building. Davenport previously built an inn that had burned down. He was so well-regarded and trusted in the community that people loaned him the money needed to construct a new building, interest-free for ten years. The first meeting of the Centre College Board of Trustees was held at the popular stagecoach tavern on February 1, 1819, twelve days after the Kentucky state legislature chartered Centre College. (Courtesy of Centre College Special Collections.)

Boyle County's first courthouse was erected in 1842, but it was destroyed in a fire in 1860 that devastated Danville's commercial district. Rebuilt in 1862, the courthouse was used as a Union hospital during the Civil War. The nearby Battle of Perryville ended with a strategic Union loss but a Confederate retreat in October 1862. Many private homes, churches, schools, and businesses provided shelter for the thousands of wounded and dying soldiers. (Courtesy of Michael Wiser.)

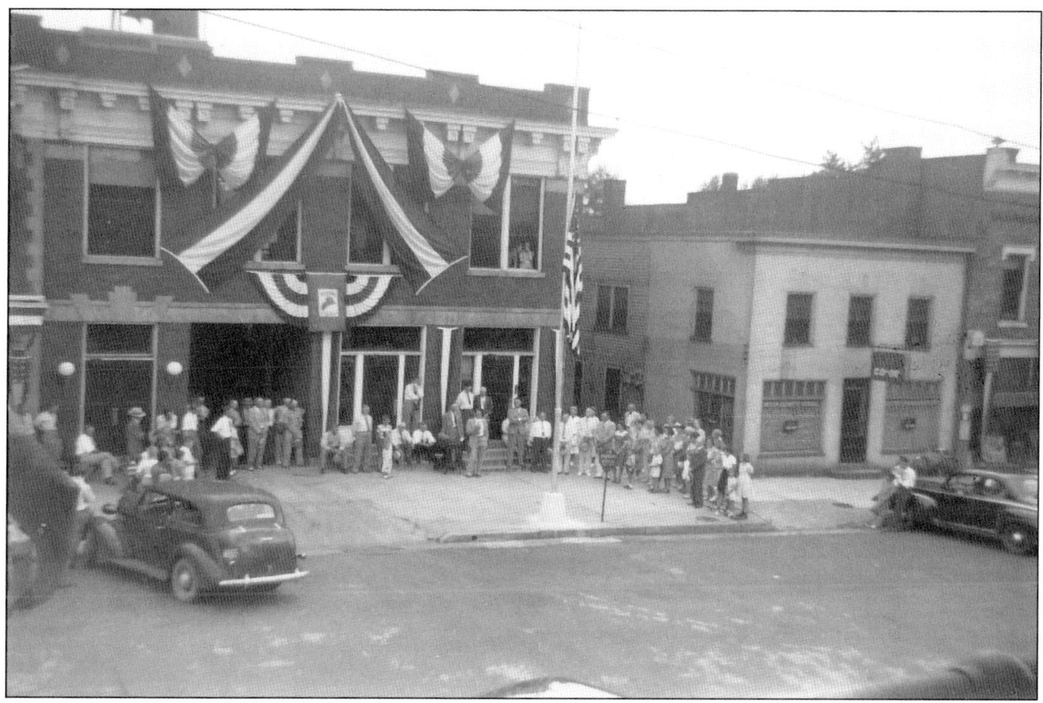

Housing both city hall offices and the Danville Fire Department, the Old Danville Municipal Building was built around 1916 near the corner of Main and Second Streets. Pictured in the 1940s (above), a crowd gathers for a ceremony in front of patriotic banners and a small welcome sign depicting a fireman's helmet. In the 1960s (below), after some minor changes to the facade, the building was razed to make way for the new fire station, which is in use by the Danville Fire Department today. (Both courtesy of Guy Ingram.)

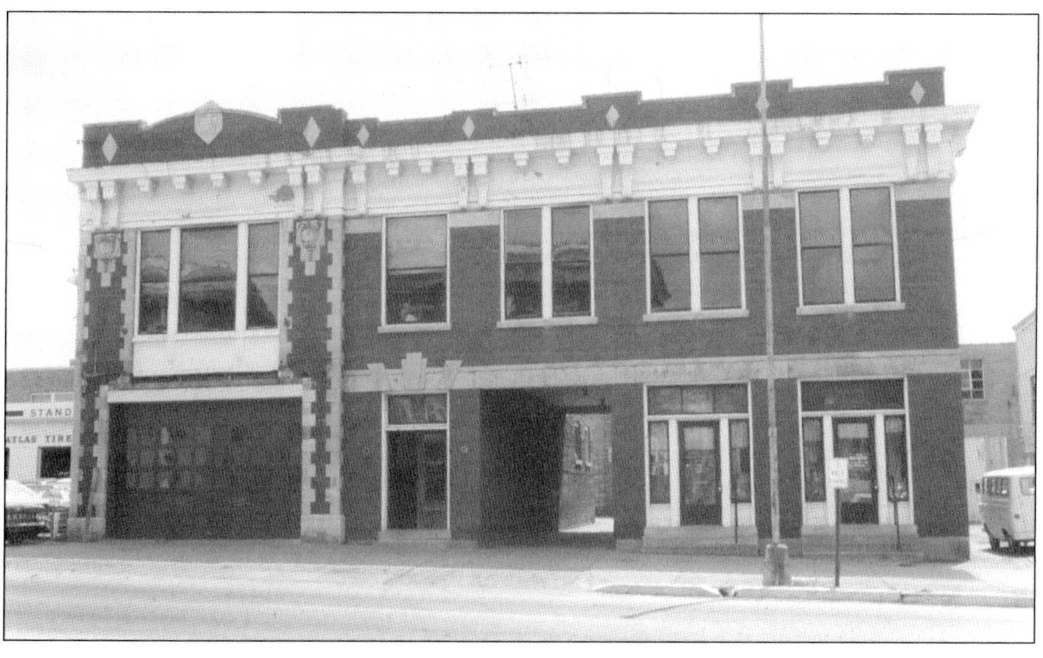

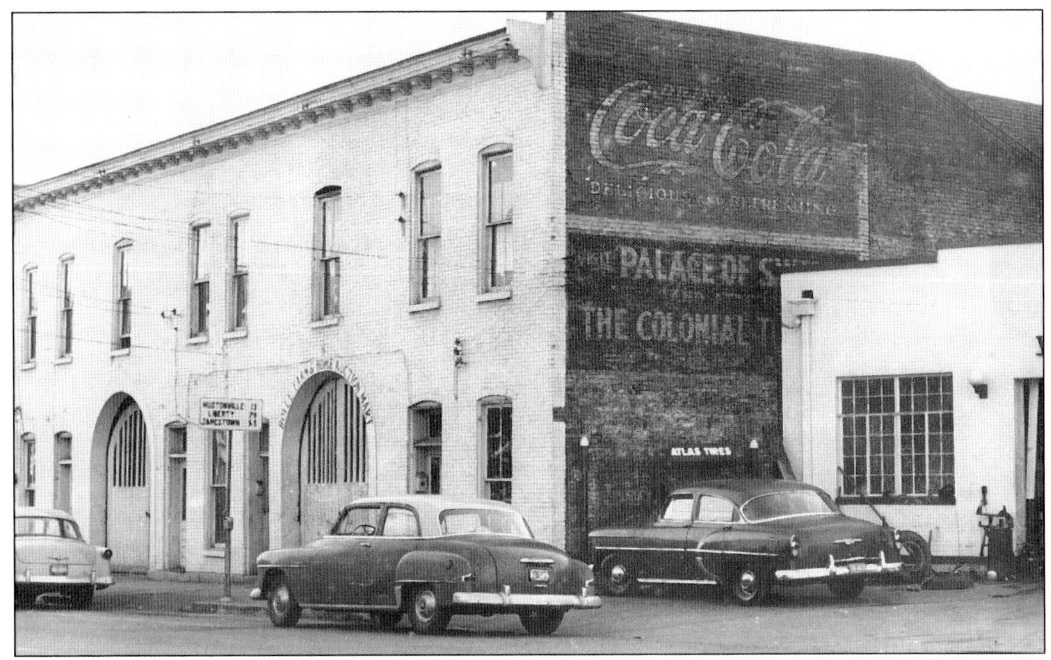


Boyle Stables was used as an auction barn until being torn down to make room for a bank. Located on bustling Fourth Street, the side of the Boyle Stables building served as an excellent spot for advertisements, such as the iconic Coca-Cola and Palace of Sweets logos visible in this early-1950s photograph. (Courtesy of Guy Ingram.)

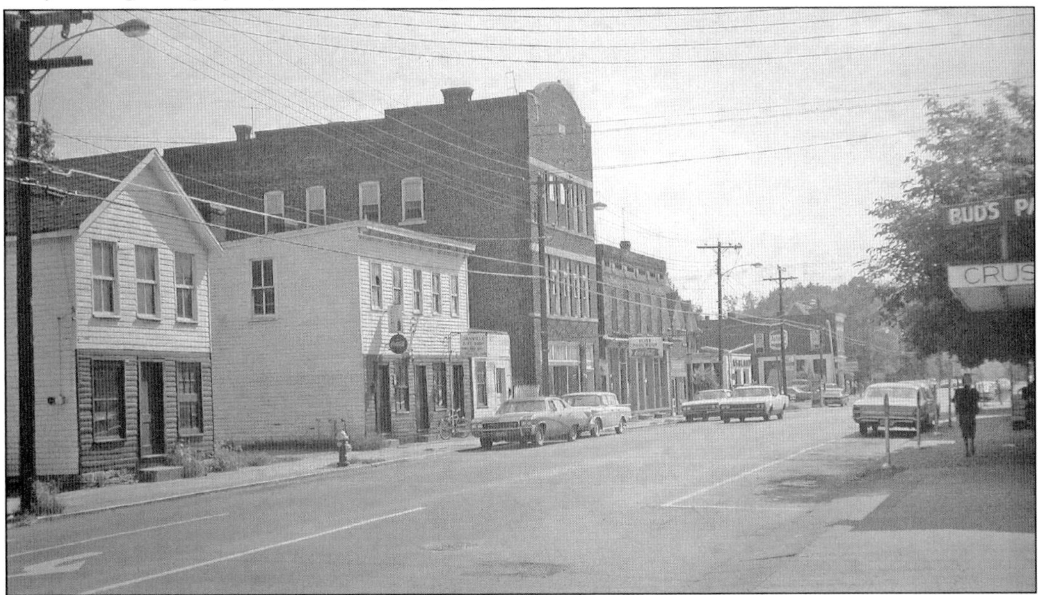


From the mid-19th century up until 1973, Constitution Square was the location of a thriving African American business district, seen here in 1966. The site also included Doric Lodge No. 18, a social and cultural center for African Americans in Boyle County that was initially founded in 1888 and moved to Second Street in 1920. During an urban renewal push, these businesses and residences were torn down, and Constitution Square was restored to how it originally appeared in the early 19th century. (Courtesy of Guy Ingram.)

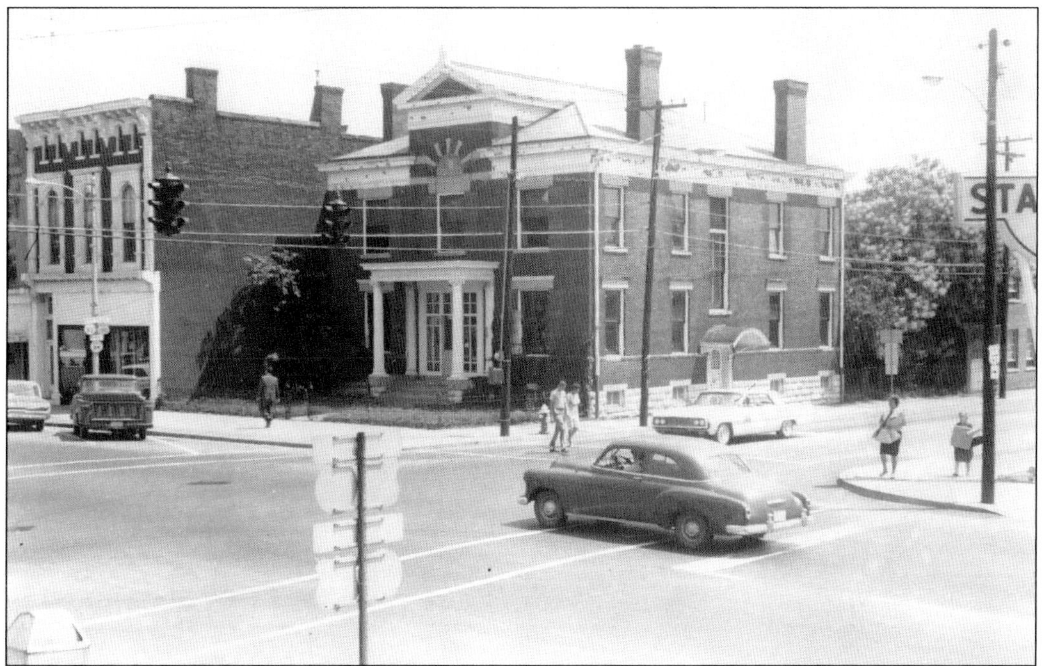

Located at 336 West Main Street, this building served as the office and sanitarium of doctors George and John Cowan. Known as the Cowan Building, it was a striking part of the town's streetscape until its demolition in the late 1960s to make room for the Central Kentucky Building and Loan Association. (Courtesy of Guy Ingram.)

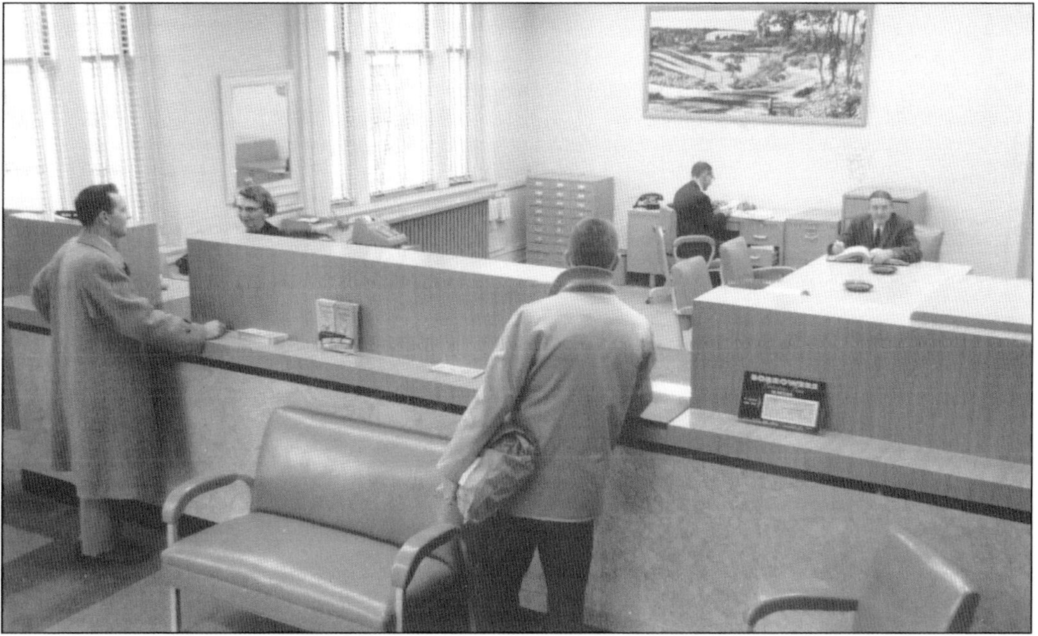

The Central Kentucky Building and Loan Association played an important role in the growth of Danville. Aspiring businessmen and homeowners would use the association to secure financial aid for the construction of new buildings. In this image taken prior to its move to Main and Fourth Streets, the association is located next to the courthouse. (Courtesy of Guy Ingram.)

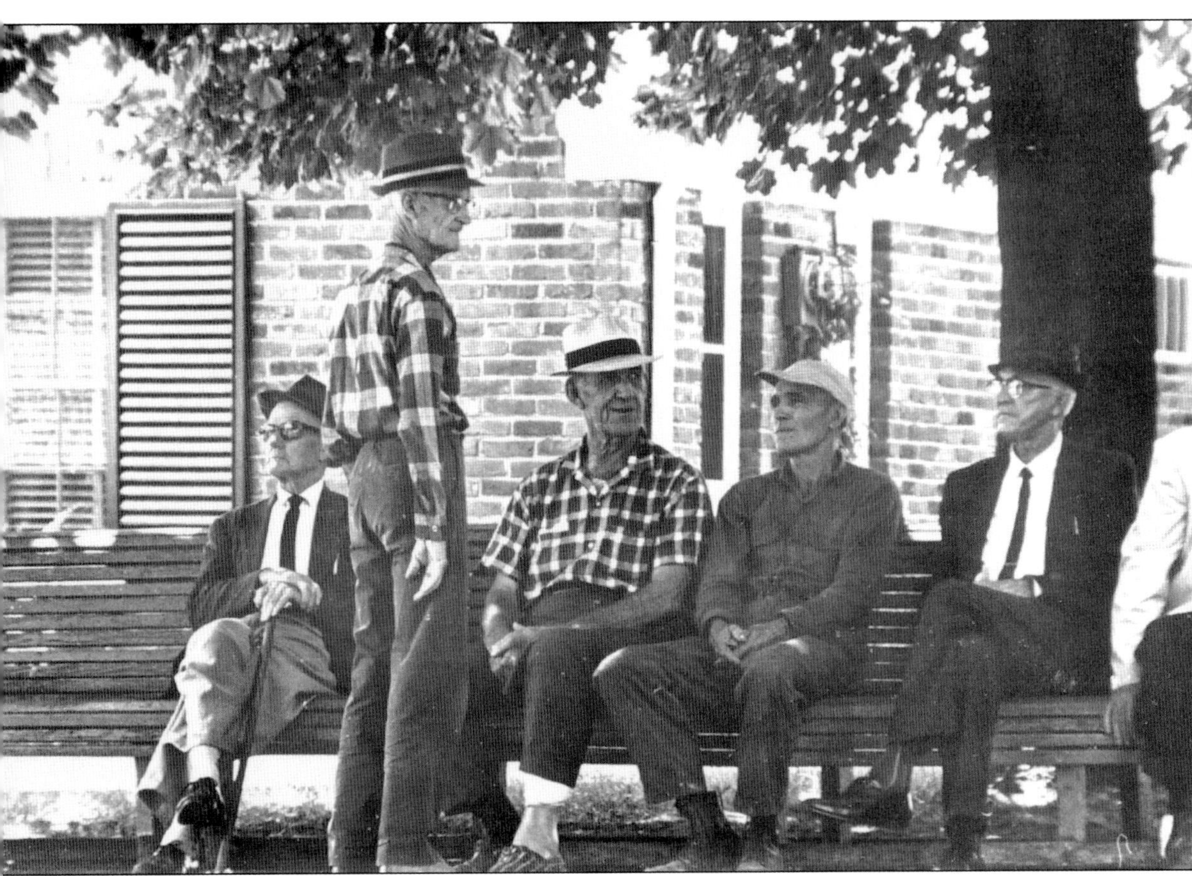

After the original Boyle County Courthouse was destroyed in the great 1860 fire that damaged a large number of buildings in downtown Danville, the town rebuilt on the same spot where the 1842 courthouse had existed. Completed in 1862, the new Boyle County Courthouse served as a meeting place for many in town, including a Baptist congregation for several years, as members

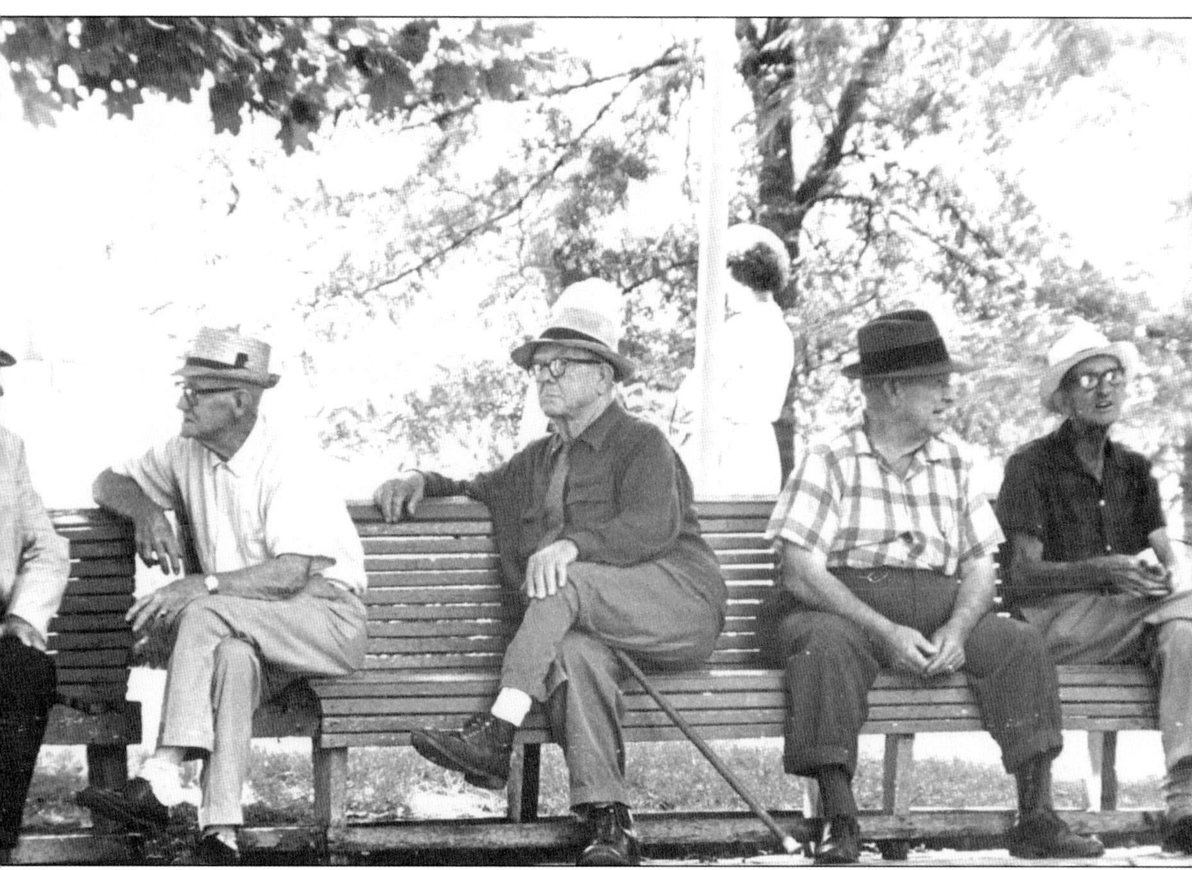

waited for their church to be built. This late-1960s photograph depicts a popular warm-weather hobby of many local residents: the benches in front of the courthouse would be full on sunny, pleasant days. (Courtesy of Guy Ingram.)

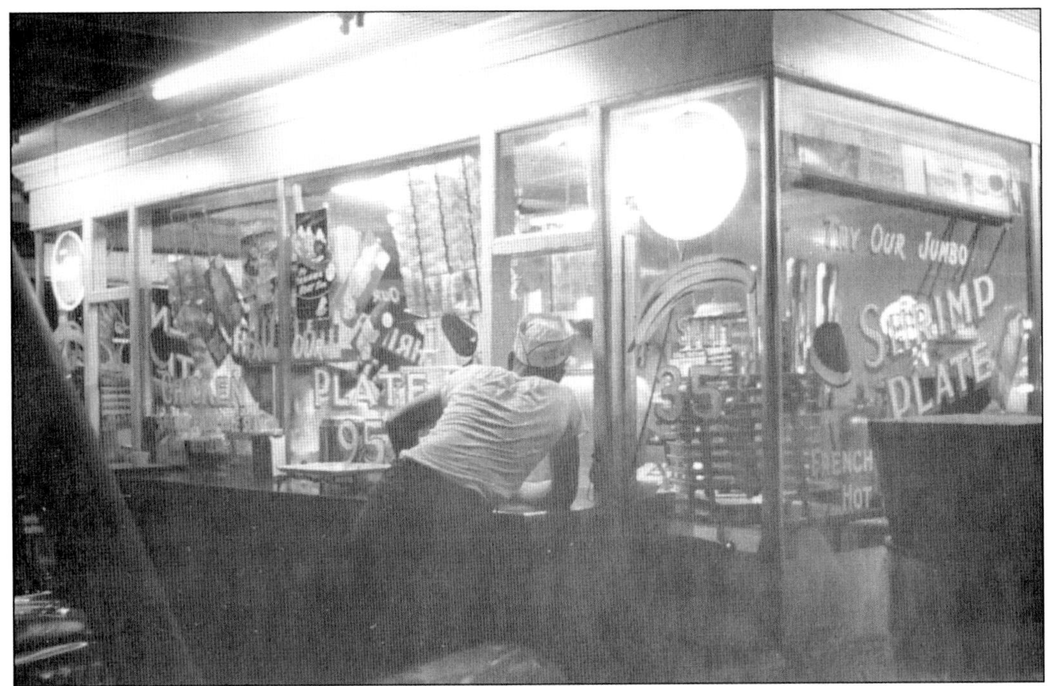


Located on North Maple Avenue, the Dairy Dip Drive-In was one of the popular early restaurants of its kind in Danville. Pictured here in the early 1960s, the Dairy Dip offered carhop service to its many loyal patrons. (Courtesy of Guy Ingram.)

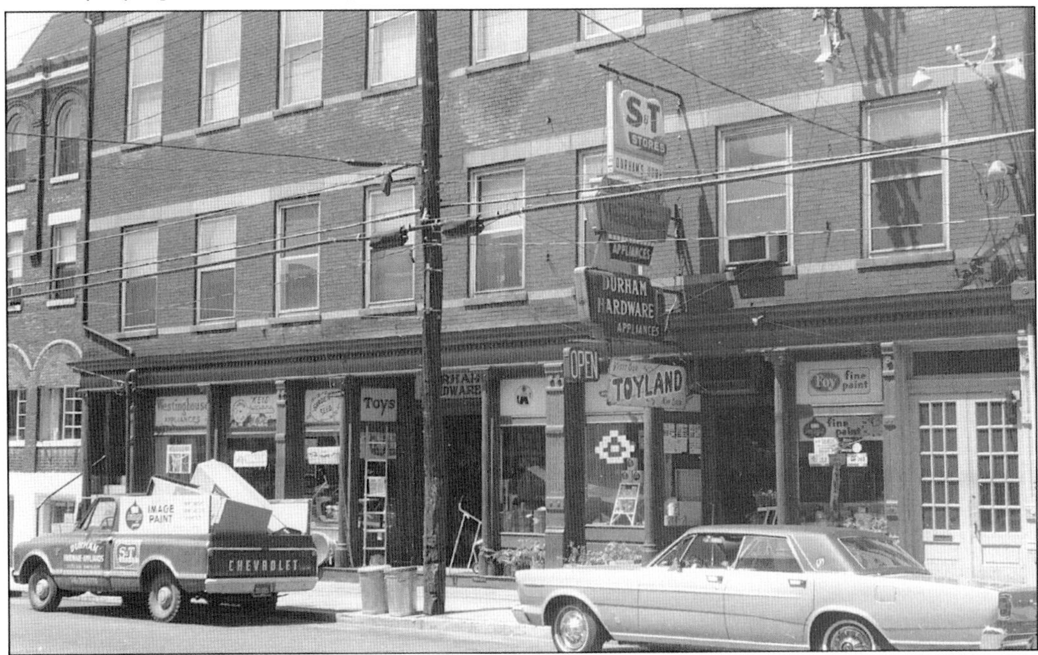


Durham Hardware, pictured here in 1967, was a staple of the Main Street business district. Initially located on Fourth Street, it was moved further down to South Fourth Street as an Ace Hardware. The original building now serves as a side entrance to Farmers Bank. (Courtesy of Guy Ingram.)

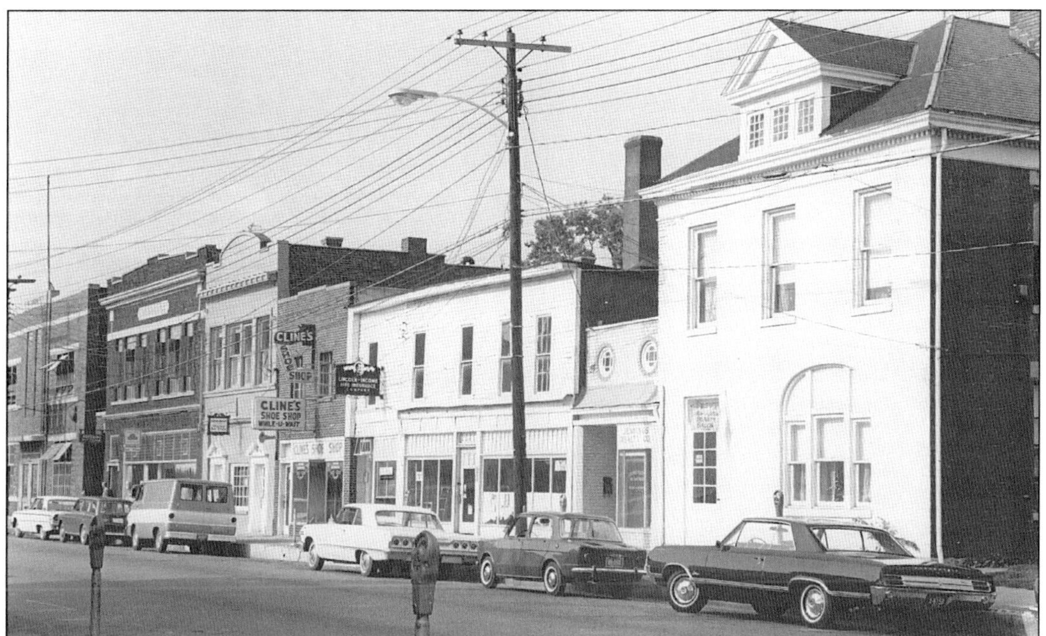


Barker's Grocery, located on North Third Street, was the last frame building in the downtown Danville business district at the time of its removal in the 1960s. North Third Street was a bustling part of town, with many popular businesses that, though long since torn down, remain favorites of longtime Danville locals. (Courtesy of Guy Ingram.)

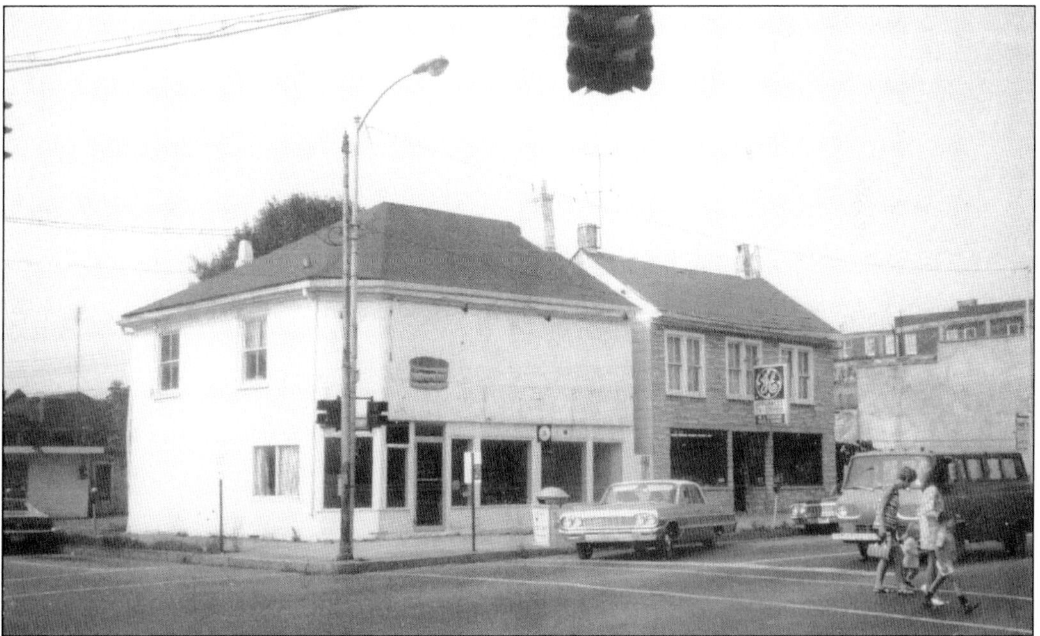

Located at the corner of Second and Main Streets, across the street from Constitution Square State Historic Site, White House Restaurant served Danville locals for several decades before being torn down to make room for office buildings. Seen in this 1971 photograph, the restaurant appears empty; it was, however, still listed in the Danville city directory as late as 1969. (Courtesy of Guy Ingram.)

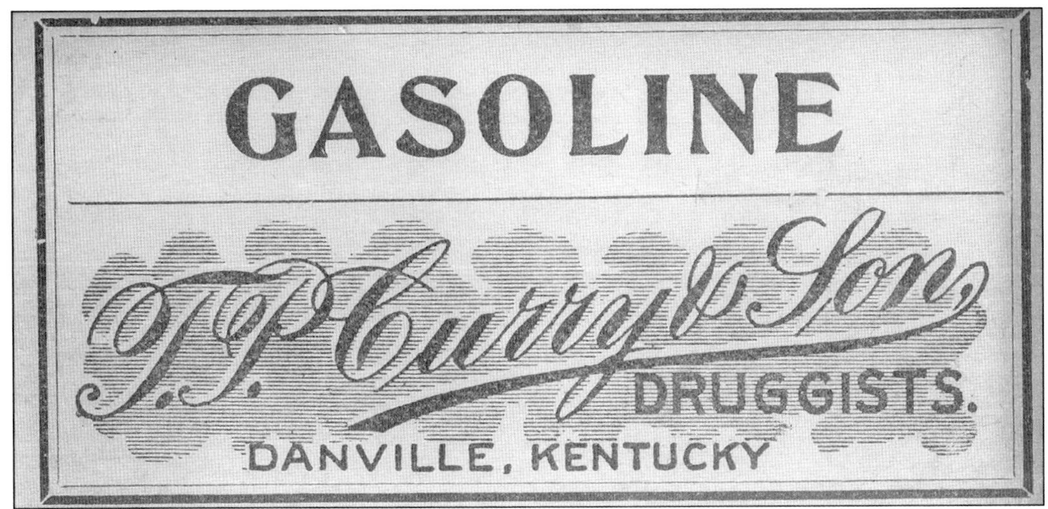


T.P. Curry, owner of the drugstore T.P. Curry and Sons, advertised himself as a "Druggist and Bookseller." His drugstore was the first in a chain of four such stores that occupied the building on Main Street. Among the many things sold at his business was gasoline, as indicated by this jar label. (Courtesy of Guy Ingram.)

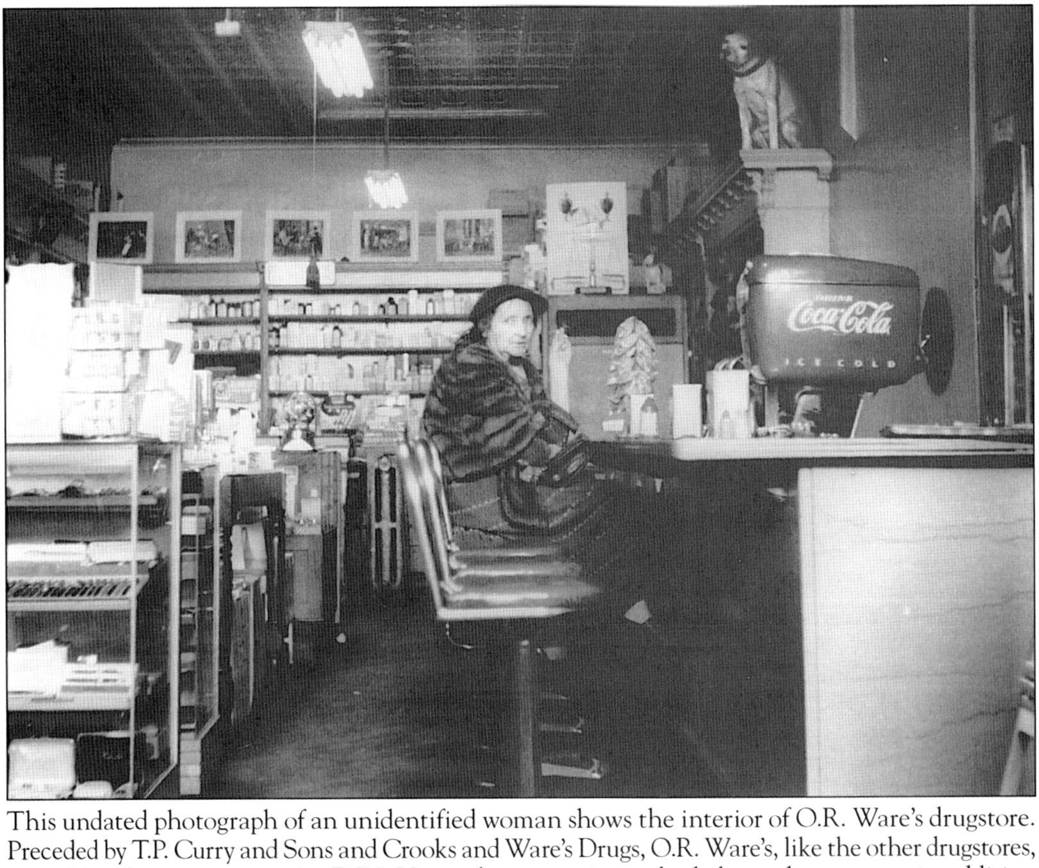

This undated photograph of an unidentified woman shows the interior of O.R. Ware's drugstore. Preceded by T.P. Curry and Sons and Crooks and Ware's Drugs, O.R. Ware's, like the other drugstores, served lunch at a counter. An RCA Victor dog statue is perched above the counter; in addition to food, medicines, and sundry items, O.R. Ware's sold records. (Courtesy of Guy Ingram.)

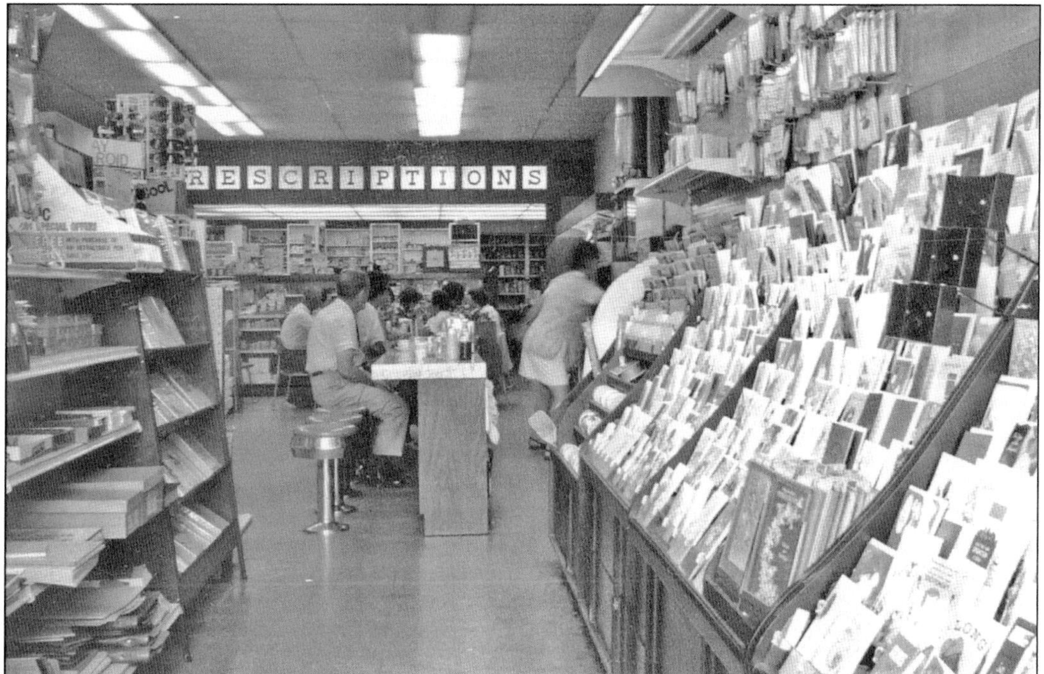


Patrons of Freeland Pharmacy sit at the lunch counter and enjoy their meals in this 1969 photograph. Freeland was the last of several druggists who owned the building in which the pharmacy was located. It was a popular lunch spot and soda fountain for locals. (Courtesy of Guy Ingram.)

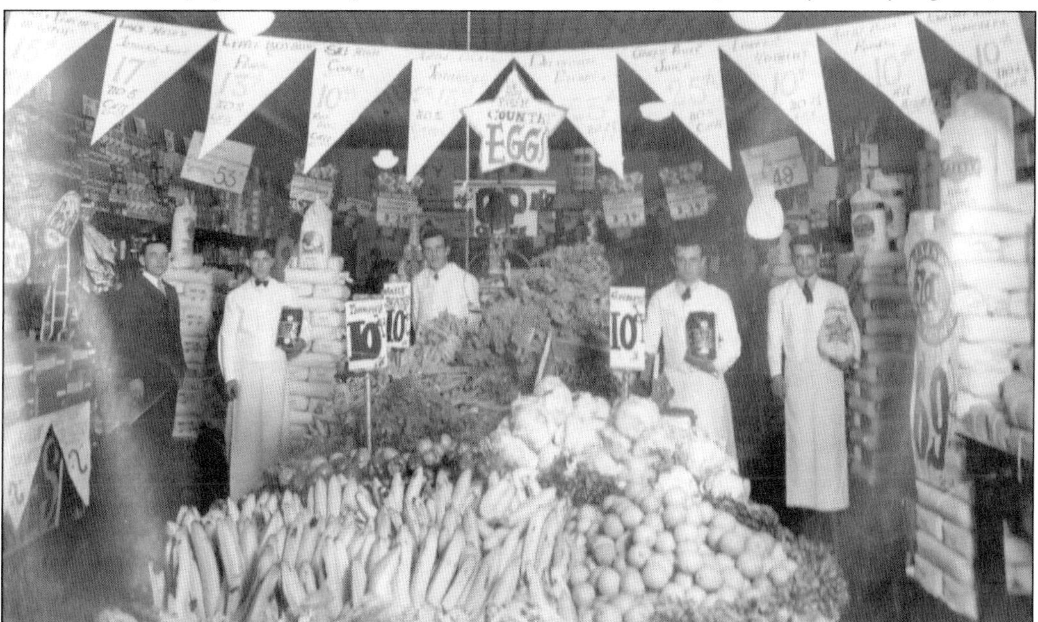

Located on West Main Street near the Trinity Episcopal Church in the 1930s and early 1940s, was the Gabbard and Pennington Grocery Store, managed by Abe Gabbard. The grocer was a favorite with locals, who enjoyed the fresh produce and canned foods offered. Abe Gabbard opened a new store in the 1940s at the corner of Walnut and Fourth Streets; this building is now in use by the Johnson and Pohlmann Insurance Agency. (Courtesy of Michael Wiser.)

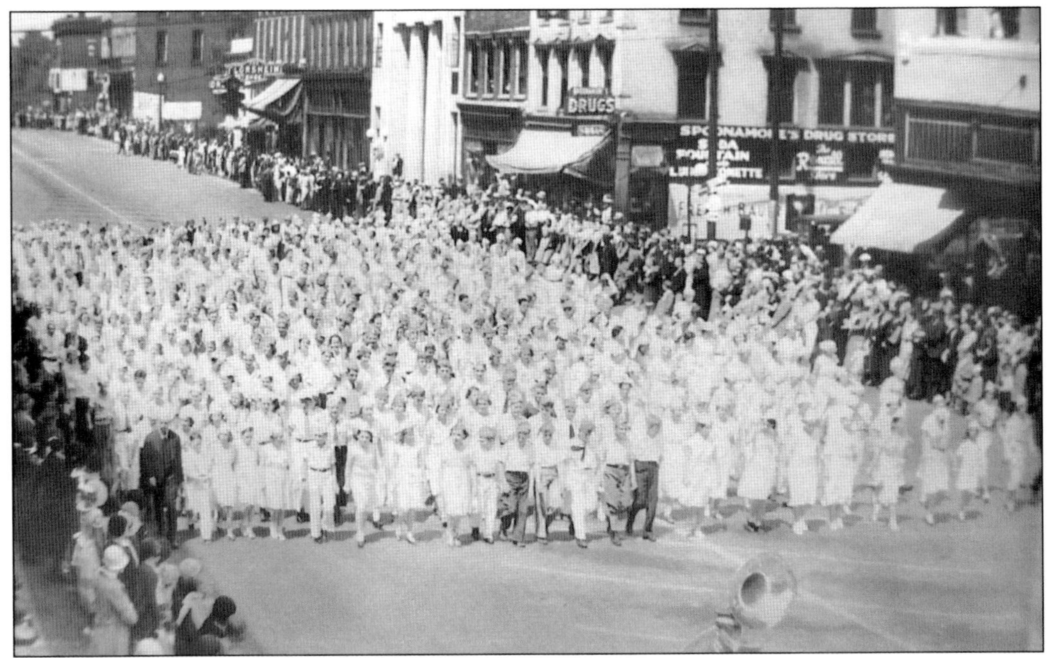


In the early 1930s, the Red Cross ran many community events and activities in Danville. The parade in these photographs was in honor of Boyle County schoolchildren who had been awarded blue ribbons for maintaining good health standards in the previous year. A fleet of Austin autos (below) was brought in by the dealer especially for the parade, a celebration in which nearly 2,000 schoolchildren of all ages participated. (Both courtesy of Guy Ingram.)

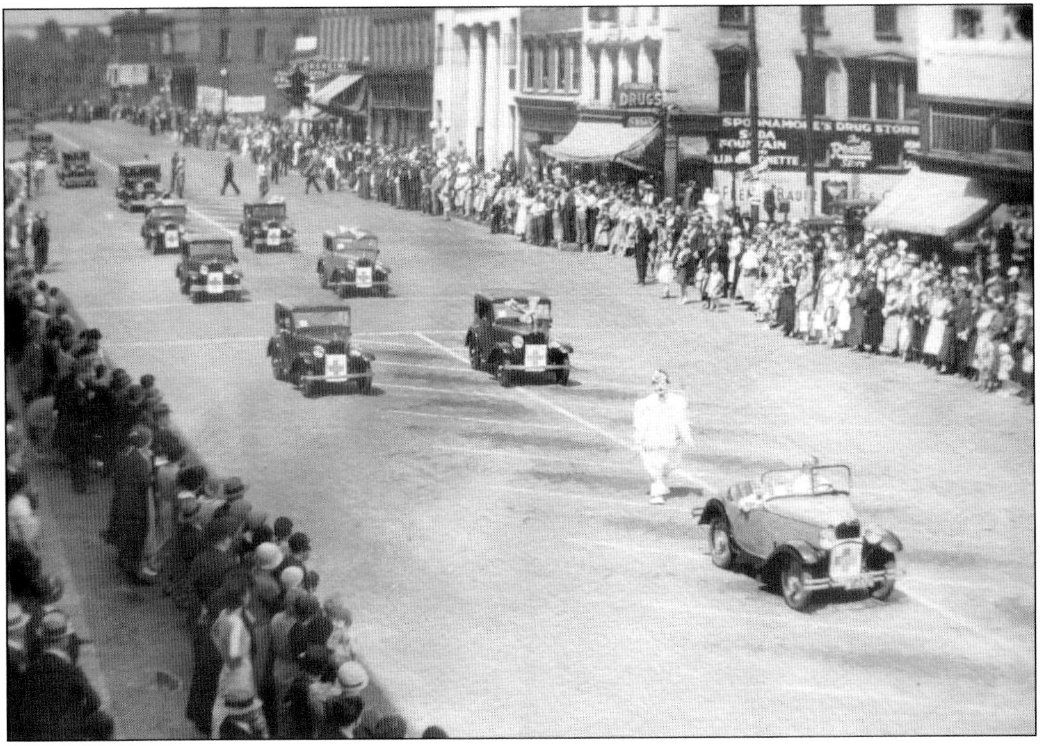

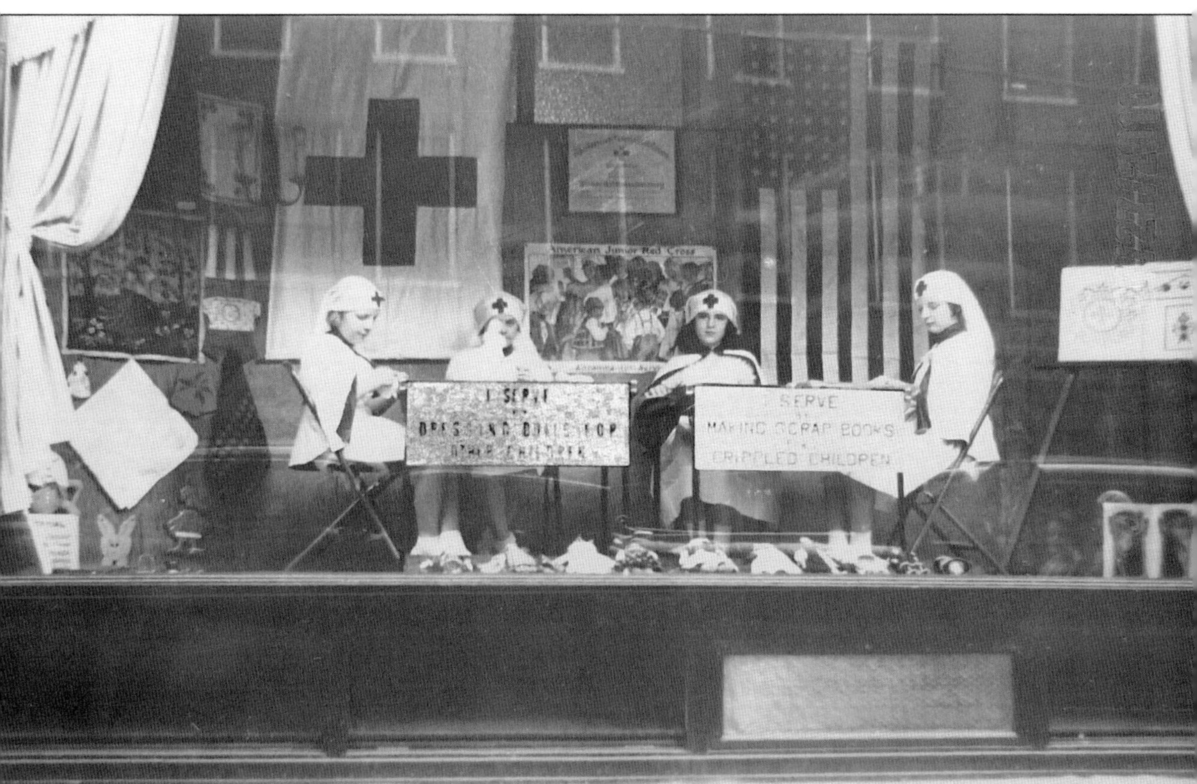


Four members of the Junior Red Cross sit in a window display in the Hub, located at the corner of Main and Third Streets. The Junior Red Cross, a service organization, was officially established by Pres. Woodrow Wilson, who asked American children after the United States entered World War I, "Is not this perhaps the chance for which you have been looking to give your time and efforts in some measure to meet our national needs?" These four young volunteers served the Danville community by dressing dolls and making scrapbooks for handicapped children. Other duties that the Junior Red Cross members performed included rolling bandages, growing victory gardens, preparing "friendship boxes" for children overseas in war-torn nations, and assisting local Red Cross chapters with their responsibilities. (Courtesy of Guy Ingram.)

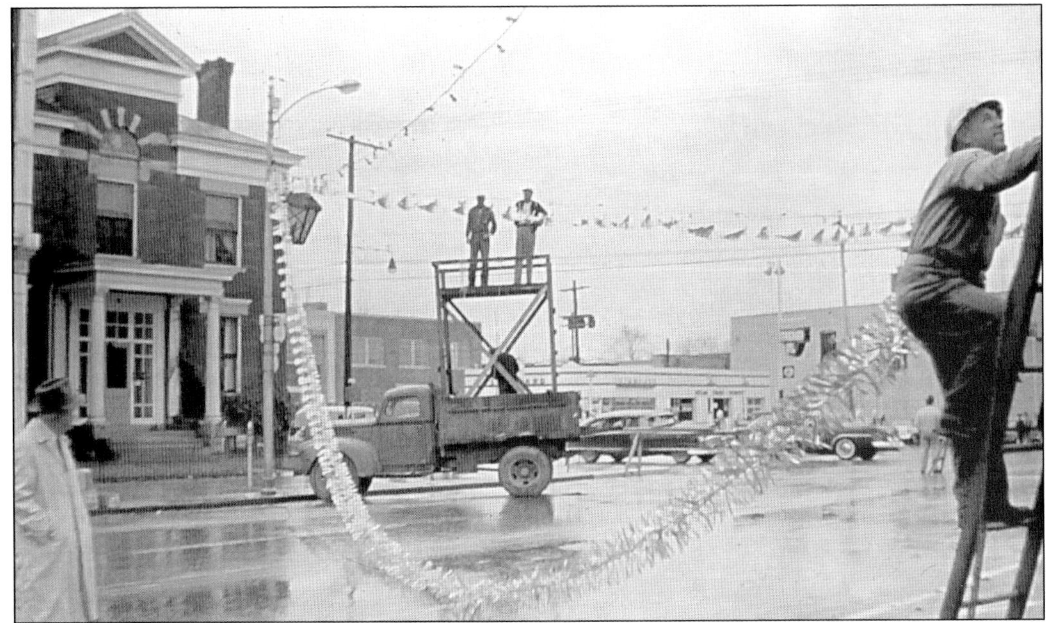

Every winter, the streets of Danville are decorated with wreathes, ribbons, and strands of lights to celebrate the holiday season. In this early 1960s photograph, city workers hang lights and garland across Main Street. In more recent years, the Danville Fire Department has assumed decoration duties, draping the trees lining the streets with lights to complement the festive adornments provided by Main Street businesses. (Courtesy of Guy Ingram.)

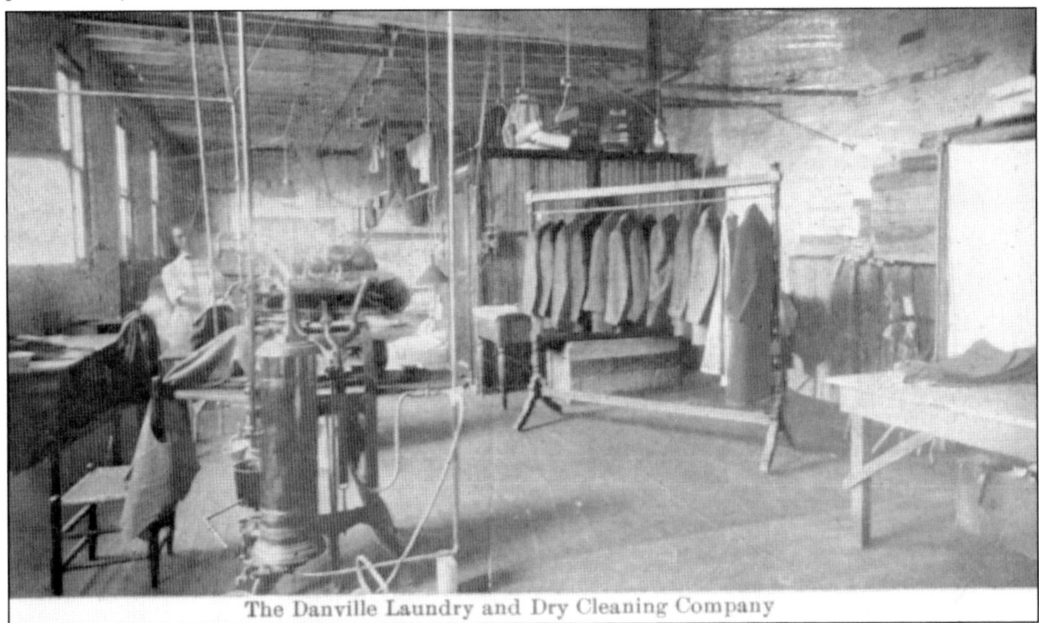

The Danville Laundry and Dry Cleaning Company

In 1895, local businessmen Henry and Samuel Lyons formed a partnership with John M. Nichols, establishing the Danville Steam Laundry. This business became one of the most successful of its kind in Kentucky, and it eventually changed its name in 1909 to Danville Laundry and Dry Cleaning. Henry and Samuel Lyons were beloved in Danville for their philanthropic activities and involvement in charities. (Courtesy of Michael Wiser.)

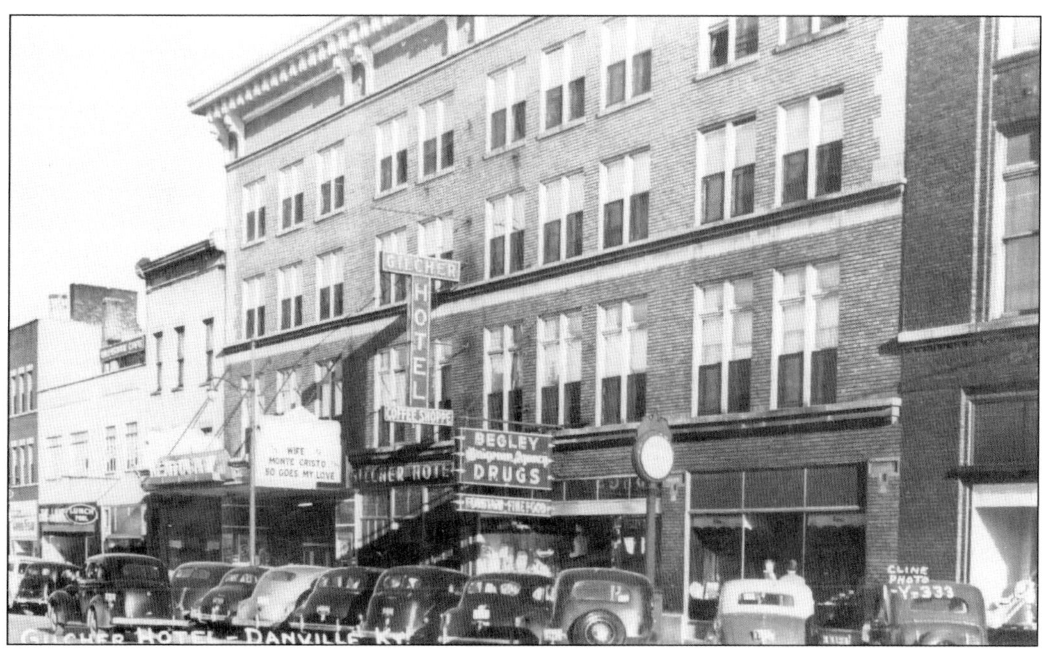


In 1875, Peter Gilcher bought property at the corner of Third and Main Streets, the hub of activity in Danville. He tore down the Henderson's building and built the Gilcher Hotel in its place. In addition to its 34 hotel rooms for paying guests, the hotel contained a kitchen, office, and dining room on the first floor as well as a confectionery and restaurant called the Sweet Shop. In 1899, plumbing was added to the building; in 1908, when Gilcher passed away, the structure was leased to new managers. The Gilcher Hotel was destroyed by a fire in 1914, but the site today contains various businesses, including an aptly named coffee shop, The Hub. (Above, courtesy of Michael Wiser; below, courtesy of Guy Ingram.)

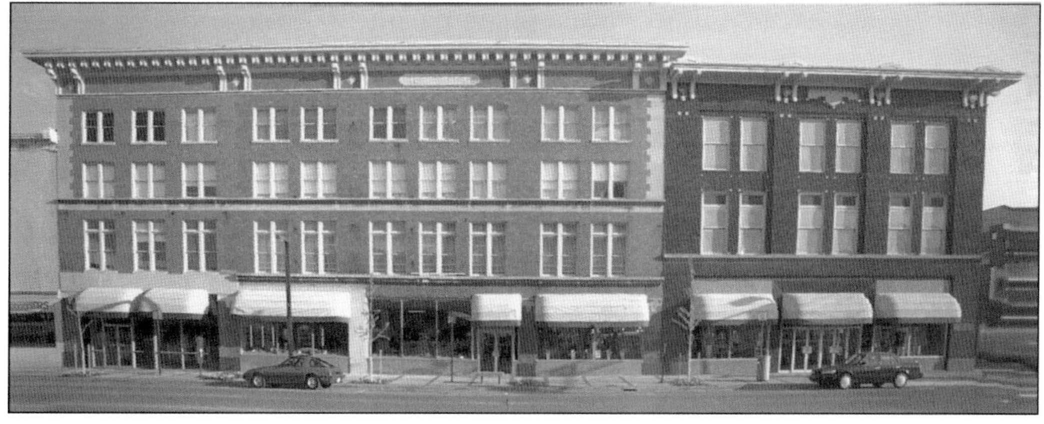

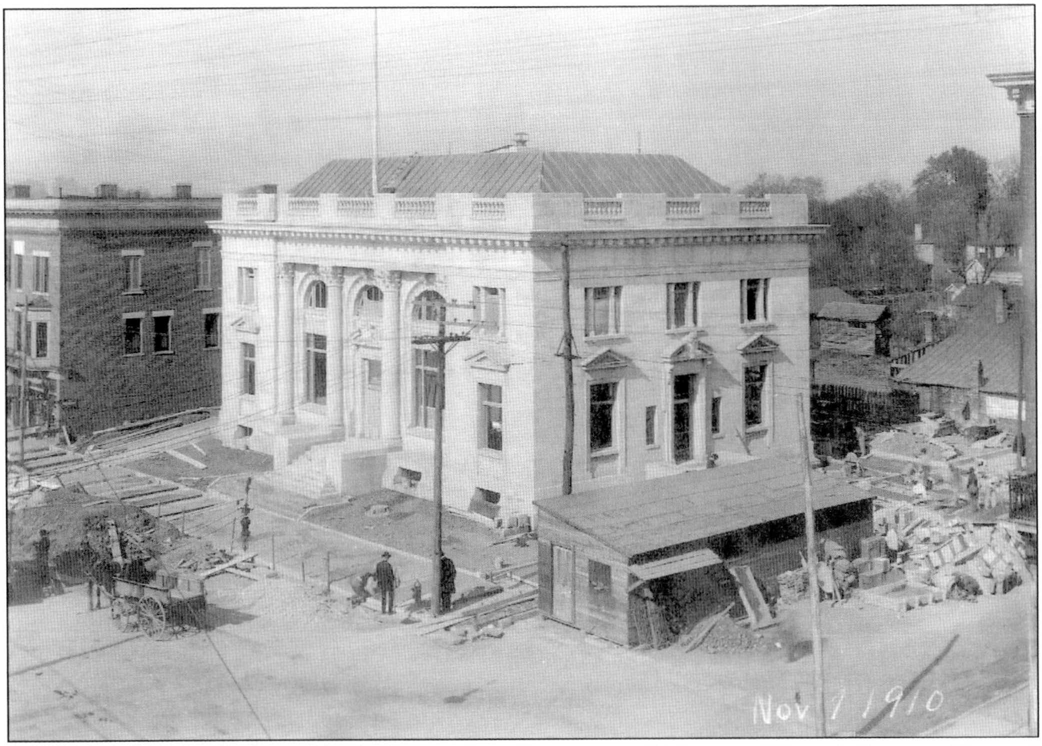

In 1909, the Danville Post Office relocated to the corner of Main and Fourth Streets. Pictured in 1910 (above) and again at a later date (below), the building was constructed in the Beaux-Arts style and served as the town's post office until 1961. After the post office relocated, the building, known then as the Federal Building, held military recruitment offices and the law offices of US Court of Appeals Judge Pierce Lively, and it currently serves as Danville's Community Arts Center. This community center houses galleries, classrooms, and studios and displays art and exhibitions created by locals. (Above, courtesy of Guy Ingram; below, courtesy of Michael Wiser.)

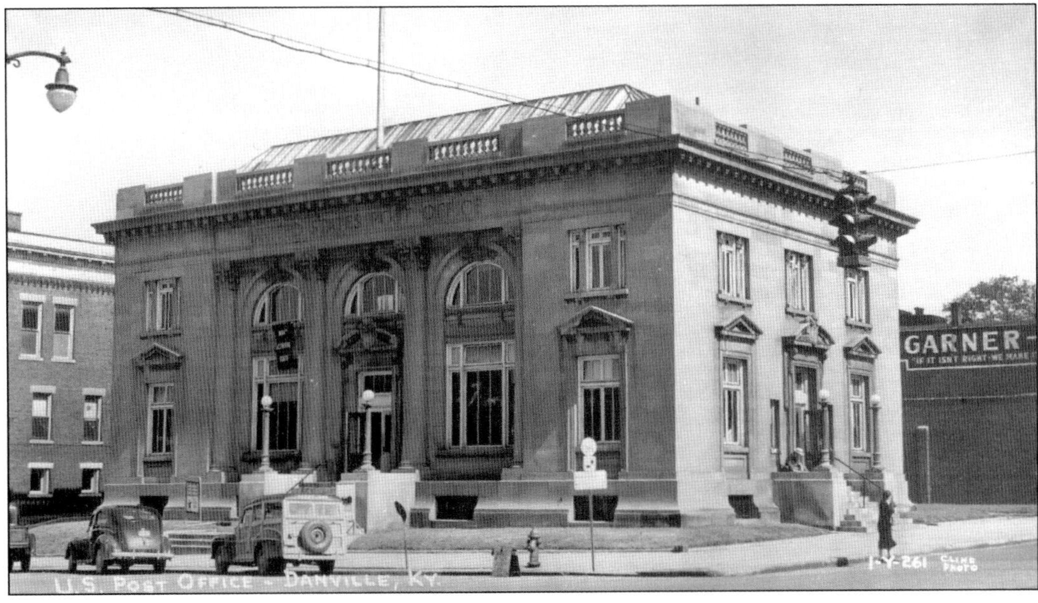

This 1953 photograph shows an eastward view of Main Street, peppered on both sides by businesses familiar to longtime Danville natives. Visible are the Gilcher Hotel, a movie theater, drugstores, and clothing stores. Parking on Main Street was initially diagonal before changing to parallel parking several years after this photograph was taken. (Courtesy of Guy Ingram.)

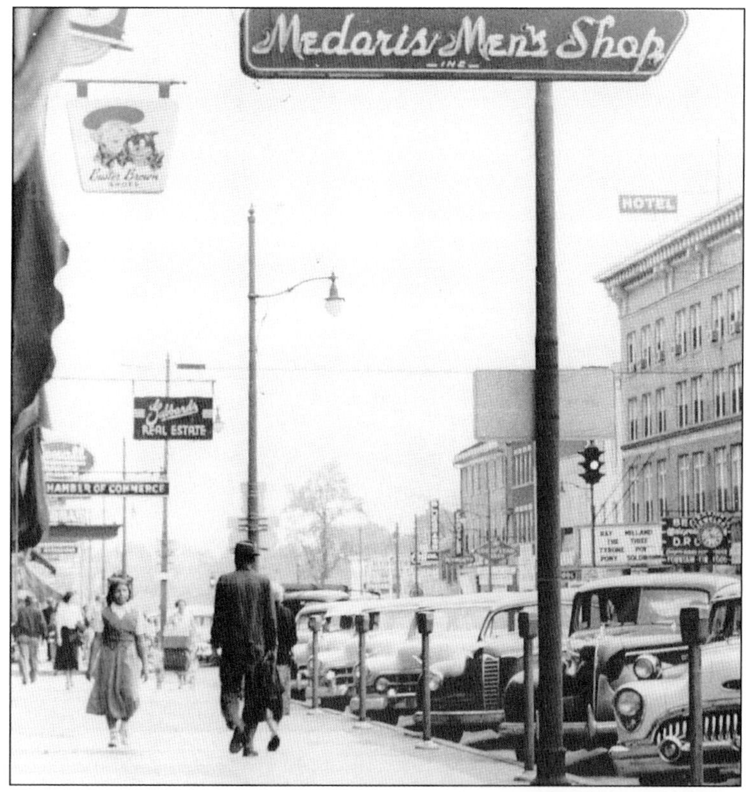


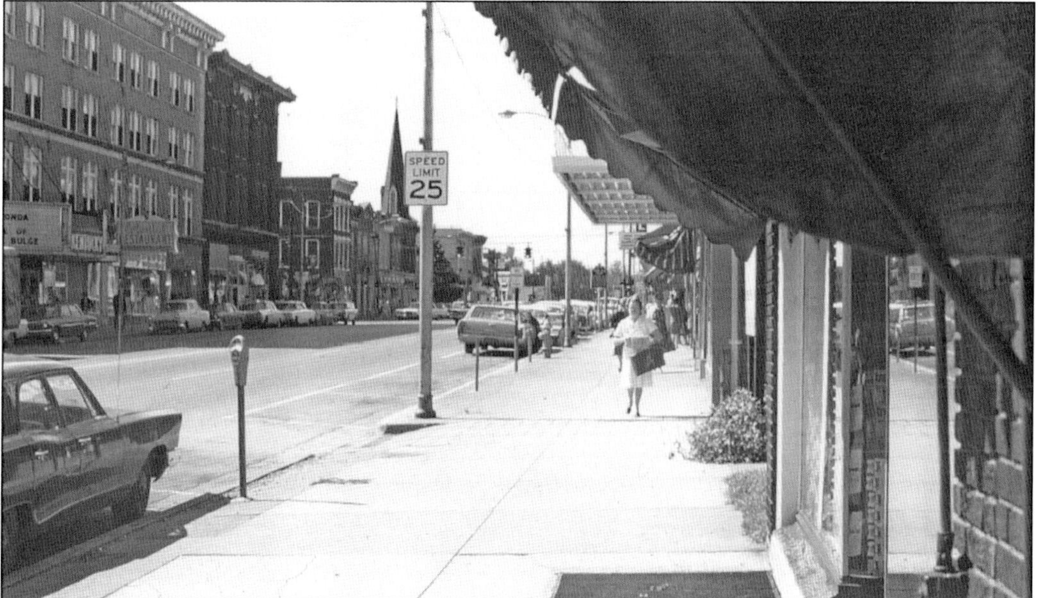


This photograph of Main Street, taken in 1966, shows the business section of town and the change from diagonal parking on the street to parallel as traffic through the downtown area became busier. On the left is the former Gilcher Hotel, which served as a variety of businesses at the time this photograph was taken. Trinity Episcopal Church's steeple is visible in the center. (Courtesy of Guy Ingram.)

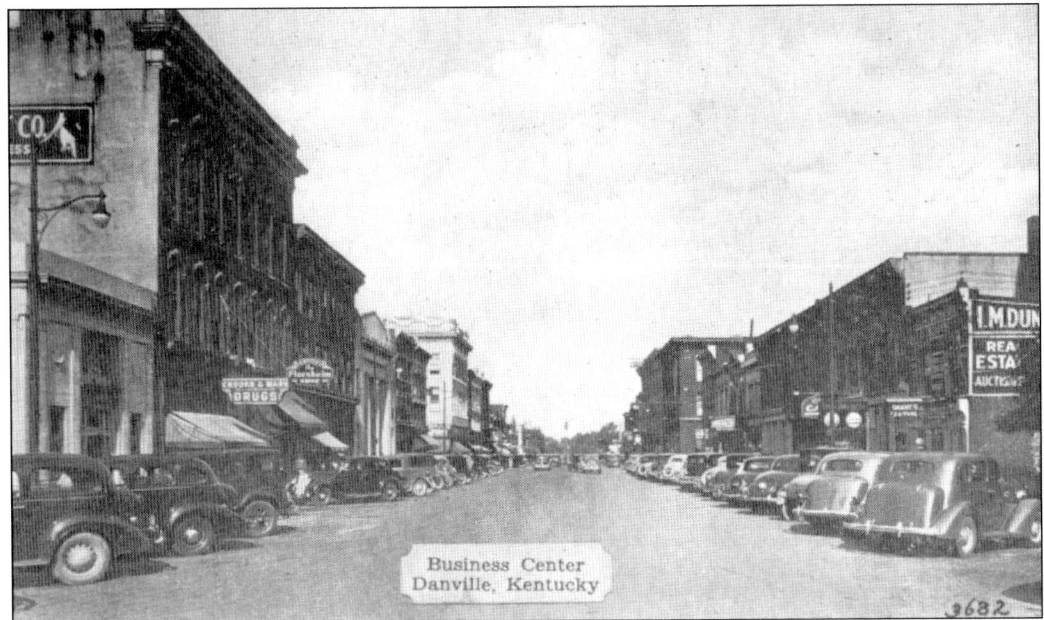


Postcards of various buildings and streetscapes in Danville were common in the early 20th century. This postcard of Main Street shows various stores that, though long gone, remain in many Danville locals' fond memories. Drugstores such as Crooks and Ware (left), served not only as pharmacies but also as gathering places where working men and women could get a hot meal at the lunch counter. (Courtesy of Michael Wiser.)

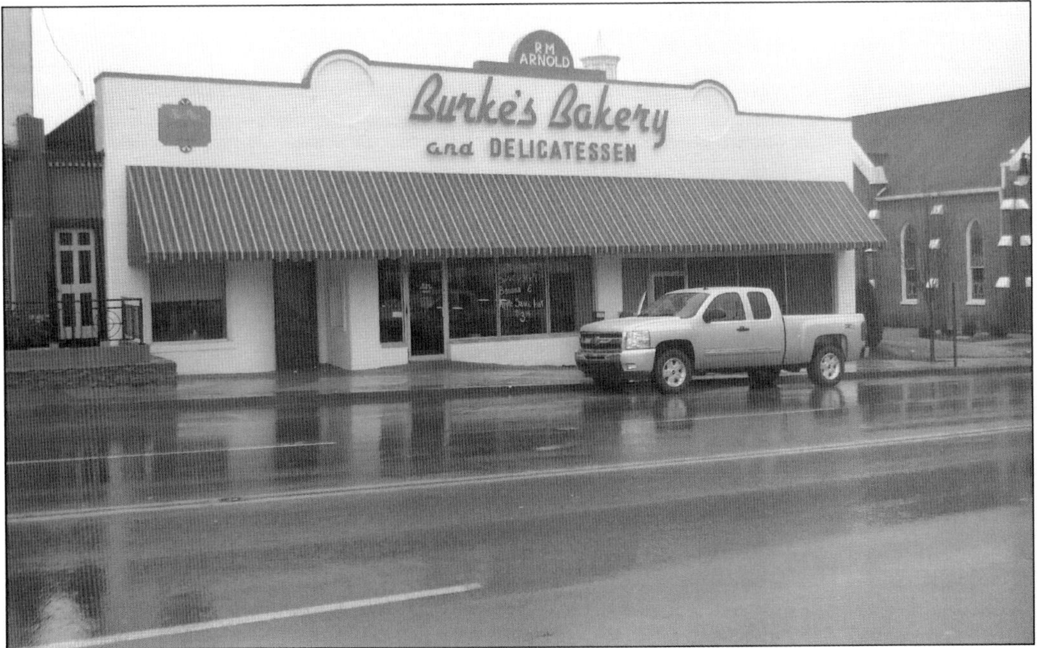


When visitors pass through Danville, locals will always ask, "Have you been to Burke's Bakery yet?" The bakery, originally started in nearby Junction City, has been a staple of the Danville streetscape for decades. Burke's is owned and operated by the fourth and fifth generations of a family that has been serving baked treats to faithful customers for many years. (Author's personal collection.)

# *Eight*

# Familiar Faces and Places

While famous people, landmark events, and important buildings contribute to the scholarly history of a town, it is the regular people and their experiences that create the personal history. From school buildings and railroad structures that no longer stand to a gentleman historian and a woman enjoying her daily routine of coffee and a cigarette at Spoonamore's, one might argue that their stories contribute significantly to the history of Danville. When asking the current generation of longtime Danville residents what they remember best about their town, they will mention the parade to celebrate the local production of the Technicolor film *Raintree County* starring Elizabeth Taylor and Montgomery Clift, the weekday visits of "Candy Man" Huss Steinberger to Danville High School where he sold sweets, the 5¢ ice cream cones at Swiss Sanitary Milk, or the beautiful antebellum mansions that were passed down through generations of families. There is a great appreciation for the over 225 years of history in Danville and a drive to preserve it for the education and enjoyment of future residents and visitors.

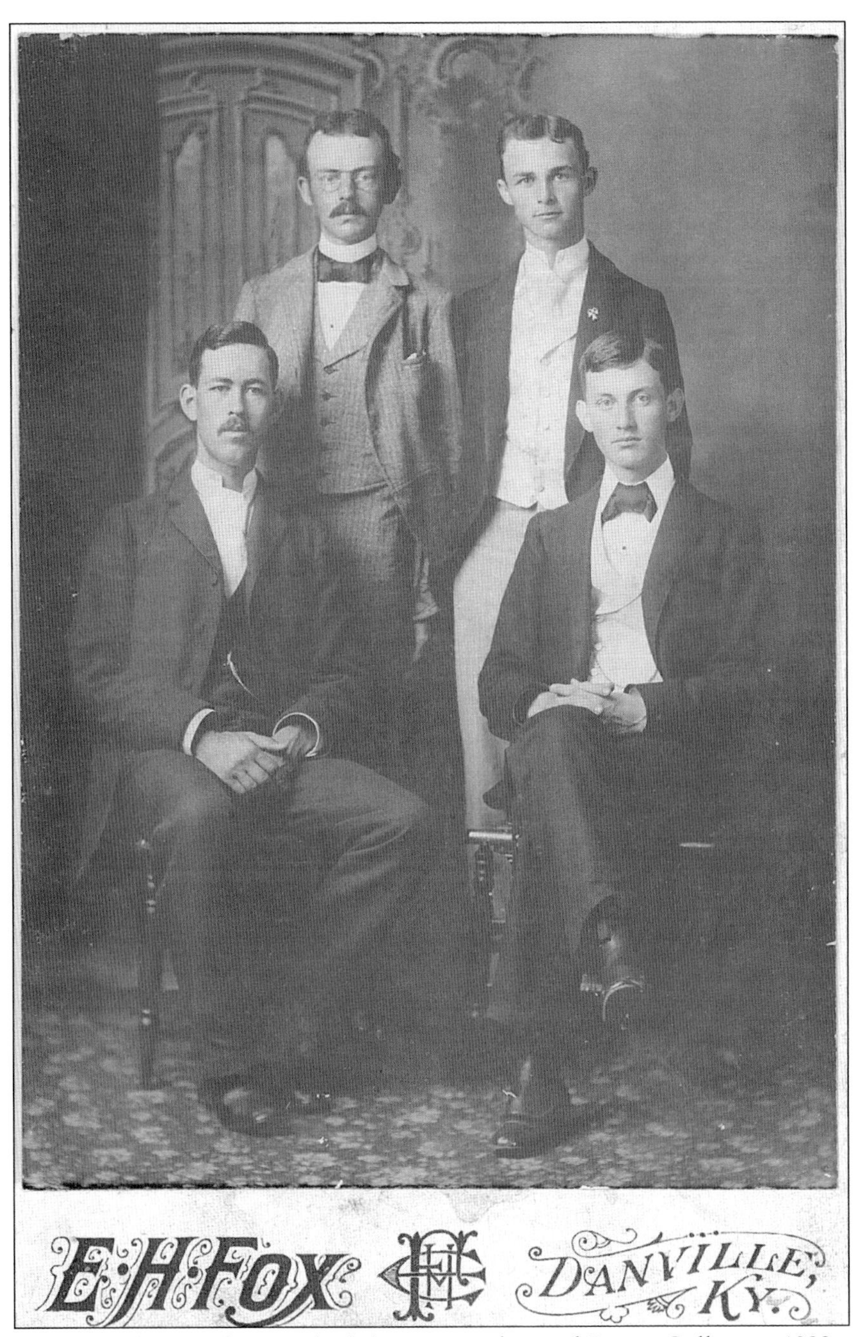


Calvin Morgan Fackler, standing on the left, was a graduate of Centre College in 1892 and of the University of Louisville Law School in 1894. Born in Boyle County in 1872, Fackler worked as a lawyer and became deeply involved in the Danville community; he was active in local church groups, educational programs, and charities. Fackler considered his hobbies to be "history and genealogy" and dedicated much of his free time to the research of Danville's history. In 1941, he published *Early Days in Danville*, which covers the history of the town from its pioneer days through the Civil War. His elegant and often witty writing remains a favorite of local historians, and his book is considered the benchmark of Danville history books. (Courtesy of Guy Ingram.)

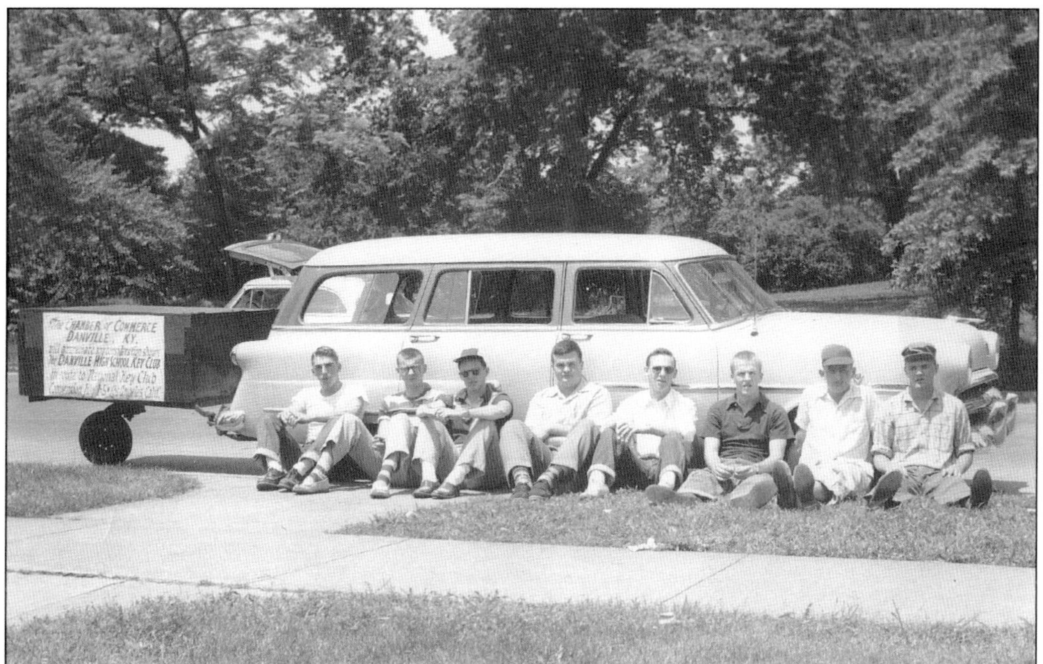


Operating from 1918 until 1963, the old Danville High School was located next to Centre College's campus. The building was demolished in 1971 to make room for the Norton Center for the Arts. The 1953 photograph above depicts Danville High School Key Club members preparing for a trip to the National Key Club Convention in Los Angeles, California. Below, another local marching band from Perryville High School performs in Centre College's 1954 Homecoming Parade down Main Street. (Both courtesy of Guy Ingram.)

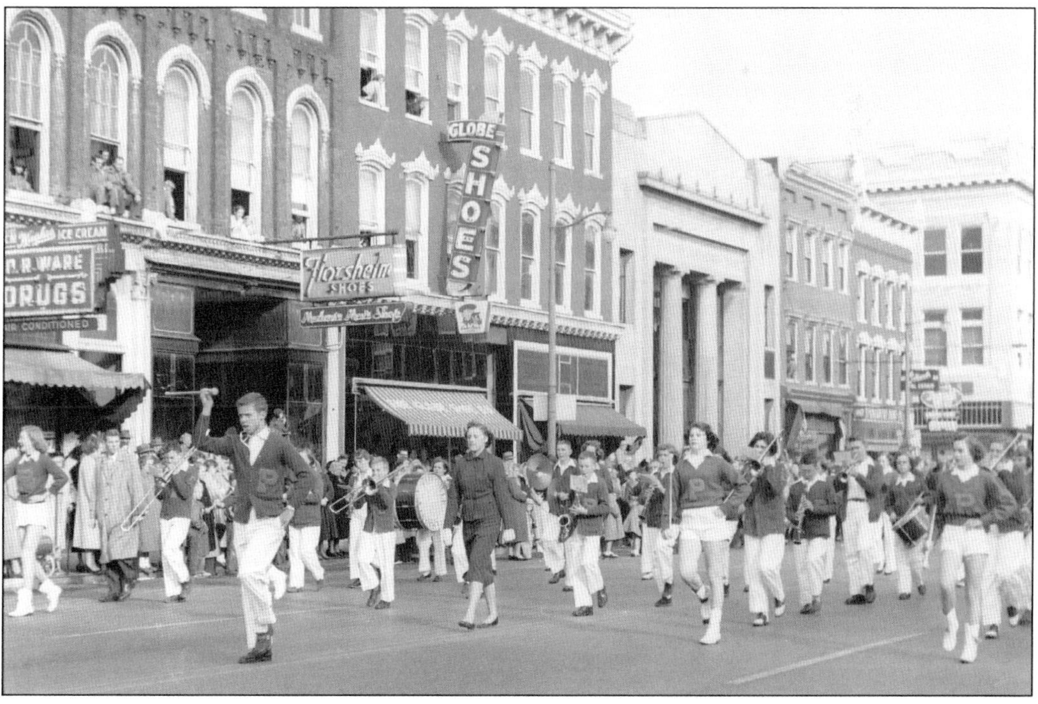

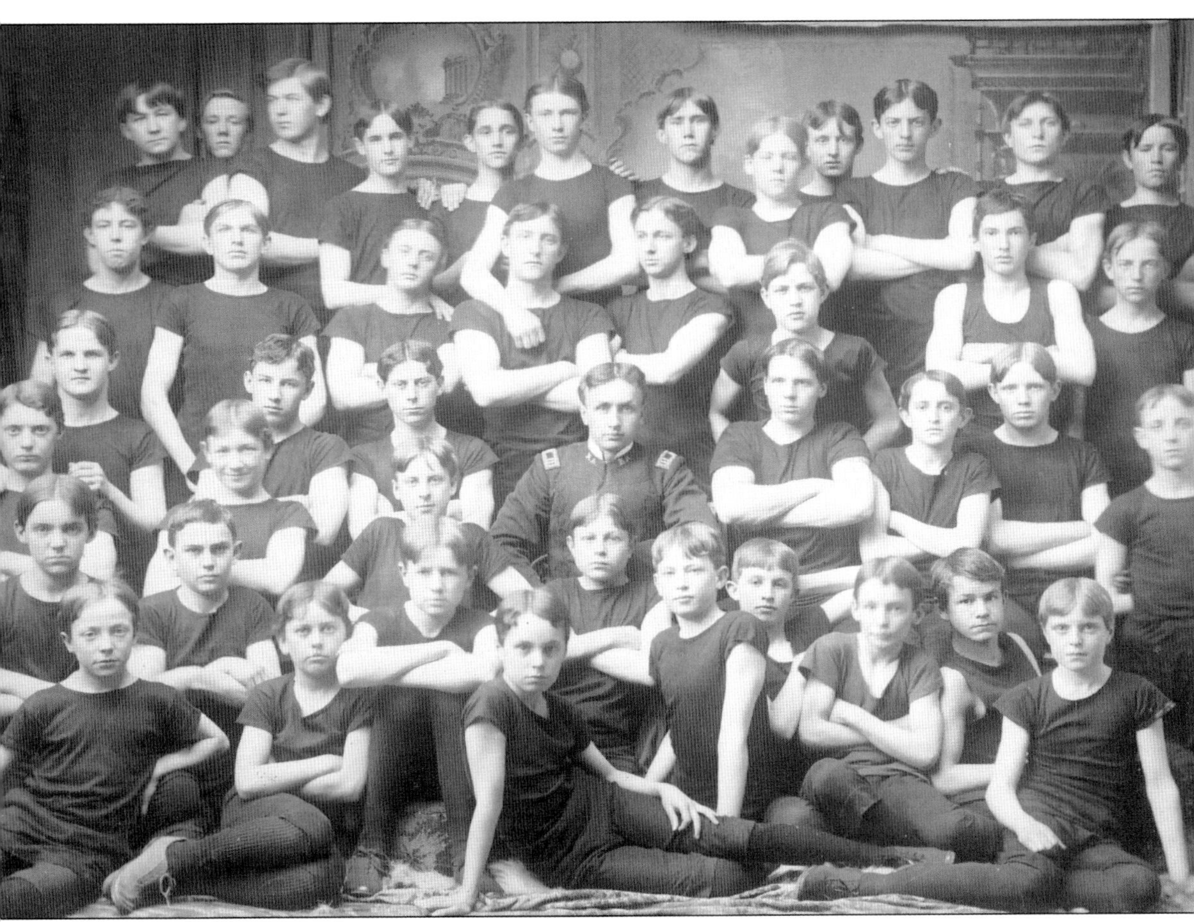

Hogsett School, opened by Centre College alumnus John James Hogsett in 1889, served as a military academy for the Danville area. Hogsett, valedictorian of the Centre College class of 1872, ran an academy in Harrodsburg for several years before moving to Danville to open Hogsett School with his brother Samuel, an 1886 graduate of Centre College. John served as its head until his death in 1891, after which the school became a military academy. The academy's gymnasium class poses in this 1895 studio portrait; Walter D. Berry, seated in the middle in his uniform, is surrounded by unidentified students. In 1899, Centre College considered merging its preparatory school with Hogsett, but for unknown reasons the institutions did not consolidate, and the Hogsett Military Academy closed in 1901. (Courtesy of Centre College Special Collections.)

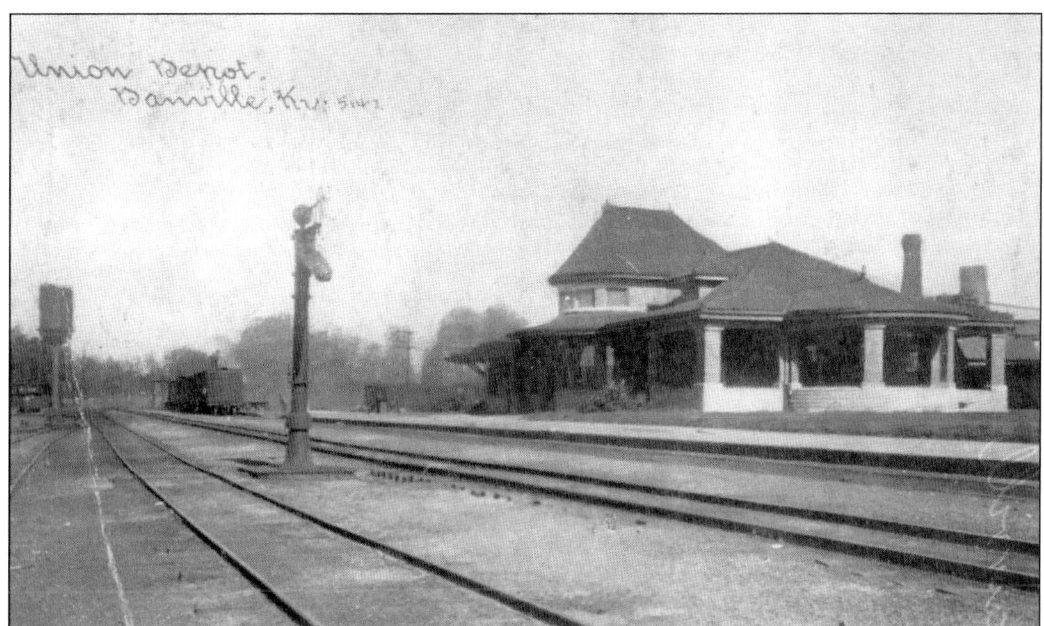


Danville became a major link in the Southern railroad system in 1877 when High Bridge was built over the Kentucky River. Many businesses built around the railroad in Danville, including Danville Roller Mills and Grain Elevator, Samuel Harding Lumber Company, and the Potts, Proctor & Company Eclipse Roller mills, among others. The Danville Train Depot, pictured here on a postcard, was built in 1908. (Courtesy of Michael Wiser.)

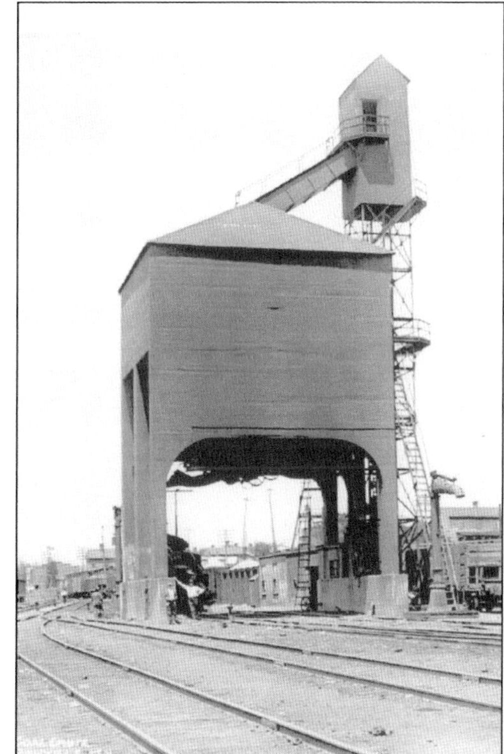

Kentucky was and remains a key player in the nation's coal industry, producing roughly 120 million tons of the resource every year. Nearly 80 percent of all coal mined in Kentucky is sent to other states, mostly via rail. This coal chute, located next to the railroad in Danville, allowed for easy loading of boxcars to transport coal to other destinations. (Courtesy of Michael Wiser.)

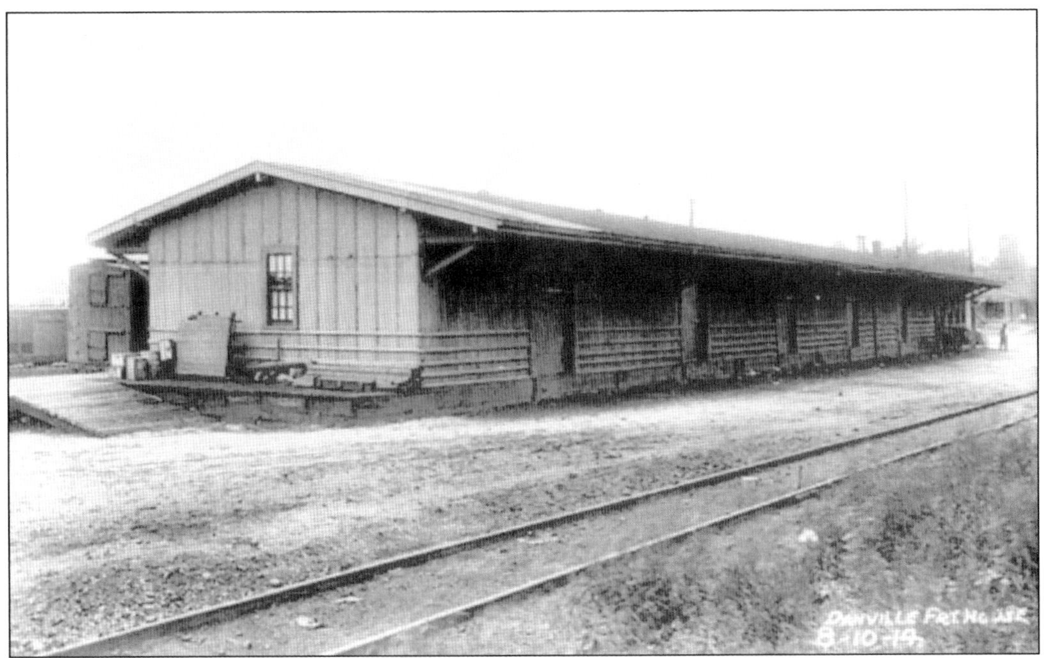


Numerous businesses such as mills, lumber companies, and farms shipped their products around the country via Danville's railroad. The freight house, pictured in this undated photograph, was used to receive and store the transported goods. (Courtesy of Michael Wiser.)

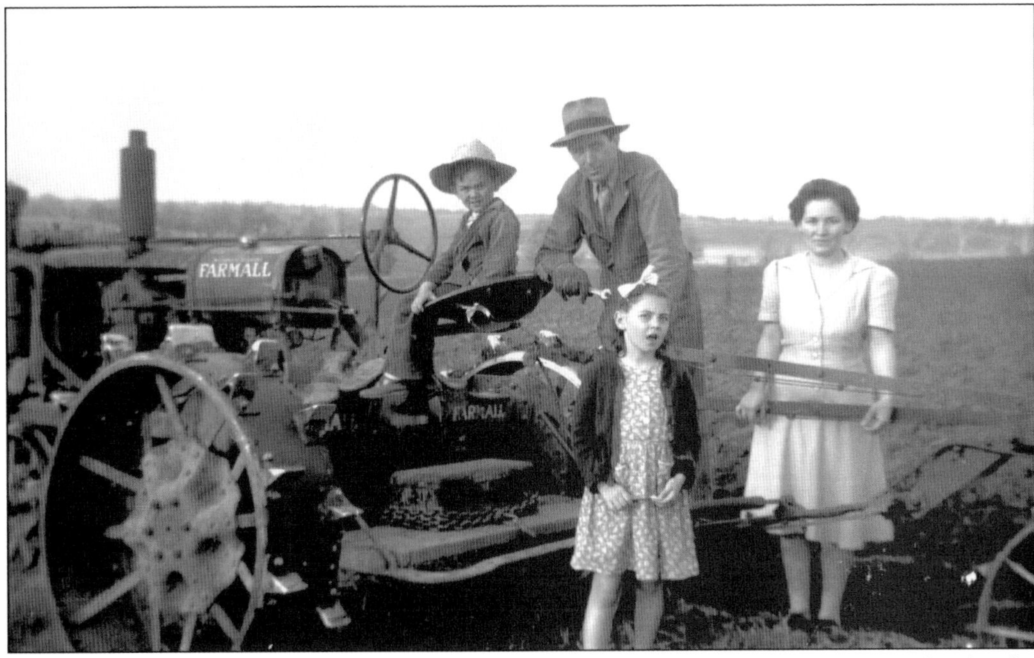


The Salt River originates in Danville and flows 140 miles to the Ohio River on Kentucky's border with Ohio. When the area around the river was settled in the late 18th century, pioneer families found it to be good farmland. Even into the 20th century, farmers worked the land around the river. Pictured above on their family farm in 1947 are Marcus and Gladys Russell with their two children, Nathan and Anna Mae. (Courtesy of Guy Ingram.)

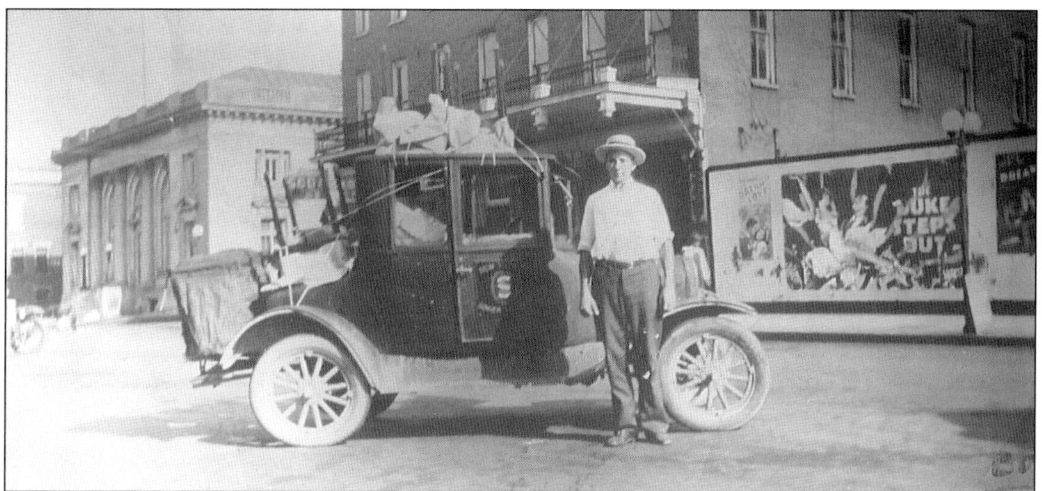


Ed Fraysur, manager of the Singer Sewing Company in the western counties of Kentucky, had a store and office in Danville. He is pictured in 1928, standing with his car in front of the Palace of Sweets and the Colonial Theatre. Both of these businesses burned down in the early 1930s. (Courtesy of Guy Ingram.)

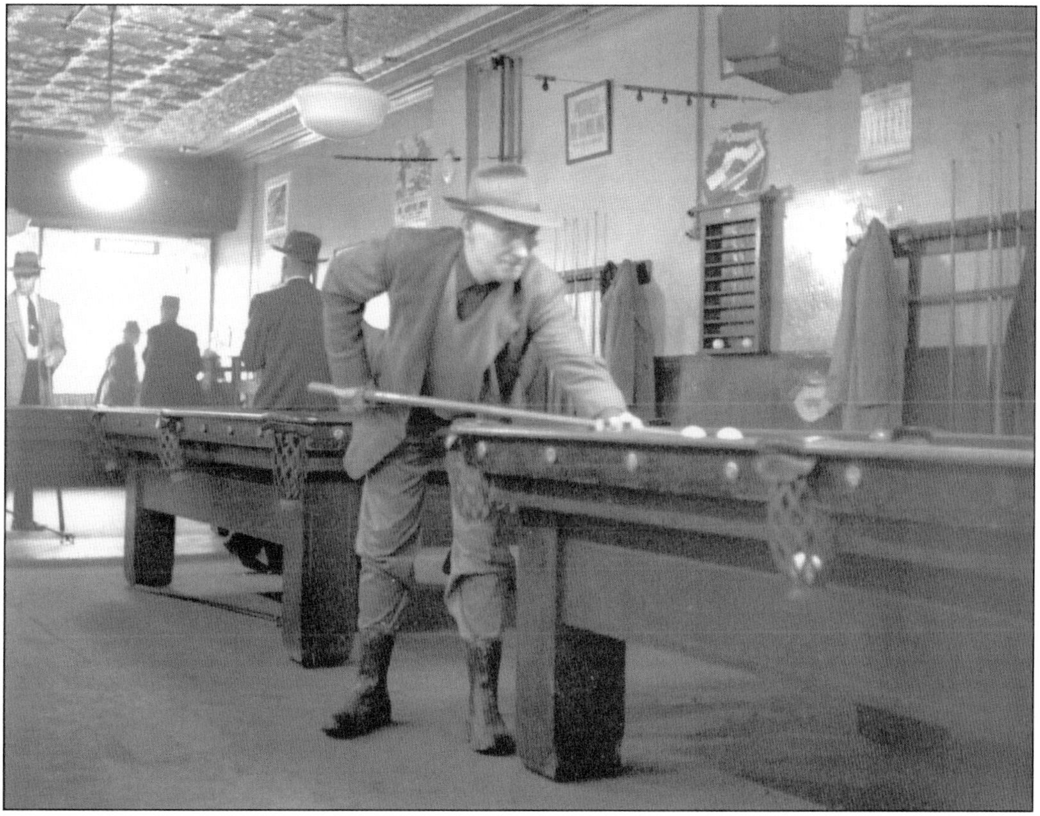

In this 1953 photograph, fire chief Alex Upton prepares for a shot in the Kreiner and Hunt Pool Hall, located at 303 West Main Street. Beloved by many generations in Danville, the pool hall was the second oldest business on Main Street at the time of its closing in the fall of 2010. (Courtesy of Guy Ingram.)

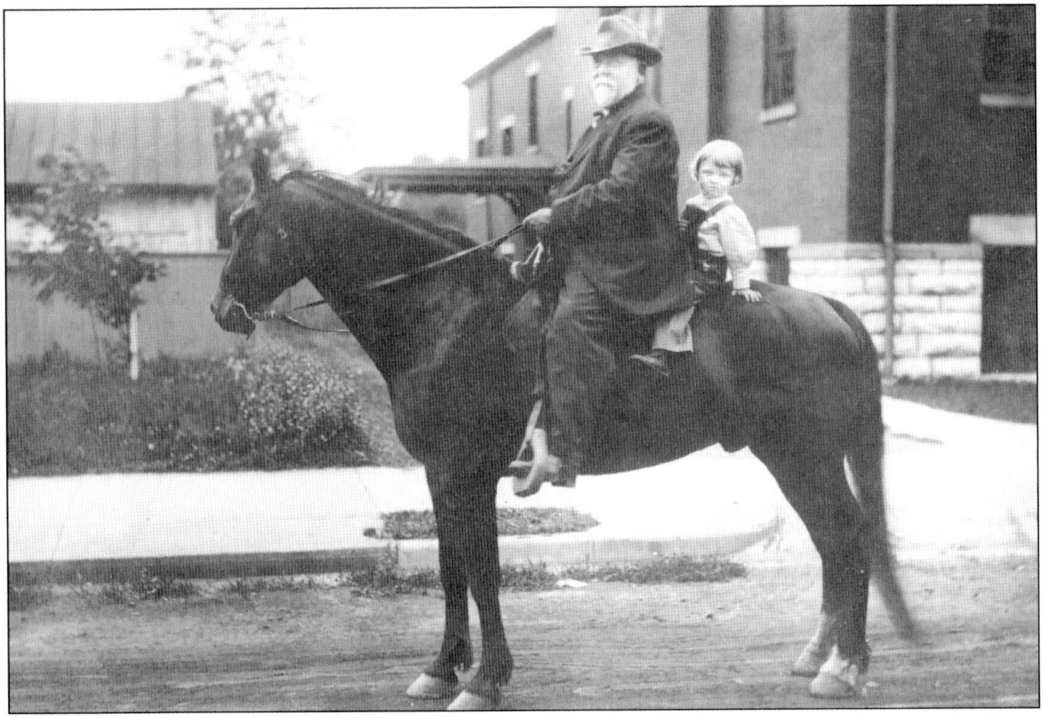

Danville residents J. Perkins Ingram and his granddaughter Kathryn pose in the street in front of the Broadway Baptist Church around 1909. This church has since been removed to expand the Boyle County Library. (Courtesy of Guy Ingram.)

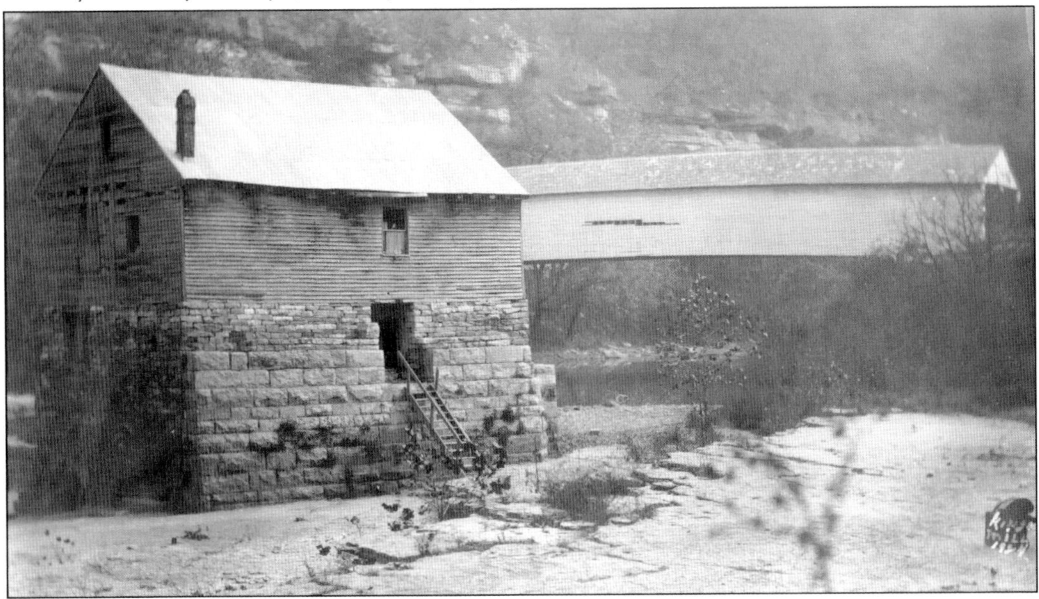

Northwest of Danville, near the line between Boyle and Garrard Counties, King's Mill Covered Bridge once spanned the Dix River, a tributary of the Kentucky River. In 1925, the Dix River was dammed to generate hydroelectric power, creating the man-made Lake Herrington. The old mill and 175-foot bridge, pictured here in 1924, were left in place and covered by the rising waters. (Courtesy of Michael Wiser.)

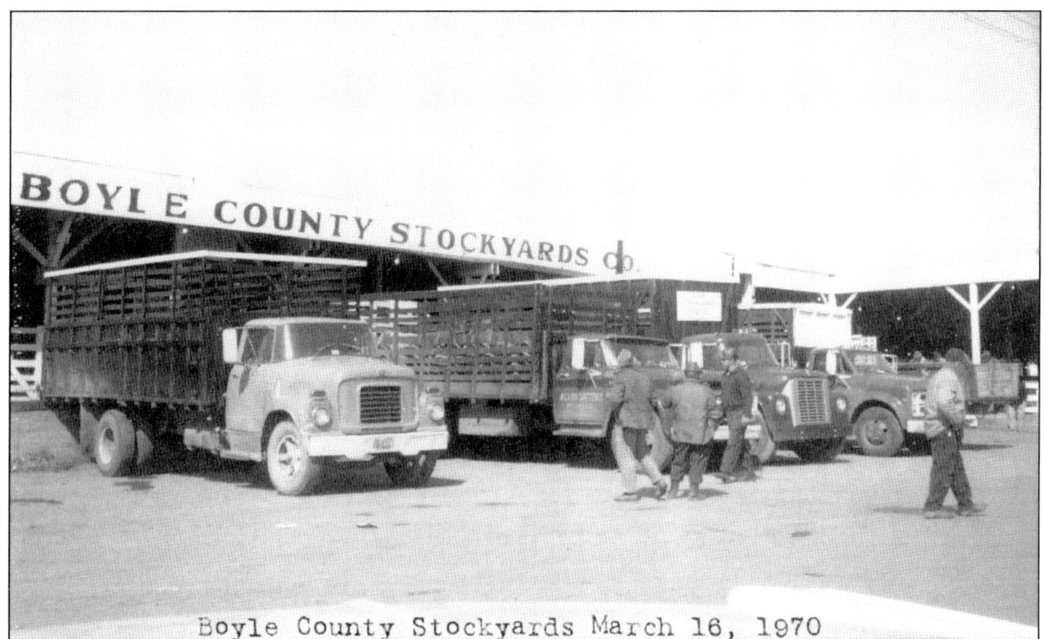


The Boyle County Stockyards, seen here in the spring of 1970, played a key role in the agriculture industry in Danville and surrounding regions. Located behind Centre College's campus, the stockyards were a place where cattle could be sold to vendors. (Courtesy of Guy Ingram.)

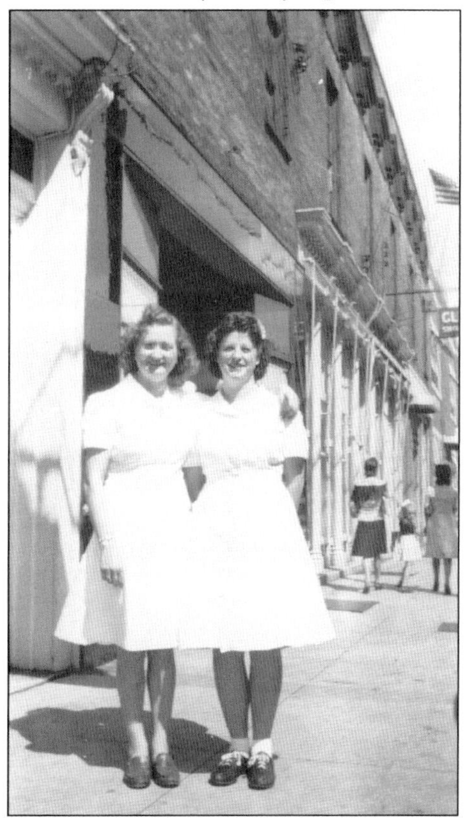

Star Grill waitresses Addie and Minnie pose in front of Cline's shoe store on Third Street. Cline's was a favorite of many in town, but it closed down and was replaced by Melody Music. The new music store offered lessons and sold a variety of instruments, including some exotic-looking pianos from Japan. (Courtesy of Michael Wiser.)

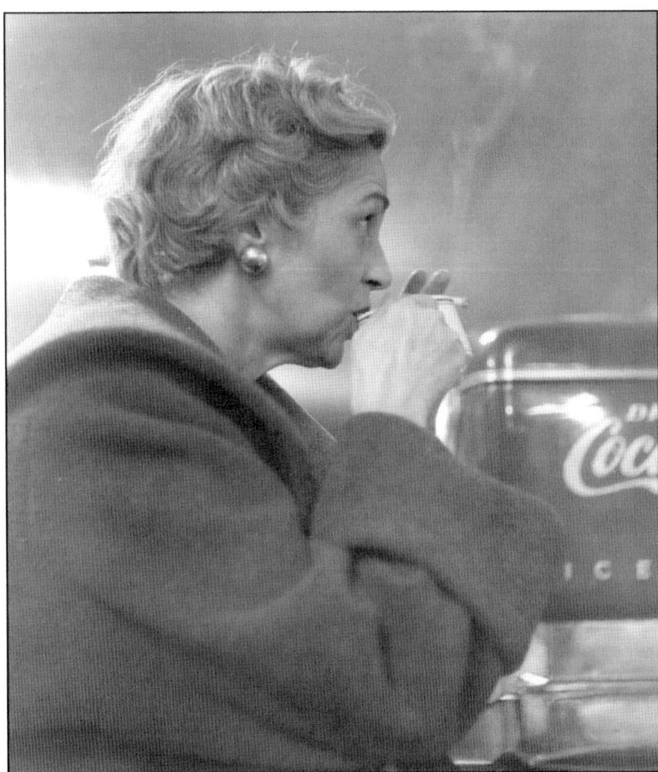

Elizabeth Ingram takes a coffee and cigarette break at Spoonamore's Drug Store in this undated photograph. Spoonamore's, located at the corner of Main and Third Streets, was a popular pharmacy in Danville and offered lunch-counter service for its patrons. (Courtesy of Guy Ingram.)

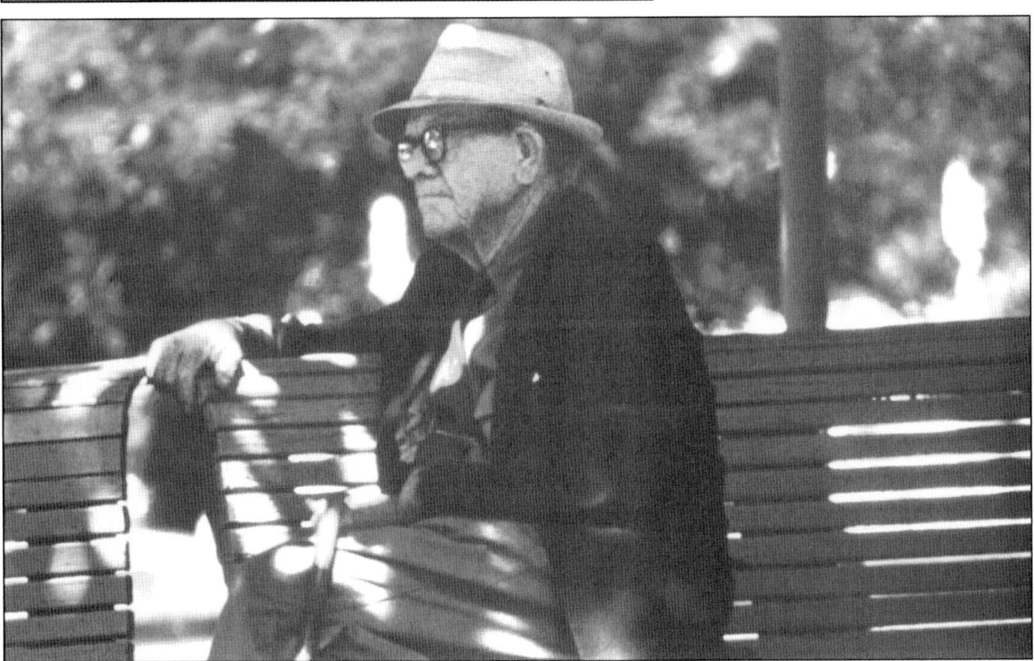

Danville resident Huss Steinberger, known affectionately as Candy Man Huss, sold candy to passersby in front of Danville High School in the 1940s and 1950s during school hours. In 1901, the *Kentucky Advocate* wrote about young Steinberger's well-known phrase, "Give me a copper." He was a beloved member of Danville's community for many decades. (Courtesy of Guy Ingram.)

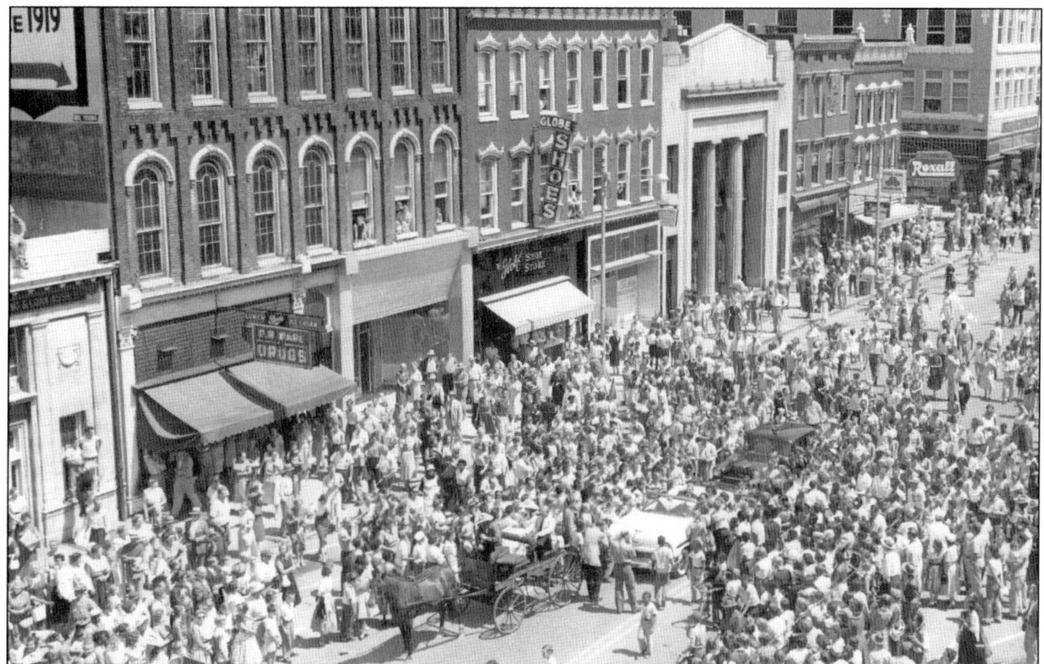


*Raintree County*, a 1957 Technicolor drama about the Civil War, was filmed in and around Danville as well as in several other locations in Kentucky. The film starred Hollywood legends Montgomery Clift, Elizabeth Taylor, Eva Marie Saint, and Lee Marvin. Danville citizens lined Main Street for a parade (above) welcoming the cast and crew, who spent six weeks in the area for filming. Elizabeth Taylor, nominated for the Academy Award for Best Actress for her role as Susanna Drake, was seated in the first car in the parade, and addressed the crowd (below). (Above, courtesy of Guy Ingram; below, courtesy of Michael Wiser.)

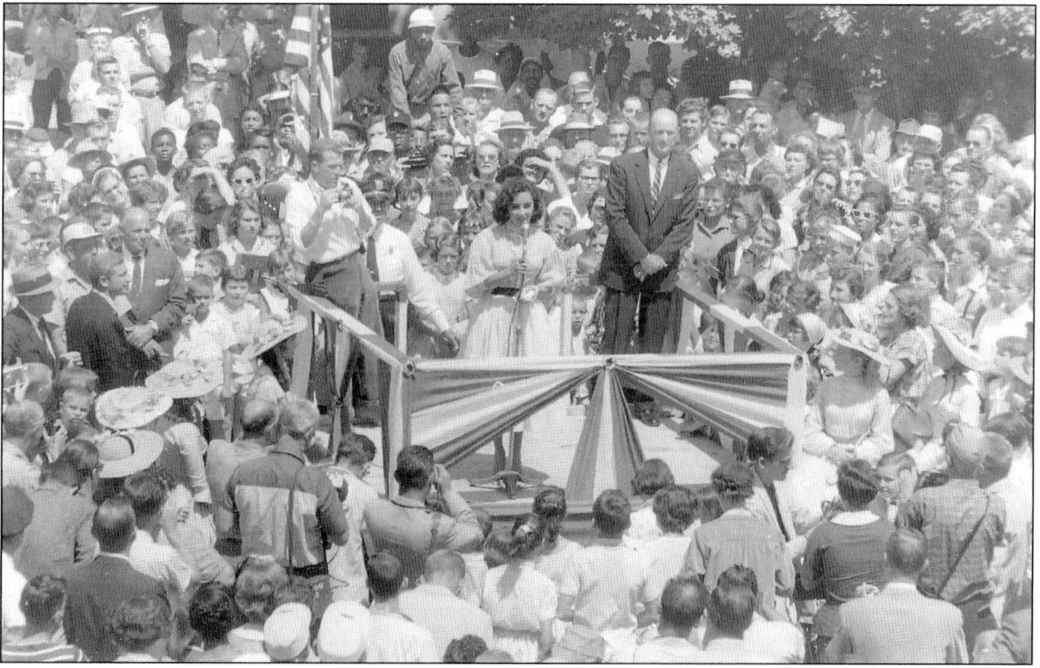

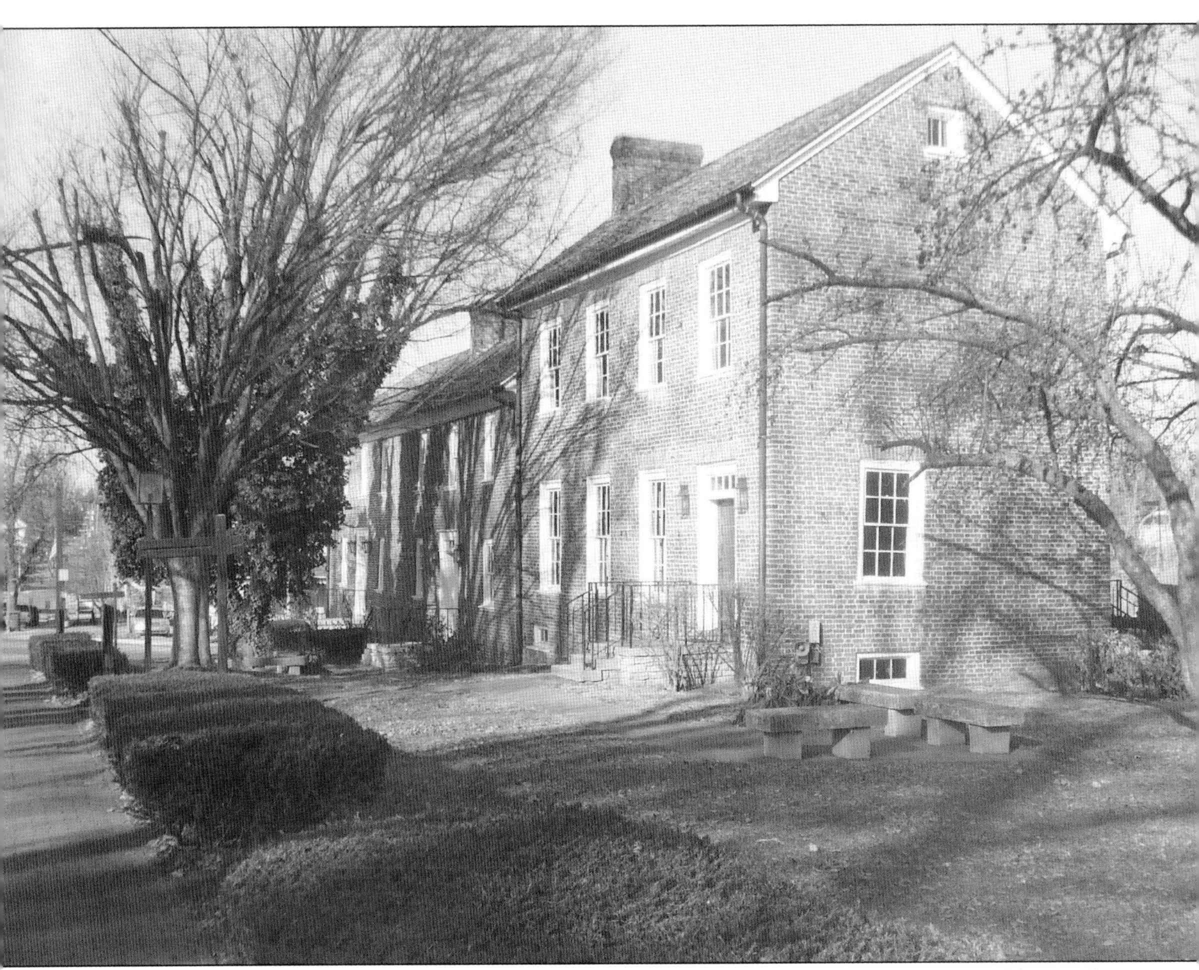

The Watts-Bell House (right) was built by William Watts around 1816–1817 for Danville merchant David Bell. Joshua Fry Bell, grandson of David Bell, grew up in the Watts-Bell House before becoming a lawyer, statesman, US congressman, and Kentucky secretary of state under Gov. John J. Crittenden. The Danville Literary and Social Club, now known as the Anaconda Club, was formed in 1839 and met from time to time in the house; it is the oldest club of its type west of the Allegheny Mountains. The Watts-Bell House was built in the Flemish Bond pattern, like Fisher's Row houses (left), with which it shares a common wall. The Fisher's Row houses were constructed by Jeremiah Fisher for use as rental properties. The two buildings recently housed the Wilderness Trace Art League, an education center, and the Danville-Boyle County Historical Society, but both are currently empty. (Author's personal collection.)

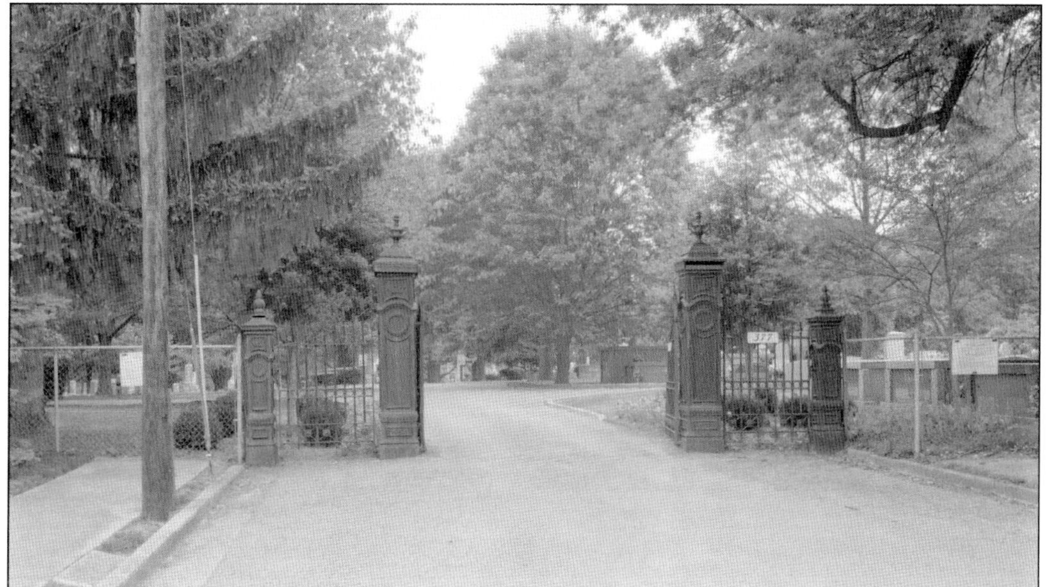

Danville National Cemetery is one of 146 national cemeteries, so designated for their historical importance. Located in the northwest corner of Bellevue Cemetery on North First Street, the national cemetery received its designation in 1862 after the federal government appropriated 18 lots in what was then known as Danville City Cemetery. During the Civil War, Union soldiers who died in Danville military hospital were the original interments; a Confederate lot with 66 graves adjoins the national cemetery. The site is 0.3 acres, and its boundaries are marked by square limestone posts with "U.S." carved on the faces. (Both courtesy of the NPS Historic American Buildings Survey.)

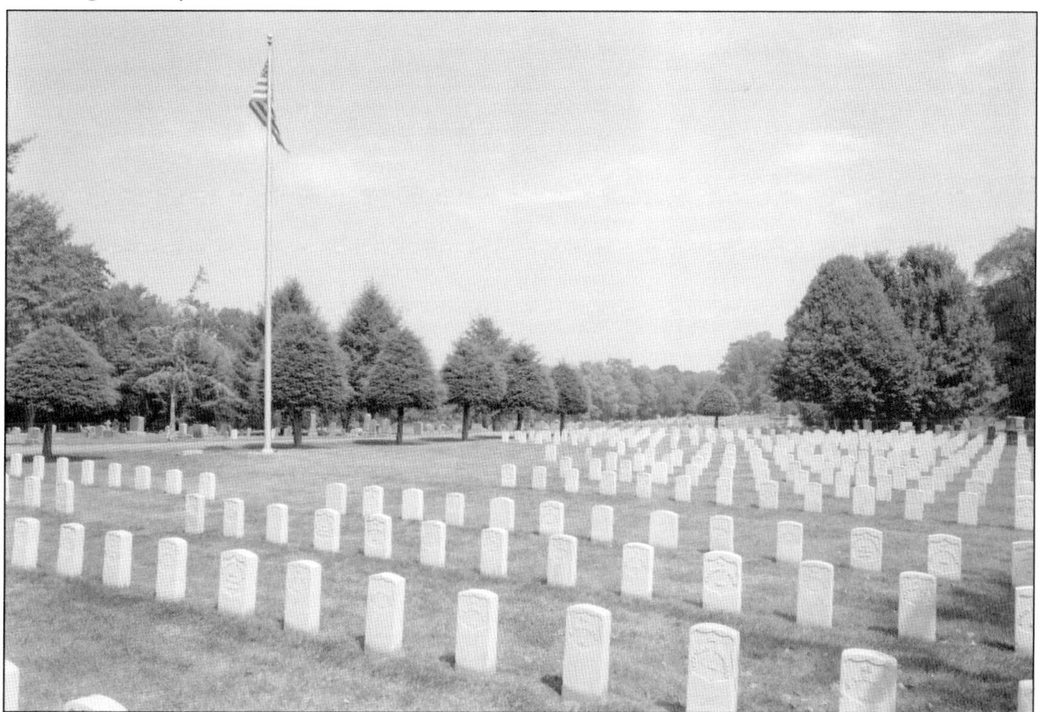

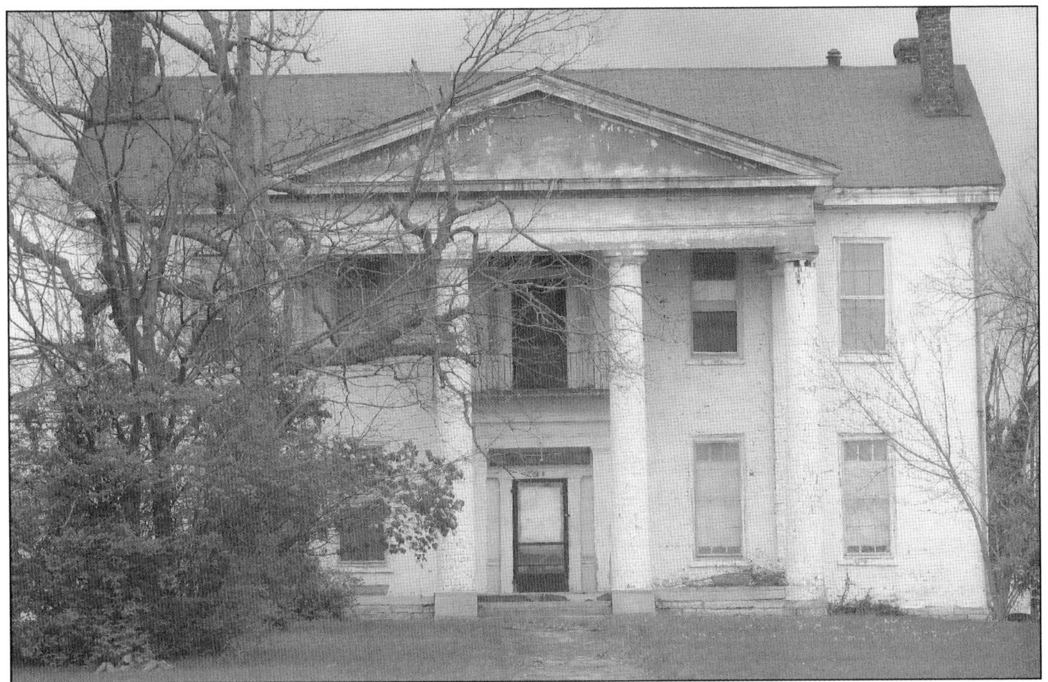

Robert Russell Junior, who built several historic houses in Danville, completed the Fisher-Byington House (above) around 1845. The home, located at 805 South Fourth Street, was included in the Heart of Danville's 2007 list of most endangered properties in the city. The Rochester-Farris mansion (below), another of Russell's creations, was built around 1832 on a hill overlooking the Wilderness Road. The mansion, known locally as Mount Airy, was razed in 1957 to make way for Jennie Rogers Elementary School. (Above, courtesy of Guy Ingram; below, courtesy of the NPS Historic American Buildings Survey.)

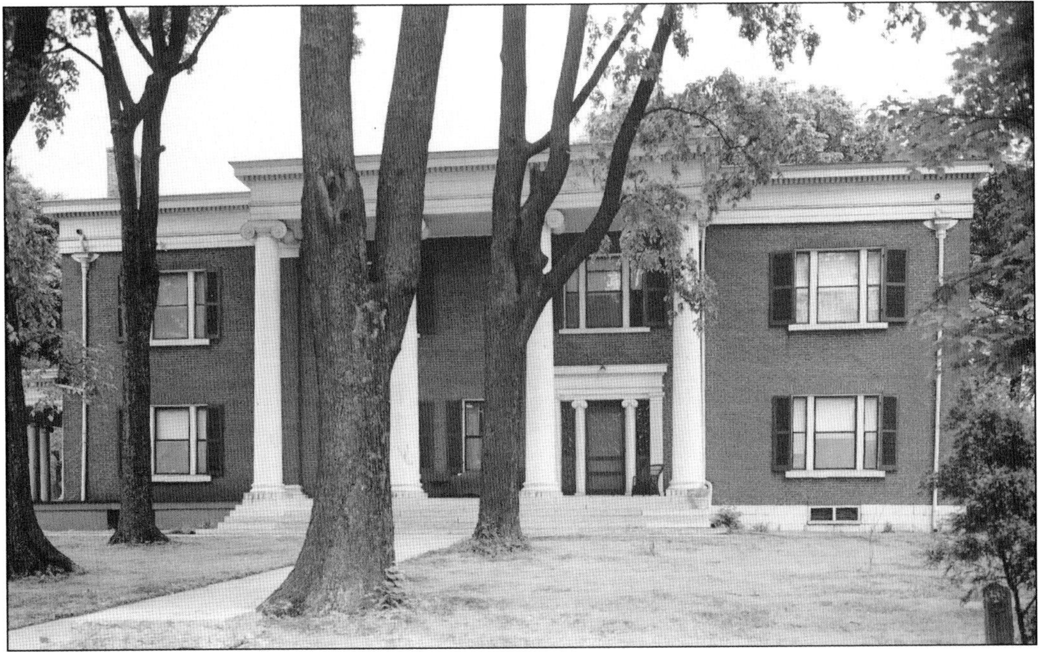

One of the most elaborate and recognizable Gothic structures in Danville is Mound Cottage, located on Maple Avenue. It was built in 1856 for Jeremiah Tilford Boyle, son of Judge John Boyle, the namesake of Boyle County. Jeremiah Boyle was a lawyer and served as a Union officer during the Civil War. (Courtesy of the NPS Historic American Buildings Survey.)

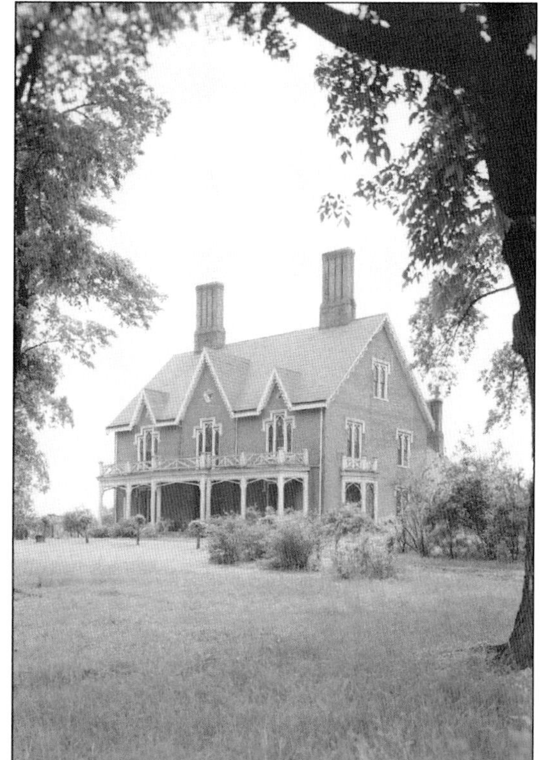

Cecilian Park, owned by Granville and Charles P. Cecil, was a prominent horse breeding business in Danville that was originally known as Melrose Stock Farm. The Cecil brothers produced a four-times leading sire of America in Gambetta Wilkes, pictured here with his attendant Paul Helm in 1908. (Courtesy of Michael Wiser.)

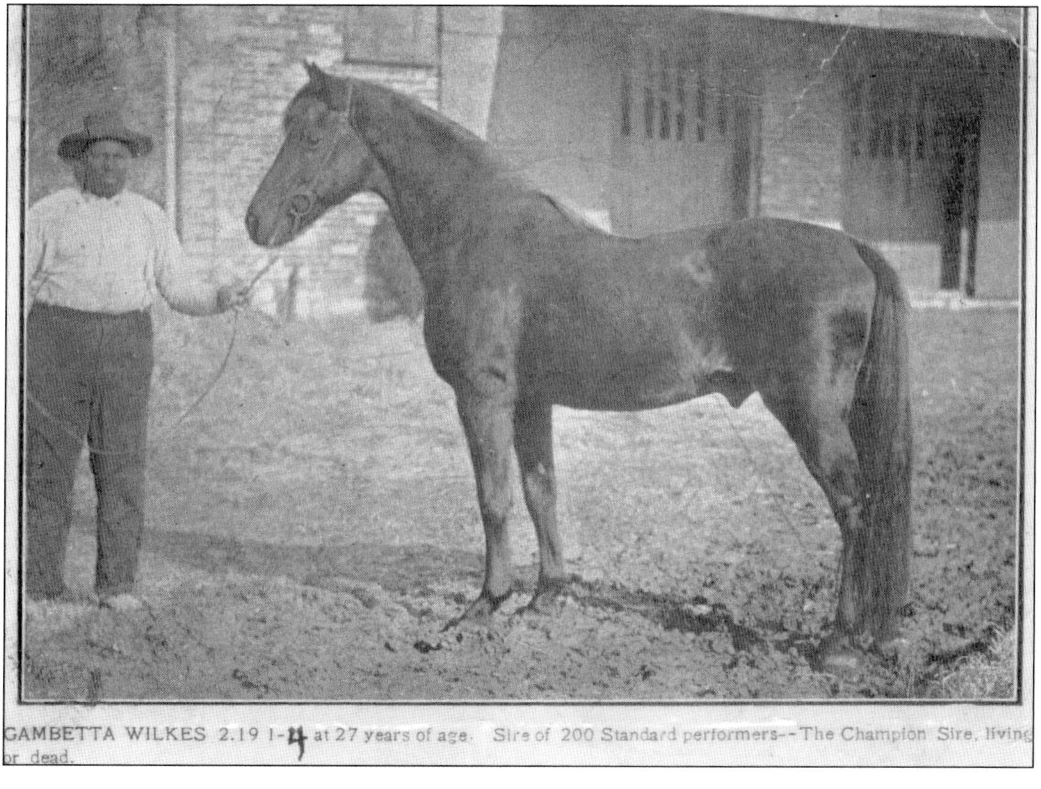

GAMBETTA WILKES 2.19 1-4 at 27 years of age. Sire of 200 Standard performers--The Champion Sire, living or dead.

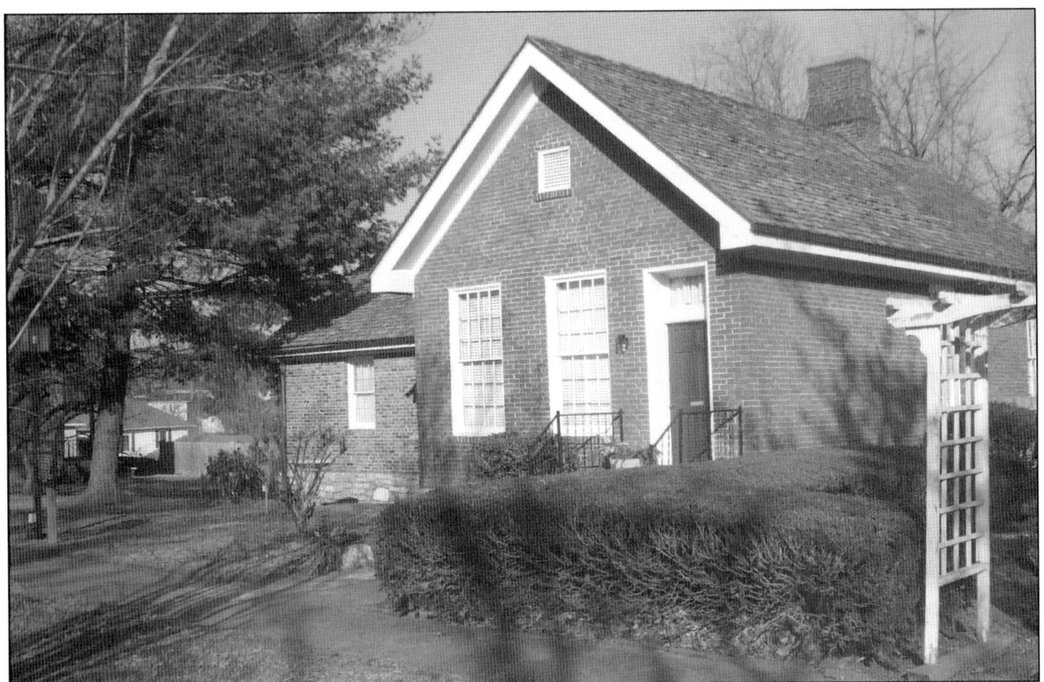

The first brick schoolhouse in Danville was built in the public square around 1820, between Grayson's Tavern and the Watts-Bell House and Fisher Row. It had only two rooms, but the structure has since been enlarged and was renovated in 1975. (Author's personal collection.)

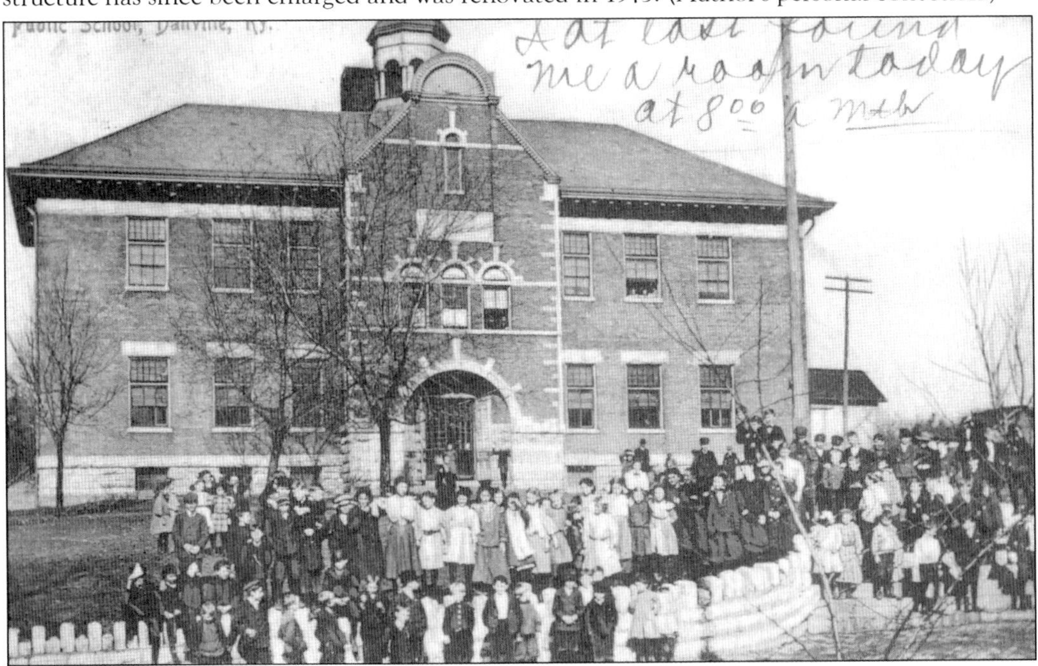


Students line up outside of the Broadway School, located on East Broadway Street between First Street and Wilderness Road. Well-recognized for its stone arches and bell tower, the Broadway School burned down in 1950, and the Danville employment office now sits on the school's former site. (Courtesy of Michael Wiser.)

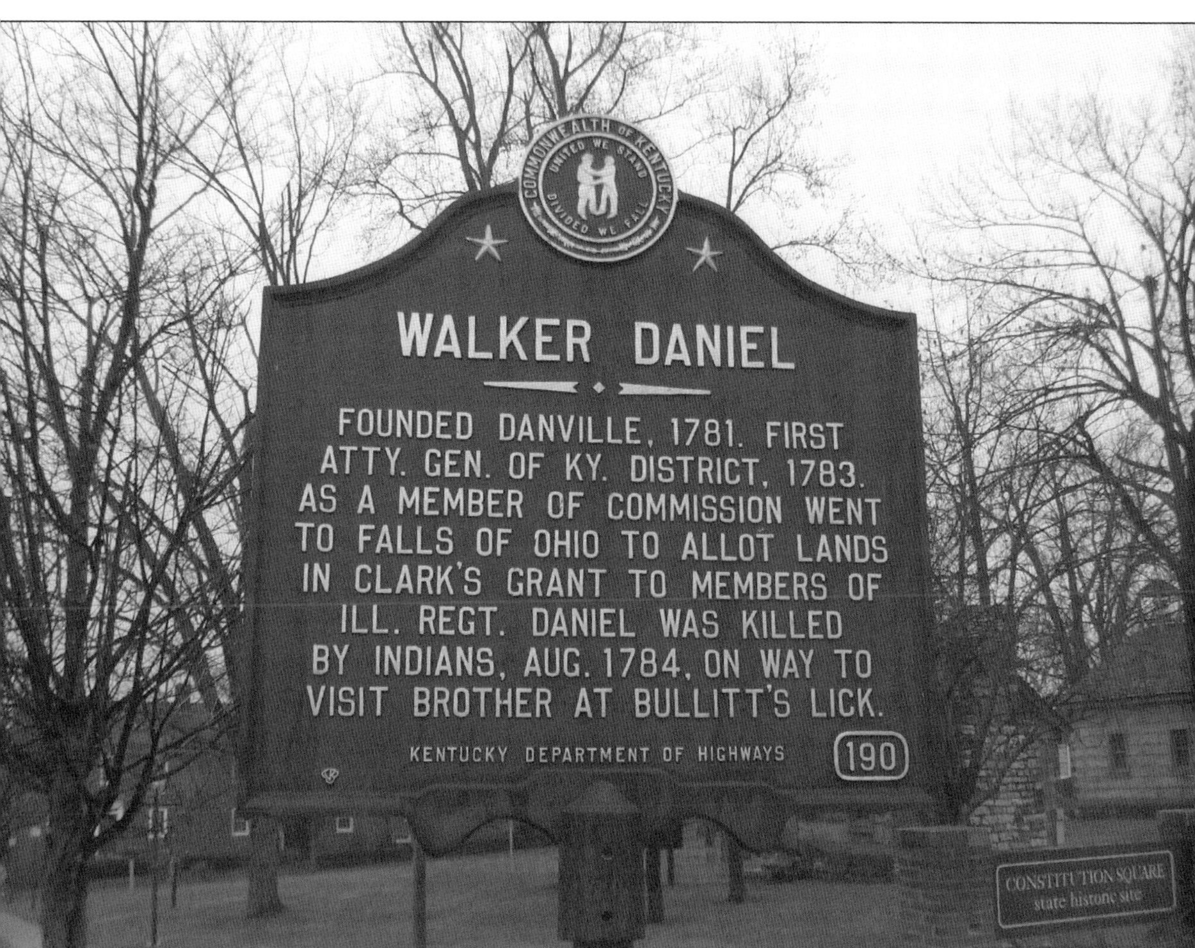


It is unlikely that Walker Daniel could ever have imagined his small plot of land growing to the town it is today. Killed by Native Americans in 1784, Daniel did not live to witness the constitutional conventions crucial to Kentucky's statehood being held in the public square, nor did he see the magnificent educational institutions and beautiful churches that were founded in the town named for him. Though relatively small, Danville has over 225 years of fascinating history that still resonates today, intriguing residents and historians alike. (Author's personal collection.)

# About the Organization

The author is privileged to work at the Ephraim McDowell House and Apothecary Shop Museum in Danville, located at 125 South Second Street, across from the Constitution Square State Historic Site. The museum's mission reflects Danville's dedication to protecting historically significant structures and sites from deterioration and new developments, sharing pieces of material culture that tell the story of this town, and promoting the teaching of history to younger generations. One of the most wonderful things about Danville is how important its history is to its residents. It is truly a delight to see original 18th- and 19th-century structures cared for, appreciated, and still standing today. The respect for Danville's history is evident in the McDowell House Museum's staff and docents, who dedicate their time, energy, and expertise to teach visitors about the small town and to preserve its history. Whether someone has lived in Danville his whole life or is simply passing through, it is worthwhile to take the time to explore this beautiful City of Firsts and all it has to offer.

# BIBLIOGRAPHY

*CentreCyclopedia*. Centre College Encyclopedia. Centre College Special Collections. www.centre.edu/web/library/ency/open.html.

Brown, Richard C. *The Presbyterians: 200 Years in Danville, 1784–1984*. Danville, KY: Presbyterian Church, 1983.

Fackler, Calvin Morgan. *Early Days in Danville*. Louisville, KY: Standard Printing, 1941.

Joseph, Mary J. and Janet Hamner. *Danville and Boyle County in the Bluegrass Region in Kentucky*. Paducah, KY: Turner Publishing, 1999.

Kleber, John E., Thomas D. Clark, Lowell H. Harrison, James C. Klotter. *The Kentucky Encyclopedia*. University Press of Kentucky, 1992.

Schachner, August. *Ephraim McDowell, "Father of Ovariotomy" and Founder of Abdominal Surgery, with an Appendix on Jane Todd Crawford*. Philadelphia, PA: J.B. Lippincott, 1921.